W9-BPE-649
R. POPE
this book is a gift from the
SMALL PRESS EXPO
@SPXCOMICS ~ WWW.SMALLPRESSEXPO.COM

Walt Disney
UNCLE $CROOGE
and
Donald Duck

The

Library

Volume Seven

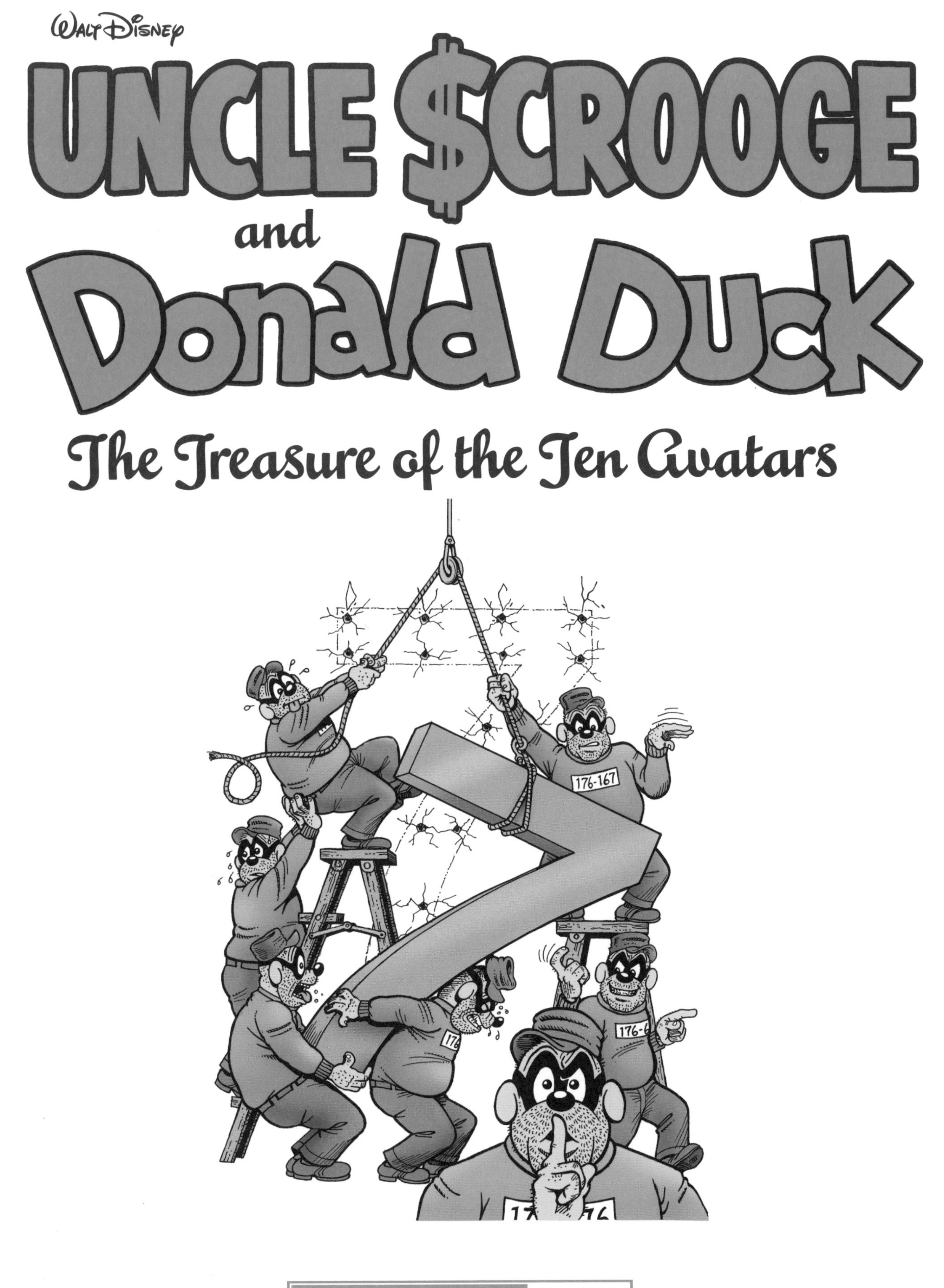

FANTAGRAPHICS BOOKS

Fantagraphics Books
7563 Lake City Way NE
Seattle, Washington 98115

Editor: David Gerstein
Supervising Editor: Gary Groth
Color Restoration: Scott Rockwell, Erik Rosengarten, and Digikore Studios
Series Designer: Tony Ong
Designer: David Gerstein
Production: Paul Baresh and Preston White
Associate Publisher: Eric Reynolds
Publisher: Gary Groth

For a free full-color catalogue of comics and cartooning, call 1-800-657-1100. Our books may be viewed–and purchased–on our website at www.fantagraphics.com.

The Editor would like to thank: John Clark, Jacques Echegaray, Joakim Gunnarsson, Stein Hjelmerud, Raimo Hyvonen, Aki Hyyppä, Janet and Al Jamison, Thomas Jensen, Anne Marie Mersing, Erik Rosengarten, Dan Shane, Matteo Sonz, Solveig Thime, and Germund von Wowern.

First Fantagraphics Books edition: June 2017

ISBN 978-160699-961-5

Printed in Korea

Table of Contents

All stories and text features written and drawn by Don Rosa.

Preface

By Don Rosa

The most unique story in this *Don Rosa Library* volume is the first of a series of "official anniversary" stories that I was asked by my editors to create for various Carl Barks characters; the other such stories will be in the next volume. But my first such story was in 1997 for the fiftieth anniversary of Barks' creation of this Scrooge McDuck guy whom I love so dearly! As I am, first and foremost, merely a comics fan, I very much enjoyed the opportunity to create this special story that honored the first appearance of such a classic character of comicdom!

But "anniversary stories" are difficult projects to undertake. I needed to create a plot that had some sort of very *special* quality about it... something *never* done before. Yet, as with any Duck story, it could *never* be a plot that would *change* any element of the Barks Duck universe. When superhero comics need a special publishing event, they will kill Superman or have Spider-Man get married. But this Duck universe is more precious than that, nor would any of us ever want to see it changed so dramatically. So, since I couldn't change the way anything *was*, I figured the only options for a "special" story would be for me to show *how* things got to *be* that way—a so-called "origin" tale—or else a simple celebration of when the anniversary character entered our lives. The latter path was the one I took for my Uncle Scrooge anniversary story, "A Little Something Special." As critical as I am of my own work (and there are some stinkers in this volume), I thought I did perhaps one of my best stories in my celebration of Scrooge McDuck's first appearance.

I always had the most trouble creating short "gag" stories... my enthusiasm was just too much to limit myself to something short; I found it much easier to create long and complex plots, as paradoxical as that may seem. I was glad that other writers could do a much better job on these short stories—which are the real backbone of the Egmont Duck comic books—leaving me free to indulge myself in the long adventures. But this volume contains what I think is perhaps one of my best short stories! I've heard from some readers who think "A Matter of Some Gravity" is my best short story; others have said it's my best story of any length; and still others claim it's their favorite, funniest Duck story *ever*! Well, I hope you'll at least find it better than a poke in the eye with a sharp stick.

Then there's a story I *don't* like. My plot for "The Once and Future Duck" may have made a good story for my fanzine characters twenty years earlier, but when I forced Barks' characters into this old King Arthur plot, I didn't think the resulting adventure had the proper tone or basis.

But I actually like the other stories featured here. When my editor wanted an "outer space" adventure, that worried me, since—as with time travel—I don't think the Duck characters should be featured in stories that portray space travel as if it were commonplace. But I managed to have our heroes thrust into outer space, anyway, by forces beyond their control in a plot that's reminiscent of an old-fashioned 1950s "monster from outer space" movie. However, the fearsome creatures referred to in "Attack of the Hideous Space Varmints" are our Ducks, not the friendly alien farm family.

Then there's this book's title story, "The Treasure of the Ten Avatars," which was one of my better Scrooge quests for a treasure of antiquity. And rounding out this volume is another B-chapter in my "Life and Times of Scrooge McDuck," and you *know* I always loved doing those! •

The Stories

Drawing made for *Joakim Von And: Her er dit liv* ("Scrooge McDuck: This Is Your Life"), a 1997 Danish anthology of Rosa's *Life and Times of Scrooge McDuck* series. Color by Susan Daigle-Leach.

The illustration idea came from Italian Disney artist Marco Rota, who had drawn a similar pose of Scrooge for the long-running Italian Disney magazine *Zio Paperone*.

A modified version of Rosa's drawing—with Scrooge's eyes redirected at the photo album—has more recently been used on the intro page to many *Don Rosa Library* volumes' "Rosa Archives" section. (You can find it in this volume on page 207.)

Walt Disney's DONALD DUCK
"The Once and Future Duck"
VOOM!
VOOM!
CRACKLE!
VZT! VZT!
HEAR THAT? SOUNDS LIKE GYRO'S HAD ANOTHER BRAINSTORM!
PATENT REFUSED
GYRO GEARLOOSE
Insolvable Problems Solved
STAND BACK! GENIUS AT WORK
SPECIAL SALE! BARREL-O'-INVENTIONS 5 BUCKS
U.S. MAIL
PATENT PENDING
PATENT APP. FOR
≥GULP!≤ LET'S HURRY PAST!
YEAH! IT'S NOT WISE TO BE AROUND WHEN GYRO'S WORKING ON ONE OF HIS WACKY EXPERIMENTS!
D 95079 A
BLAM!
ZOW!
OOOH... MY POOR BACK!
HEY! QUICK! IS IT LAST WEEK OR ONLY YESTERDAY?
IT'S... ER... TUESDAY, UNCA DONALD! WHY?
DRAT! THAT MEANS IT'S STILL TODAY! GYRO'S BLOWN ME UP FIVE TIMES AND HE STILL HASN'T SENT ME THROUGH TIME!
!
THROUGH TIME?!!
YEAH! AND IF HE EVER GETS IT RIGHT, I'LL BE RICH!

YOO-HOO...DONALD! ARE YOU IN HERE NOW OR YESTERDAY?
BAD NEWS, GYRO! WE'LL HAVE TO TRY AGAIN!
ER... TRY WHAT AGAIN?
WHY, MY NEW INVENTION, BOYS—A MINIATURE PERSONAL TIME-TRAVEL HELMET! IT'S FOR SHORT TIME-HOPS AROUND THE HOUSE!
OH, SO?
CONSIDER THE HOUSEWIFE WHO GETS SO CAUGHT UP IN A SOAP OPERA THAT SHE BURNS DINNER! WITH THIS HELMET, SHE CAN POP BACK ONE HOUR AND TAKE THE ROAST OUT ON TIME!
OR THE GUY WHO OVERSLEEPS BECAUSE HE STAYED OUT TOO LATE AT THE BOWLING ALLEY! WITH THIS HELMET, HE CAN POP BACK IN TIME A FEW HOURS AND LEAVE FOR WORK ON TIME—WHILE HE'S STILL ASLEEP!
Z
VERY FUNNY, UNCA DONALD! BUT TIME TRAVEL IS A SERIOUS SCIENCE!
I KNOW THAT, YOU LITTLE KILLJOYS...
USED ELECTRICITY
...AND I'M GOING TO BE SERIOUSLY RICH! IN RETURN FOR HELPING GYRO TEST THE HELMET, I GET EXCLUSIVE RIGHTS TO SELL IT!
SELLING'S NO FUN! I'M ONLY INTEREST IN MAKING THE HELMET WORK!
BUT I CAN'T SEEM TO WORK OUT THE BUGS IN THE POWER GRID! AN ENERGY SURGE COULD RESULT IN A MUCH LONGER TIME HOP THAN IS SAFE!
THAT'S NOT YOUR ONLY PROBLEM, UNCA DONALD! IT'S DANGEROUS TO JUMP THROUGH TIME WITHOUT BEING INSIDE A TIME MACHINE!
NOW WHAT ARE YOU BABBLING ABOUT?

WITHOUT THE PROTECTION OF A VEHICLE, YOU MIGHT MATERIALIZE AT A TIME WHEN SOMETHING ELSE OCCUPIED THAT SAME SPOT!
YEAH? SO?
WELL, WHAT IF YOU WENT BACK A MONTH AND GYRO HAD A WORKBENCH STANDING THERE? OR IF A POWER SURGE SENT YOU BACK A FEW YEARS TO WHEN A TREE WAS GROWING IN THAT SPOT?
YOU'D MATERIALIZE INSIDE THE OBJECT! IT MIGHT NOT BE... HEALTHY!
GRACIOUS! HE MIGHT EVEN EXPLODE!
EXPLODE?! ACK!!!
I CAN SEE NOW THAT WE'LL NEED TO CONDUCT THESE EXPERIMENTS IN A PLACE SURE TO BE CLEAR OF OBSTRUCTIONS, NO MATTER HOW FAR BACK IN TIME THE SUBJECT TRAVELS!
THE "SUBJECT" AGREES! HOW ABOUT THE MIDDLE OF A FIELD?
THERE MIGHT HAVE BEEN A FOREST THERE A FEW HUNDRED YEARS AGO!
A MOUNTAINTOP?
A MOUNTAIN MIGHT HAVE ERODED AWAY A DUCK-HEIGHT'S WORTH IN A FEW CENTURIES!
GYRO, WHAT'S THE MAXIMUM RANGE OF YOUR MACHINE, EVEN WITH THE WORST MALFUNCTION?
OH, ABOUT 5,000 YEARS!
THEN THE ONLY SAFE SPOT IS... STONEHENGE!
STONE-WHICH?
IT'S AN ANCIENT CIRCLE OF STONE MENHIRS BUILT IN ENGLAND OVER 50 CENTURIES AGO! IT WAS PROBABLY A SOLAR OBSERVATORY DESIGNED TO MARK THE PASSING OF THE SEASONS!
STONEHENGE
SURELY NO TREE OR STRUCTURE WOULD HAVE BEEN INSIDE THE CIRCLE IN ALL THAT TIME!
BUT MOVE ALL THIS EQUIPMENT TO ENGLAND?
GULP! I'LL PAY TO MOVE IT! I'D RATHER BE BROKE THAN EXPLODED!

WE NOW TRAVEL AHEAD ONE WEEK IN OUR OWN INSTANT TIME MACHINE, TO A PRE-DAWN MORNING ON THE SALISBURY PLAIN IN SOUTHERN ENGLAND...
...TO STONEHENGE, WHERE PREHISTORIC BRITONS CELEBRATED MYSTIC RITUALS NOW LOST IN THE HAZE OF 50 CENTURIES!
HMPH! IT'S STILL TOO DARK TO SEE!
YES, BUT YOU CHAPS PROMISED TO BE DONE WITH YOUR EXPERIMENTS BEFORE THE TOURISTS START ARRIVING!
WHAT WILL YOU USE TO POWER THAT GIZMO?
THIS SOLAR COLLECTOR WILL HARNESS THE SUN'S POWER! AND IF WE NEED MORE, I HAVE A GENERATOR IN MY MOBILE LAB OUT THERE!
DO YOU GET A LOT OF TOURISTS HERE?
BLIMEY, YES! AND NOT ONLY TO SEE STONEHENGE, EITHER! THIS IS ALSO THE REGION WHERE KING ARTHUR LIVED!
REALLY?
QUITE SO! KING ARTHUR AND HIS GALLANT KNIGHTS OF THE ROUND TABLE, IN THEIR SHINING ARMOR, ONCE GALLOPED ON MAGNIFICENT STEEDS OVER THIS VERY COUNTRYSIDE, PERFORMING LEGENDARY DEEDS OF VALOR!
CAMELOT IS SAID TO HAVE STOOD ON CADBURY HILL, JUST WEST OF HERE! FROM THERE, THE KING OF ALL THE BRITONS LAUNCHED HIS QUEST FOR THE HOLY GRAIL!
WOW!
THE LEGENDS SAY THAT STONEHENGE ITSELF WAS MAGICALLY BUILT BY MERLIN, THOUGH ACTUALLY IT WAS ALREADY 3500 YEARS OLD IN ARTHUR'S DAY!
OKAY... WE'RE ALL SET!

REMEMBER, IF WE DO SUCCEED IN SENDING YOU THROUGH TIME, THE HELMET IS SET TO AUTOMATICALLY RETURN YOU IN FIVE MINUTES!
WE STILL DON'T THINK THIS IS A GOOD IDEA!
ONCE YOU'VE ARRIVED, CHECK THE DATE ON THE HELMET'S CHRONOMETER SO YOU'LL KNOW WHEN IT IS! TODAY'S SEPTEMBER 22!
THE AUTUMNAL EQUINOX! AN INTERESTING DAY TO VISIT STONEHENGE!
I'LL ADJUST THE SOLAR COLLECTOR SO WE'LL HAVE POWER AS SOON AS THE SUN RISES!
HERE IT COMES!
AND WITH IT COMES THE ERA OF AFFORDABLE TIME MACHINES, EXCLUSIVELY AVAILABLE FROM "DONALD DUCK & CO."!
THROW THE SWITCH, GYRO!
WE'RE ALMOST AT FULL POWER! THREE...TWO...
...ONE...
...ZERO!
BZZT!
PTHZAK!
WELL, I FELT SOMETHING, BUT I DON'T SEEM TO HAVE GONE ANYWHERE!
?
DRAT! YOU'RE STILL HERE! I'VE FAILED AGAIN!
WHEW! THANK GOODNESS!
MAYBE IF I HOOK UP THE GENERATOR AND—HEY! WHERE'S MY MOBILE LAB AND ALL MY INVENTING TOOLS?
AND WHERE'D THAT KNOW-IT-ALL GUIDE RUN OFF TO?

HE MUST HAVE HOPPED IN YOUR LAB TRUCK AND TAKEN OFF! THE CROOK!
BUT WHERE'S HIS JEEP? HE COULDN'T DRIVE BOTH VEHICLES!
SNAP
MAYBE HE HAD AN ACCOMPLICE! C'MON—LET'S GET AFTER THEM! NO ONE'S GONNA WRECK MY CHANCE TO GET-RICH-QUICK SO... QUICK!
VAROOM!
UH... WHERE'S THE MAIN ROAD WE CAME IN ON?
AND WHERE'S THE FENCE?
AND THE PARKING LOT?
AND THE TOURIST CENTER?
YOU MUST HAVE DRIVEN OUT THE BACK EXIT, GYRO! PULL OVER AND ASK THAT FARMER FOR DIRECTIONS!
HEY, BUDDY! WHAT'S THE QUICKEST WAY TO THE MAIN HIGHWAY TO AMESBURY?
SCREECH!
YAAAAH!!!
GULP! I HAVE A BAD FEELING ABOUT THIS!
NO REASON FOR YOU TO FEEL BAD JUST BECAUSE THAT GUY HAS A BAD CASE OF TEA NERVES! THEY DRINK THAT STUFF LIKE CRAZY OVER HERE, YOU KNOW!

MAN, HE'S REALLY HIGH-TAILIN' IT!
SAY, MAYBE HE'S JUMPY BECAUSE HE'S THE CROOKED GUIDE'S ACCOMPLICE! WE'D BETTER FOLLOW HIM!
VROOM!
AHA! THERE'S A BUNCH WHO CAN TELL US WHERE WE ARE, WITH THEIR FANCY-SHMANCY COMPASSES AND MAP-READING MERIT BADGES!
UH...WHO ARE YOU TALKING ABOUT, UNCA DONALD?
WHY, THE LOCAL CHAPTER OF YOUR PRECIOUS JUNIOR WOODCHUCKS, OF COURSE! LOOKS LIKE THEY'RE HOLDING A WOODCHUCK JAMBOREE OVER THERE ON THAT HILL!
DON'T DRIVE UP TO IT, GYRO! IT'S AN ARMED ENCAMPMENT!
ARMED? WITH WHAT—WOODCHUCK GUIDEBOOKS? THE BRITISH EDITION CAN'T BE ANY MORE IRRITATING THAN THE DUCKBURG VERSION!
AIIEE! FROM WHENCE DID THE SAXONS GET SUCH A FEARSOME METAL CHARIOT?
RELAX! THE FOOL HAS NO FOOT SOLDIERS TO BACK UP HIS ATTACK!
OPEN UP IN THERE! WE'VE GOT SOME UMPTEEN-STAR GENERALS FROM THE COLONIES BADLY IN NEED OF DIRECTIONS!
NO, UNCA DONALD!
GLOM!
GOSH! THOSE BRITISH WOODCHUCKS ARE A ROUGH-HEWN LOT!
KINDA BIG FOR THEIR AGE, TOO!
HEY! TAKE IT EASY!

EH... KIDS... Y'KNOW WHAT? THIS IS ALL RATHER STRANGE. I'M BEGINNING TO THINK SOMETHING'S WRONG!
REALLY, UNCA DONALD?
FLOP!
WHAT'S ALL THIS, THEN?
SAXONS, M'LORD! THEY APPROACHED THE RAMPARTS OF CAMALLATE AS BRAZEN AS AN ENTIRE LEGION!
BAH! THESE ARE NOT SAXONS! NOR ANGLES, NOR JUTES, NOR ANY OF THOSE OTHER NORTHERNERS* WHO INVADE OUR LANDS LADEN WITH ALE KEGS AND THEIR WILD ORGIES! WHO BE THEY IN TRUTH?
THE QUESTION IS— WHO ARE YOU, PAL?
* PROTO-DANES/SWEDES/NORSEMEN... PICK A VIKING, ANY VIKING!
FOOL! YOU STAND BEFORE ARTORIUS RIOTHAMUS, WARLORD OF DUMNONIA, LAST DESCENDANT OF LUCIUS CASTUS OF ROME!
SILENCE, MYRDDIN! YOUR SINGING ALWAYS MAKES MY HEAD THROB!
WHAT'S IT SAY, LOUIE?
BRACE YOURSELF! THAT'S KING ARTHUR HIMSELF! THE OTHER GUY IS MERLIN, AND WE'RE IN CAMELOT! THEY'RE USING THE ORIGINAL CELTIC NAMES!
CONGRATULATIONS, UNCA DONALD—YOU'VE GONE BACK IN TIME 15 CENTURIES! WE ALL HAVE, SOMEHOW!
AND WITHOUT THE TOOLS GYRO NEEDS TO SEND US HOME AGAIN!
YOU MEAN THAT FLEABAG IN THE SMELLY BEAR RUG IS THE KING ARTHUR?!
WHAT A RUDE PERSON!
TRULY, HE IS A SAXON!
FORSOOTH! OFF WITH HIS HEAD!

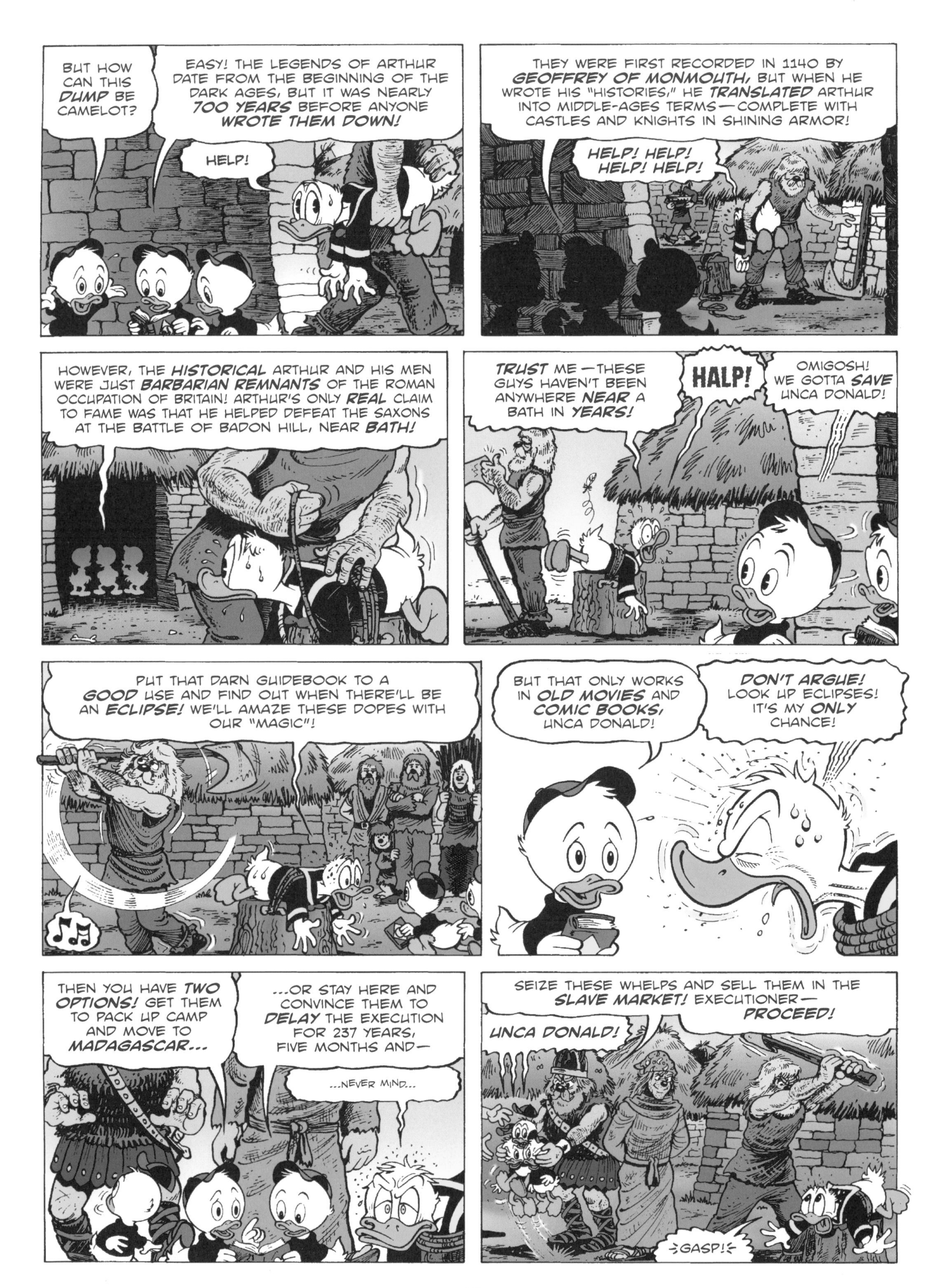

BUT HOW CAN THIS DUMP BE CAMELOT?
EASY! THE LEGENDS OF ARTHUR DATE FROM THE BEGINNING OF THE DARK AGES, BUT IT WAS NEARLY 700 YEARS BEFORE ANYONE WROTE THEM DOWN!
HELP!
THEY WERE FIRST RECORDED IN 1140 BY GEOFFREY OF MONMOUTH, BUT WHEN HE WROTE HIS "HISTORIES," HE TRANSLATED ARTHUR INTO MIDDLE-AGES TERMS—COMPLETE WITH CASTLES AND KNIGHTS IN SHINING ARMOR!
HELP! HELP! HELP! HELP!
HOWEVER, THE HISTORICAL ARTHUR AND HIS MEN WERE JUST BARBARIAN REMNANTS OF THE ROMAN OCCUPATION OF BRITAIN! ARTHUR'S ONLY REAL CLAIM TO FAME WAS THAT HE HELPED DEFEAT THE SAXONS AT THE BATTLE OF BADON HILL, NEAR BATH!
TRUST ME—THESE GUYS HAVEN'T BEEN ANYWHERE NEAR A BATH IN YEARS!
HALP!
OMIGOSH! WE GOTTA SAVE UNCA DONALD!
PUT THAT DARN GUIDEBOOK TO A GOOD USE AND FIND OUT WHEN THERE'LL BE AN ECLIPSE! WE'LL AMAZE THESE DOPES WITH OUR "MAGIC"!
BUT THAT ONLY WORKS IN OLD MOVIES AND COMIC BOOKS, UNCA DONALD!
DON'T ARGUE! LOOK UP ECLIPSES! IT'S MY ONLY CHANCE!
THEN YOU HAVE TWO OPTIONS! GET THEM TO PACK UP CAMP AND MOVE TO MADAGASCAR...
...OR STAY HERE AND CONVINCE THEM TO DELAY THE EXECUTION FOR 237 YEARS, FIVE MONTHS AND—
...NEVER MIND...
SEIZE THESE WHELPS AND SELL THEM IN THE SLAVE MARKET! EXECUTIONER—PROCEED!
UNCA DONALD!
GASP!

BUT WHAT ABOUT GYRO, WHO'S STILL WAITING OUTSIDE IN THE TRUCK?
WHAT'S KEEPING THEM?
HUH? OH, OKAY! I'LL GIVE THEM A LITTLE TOOT!
BEEEP!
ZOUNDS! SAXON WAR TRUMPETS!
NAY! 'TIS THE HORN OF GABRIEL!
OR A GAGGLE OF BANSHEES!
YOU MEAN A PRIDE OF BANSHEES!
WHATEVER!
CHOP!
WHAT A BREAK!
C'MON, UNCA DONALD! RUN FOR IT!
NO NEED TO ASK TWICE! FEET, DO YOUR STUFF!
WHAT'S THE RUSH?
JUST TURN THIS TRUCK AROUND AND PEEL OUT! WE'LL EXPLAIN LATER!
WHERE TO?
BACK TO STONEHENGE! YOU NEED TO FIX THE TIME HELMET WE LEFT BACK THERE!
VAROOOM!
THE TRUMPET CALL WAS A TRICK, M'LORD! THE SAXONS HAVE ESCAPED!
MOAN! THIS IS VERY BAD!
ENEMIES HAVE ALWAYS ATTACKED BECAUSE THEY FEAR NOT MY MEAGER TROOPS! NOW INVADERS WILL HEAR MORE NEWS OF OUR WEAKNESS!
WE MUST PURSUE THOSE SAXONS AND DESTROY THEM! TO ARMS!
THEY TOOK THE ROAD TO THAT ANCIENT STONE CIRCLE OUR PEASANTS OFT USE TO STABLE LIVESTOCK!

SOON!
SO MY TIME HELMET DID WORK AFTER ALL! I JUST HOPE I CAN FIX IT AS EASILY AS I STRENGTHEN THIS HELMET WIRE!
FIX IT, GYRO! OR WE'RE MAROONED IN THE FIFTH CENTURY!
BUT HOW?! WITHOUT ANY OF MY EQUIPMENT? I HAVE NO HYPER-TRANSISTORS, OR ATOMIC-DIODES, OR FLUX CAPACITORS, OR NUCLEAR DISCOMBOBULATORS... OR EVEN A SCREWDRIVER!
YOU'RE SAYING YOU CAN'T FIX IT?
HM? OH, SURE I CAN FIX IT! MIGHT JUST TAKE AN EXTRA HOUR OR SO!
FIRST I'LL AIM THE SOLAR COLLECTOR AT THE NOON SUN!
?
CREAK! CREAK!
WHAT DO YOU WANT? CAN'T YOU SEE WE'RE BUSY?
PREPARE TO MEET THY MAKER, SAXON DOGS!
WAK!
LET'S MAKE A RUN FOR IT! WE'VE GOT THE TIME HELMET NOW!
WE'LL PUT PLENTY OF DISTANCE BETWEEN US THIS TIME!
GREAT! OUT OF GAS!
WHERE'S THE NEAREST GAS STATION?
ONLY ABOUT THREE MILES FROM HERE...
...AND 15 CENTURIES!
RRR-RRR-RRR

THEIR HORSE SEEMS TO HAVE RUN OFF! ATTACK THE CHARIOT!
EH... YOU ATTACK IT! YOU'RE THE ONLY ONE WITH A SWORD!
WHAT A WORTHLESS ARMY I LEAD! VERY WELL, THEN— HAVE AT YOU, VARLETS!
SPLAT!
BY THE STARS! THEY ARE SITTING IN A BLOCK OF WARM ICE!
PERHAPS IT IS MERELY HARD AIR?
WE CAN STILL SEIZE THE YOUNG ONES IN THE REAR OF THE CHARIOT!
GOT YOU, SAXON BRATS!
HELP, UNCA DONALD! HELP!!!
THOSE WILDMEN HAVE GRABBED THE KIDS! I GOTTA SAVE 'EM!
BUT WHAT CAN WE DO AGAINST A HORDE OF BLOODTHIRSTY BARBARIANS?
I-I DON'T KNOW, BUT THAT SEEDY "KING ARTHUR" WILL HAVE A TRIPLE FEATURE ON HIS CHOPPING BLOCK IF I DON'T DO SOMETHING!
GACK!
TWANG!
I... SPUTTER! YOU... CHOKE!
DAGNABBIT! DROP THOSE KIDS AND GET OUTTA HERE!
CRACKLE!

PTHZAK!
?!
JEEPERS! WHAT HAPPENED?
NOW I GET IT! THIS ANCIENT STONE CIRCLE IS ACTUALLY SOME SORT OF ASTRAL BATTERY! THAT'S THE EXPLANATION FOR THE POWER SURGE THAT SENT US ALL BACK HERE!
THE SOLAR COLLECTOR TAPPED THE POWER OF THE HENGE AND FED IT INTO THE HELMET! YOU KNOCKED THOSE WARRIORS BACK WITH SHEER TELEKINETIC FORCE!
OOPS! AND MY NEPHEWS, TOO!
BY JUPITER! WHAT HIT US?
THE SAXONS REPELLED US BY MAGICK, SIRE! I SAW THE MYSTIC FORCE SEETHING AROUND THAT STRANGE OBJECT!
IT LOOKS LIKE A BOWL... A HUGE DRINKING VESSEL!
VERILY! AN ENCHANTED CUP FILLED WITH THE POWER OF GOD!
WITH A WEAPON SUCH AS THAT, YOU COULD STRIKE FEAR INTO ALL INVADERS!
YOU SAY THE SOOTH! I MUST HAVE THAT GIANT CHALICE!
ATTACK! HALF MY KINGDOM TO HE WHO CAPTURES THAT HOLY GRAIL!

HERE THEY COME AGAIN! WE CAN'T FIGHT THEM OFF FOREVER, AND YOU NEED TIME TO FIX THE TIME HELMET!
I HAVE AN IDEA! GIVE ME THE HELMET!
BY CONCENTRATING WHILE WEARING IT, I CAN MAKE THE LIGHT RAYS FROM BEHIND US BEND AROUND US! WE'LL BE INVISIBLE FROM THEIR VIEWPOINT!
DO WHICH?
PTHZAK!
ZOUNDS! THEY DISAPPEARED, HENGE AND ALL!
HA! THEY HAVE BEEN DRIVEN OFF IN FEAR OF THE TERRIBLE WARLORD, ARTORIUS RIOTHAMUS!
...
OX FRUIT! NEXT THEY'LL TURN US ALL INTO NEWTS!
RUN AWAY! FLEE LIKE BATS OUT OF HADES!!!
THAT SCARED THEM OFF! BUT THEY STILL HAVE HUEY, DEWEY AND LOUIE!
GIMME THAT HELMET! I'LL GO BEAT THOSE BUMS TO BITS WITH BRAINPOWER!
YOU CAN'T DO THAT! THE PRETERNATURAL FORCE THAT POWERS THAT HELMET EXISTS ONLY INSIDE THE RING OF STONEHENGE!
GUK!
TWANG!
GROAN! SO WHAT CAN WE DO?
OBVIOUSLY, INSTEAD OF COLLECTING SOLAR POWER, THE DISH IS GATHERING THE ASTRAL POWER OF STONEHENGE! BUT MAYBE I CAN REWIRE IT TO ALSO ACT AS A POWER TRANSMITTER!
I'LL TURN THE HELMET INTO A WIRELESS RECEIVER, AND BEAM THE POWER OF STONEHENGE DIRECTLY TO IT!
WELL, I DON'T UNDERSTAND ANY OF THIS... BUT AS LONG AS YOU DO, GET TO WORK!

SOON!
THE ANTENNA WILL RECEIVE THE TRANSMITTED ENERGY BEAM, AND THIS NEW HELMET'S ELECTRONICS WILL TRANSFORM IT INTO POWER YOU CAN USE!
WHAT'S WITH THE FULL-HELMET DESIGN?
PRNDL
IT'S TO PROTECT YOU! THOSE BRITONS COULD THROW SPEARS AT YOU FROM ALL DIRECTIONS, SO I'VE ALSO MADE YOU AN ENTIRE PROTECTIVE SUIT FROM TRUCK PARTS!
OOG! GOOD IDEA!
YOU'LL HAVE TO HURRY, THOUGH! I REALIZE NOW THAT THE ENORMOUS POWER SURGE WE HAD AT DAWN WAS THE RISING SUN STRIKING STONEHENGE ON THE DAY OF THE AUTUMNAL EQUINOX!
SINCE THE EQUINOX IS THE EXACT INSTANT WHEN THE SUN'S POWER IS BALANCED, WE CAN ONLY GET HOME WITH A RECIPROCAL POWER SURGE! OUR ONLY CHANCE IS TO LEAVE TODAY, PRECISELY AT SUNSET!
THE SURGE AT ANY OTHER TIME WON'T MATCH THE ONE THAT SENT US HERE! IT MIGHT SEND US CENTURIES OFF OUR TARGET DATE!
SAVE THE EXPLANATIONS! I'LL GET THE KIDS BACK HERE BY SUNSET!
YOU'LL NEED THIS WALKIE-TALKIE SO I CAN WARN YOU WHEN TIME IS RUNNING SHORT, BUT... HMM... IT MIGHT INTERFERE WITH THE POWER BEAM!
PRNDL
AH! I KNOW! MY HELPER CAN CARRY IT FOR YOU!
HIM?
!!!
JUST DON'T GET UNDERFOOT WHEN I START DOING MY STUFF, SQUIRT!
GET GOING! WHEN YOU GET TO CAMELOT I'LL BEAM YOU ALL THE ASTRAL POWER YOU NEED TO SAVE THE KIDS!
CRANK CRANK

THE MERCILESS SUN, UNCONCERNED WITH THE FATE OF TIME-LOST DUCKS, CONTINUES ITS RELENTLESS JOURNEY ACROSS THE SKY!
BUT SOON...
SOL IS NOW LOW IN THE WEST OVER THE ISLE OF AVALONIA! IT IS TIME TO SEND THESE SAXON WHELPS TO THE LAND BEYOND BEYOND!
THIS IS IT, MEN!
DEWEY DIES AT DUSK!
UNCA DONALD WILL SAVE US— I HOPE!
THE SOARING FLAMES WILL TELL THE GREATNESS OF ARTORIUS TO INVADERS IN EVERY CORNER OF—
THROW THAT LOUDMOUTHED BARD OUT OF HERE AND LIGHT THE PYRE!
WHAT-- WHAT IS THAT?
PTHZAK!
IT LOOKS AS IF OUR GATE HAS BEEN... ER... BREACHED!
THEE CAN SAY THAT SOOTH AGAIN!
M'LORD! 'TIS PALUG'S MONSTER CAT!
NAY! 'TIS AN ATTACK BY THE FROST GIANTS!
METHINKS 'TIS THE FEARSOME BOAR OF GLASTONBERRY!
PTHZAK!
PTHZAK!
PTHZAK
ZOUNDS! 'TIS A MAGICK METAL MIDGET!
IS IT UNCA DONALD? IS IT UNCA DONALD?
NOTHING CAN SAVE YOU FROM ME! I AM INVINCIBLE!
I AM DOOM ITSELF! SNORT!
YEP— THAT'S HIM, ALL RIGHT!
SAME OL' CORNY LINE!
ATTABOY, UNCA DONALD! HOO-HAH!

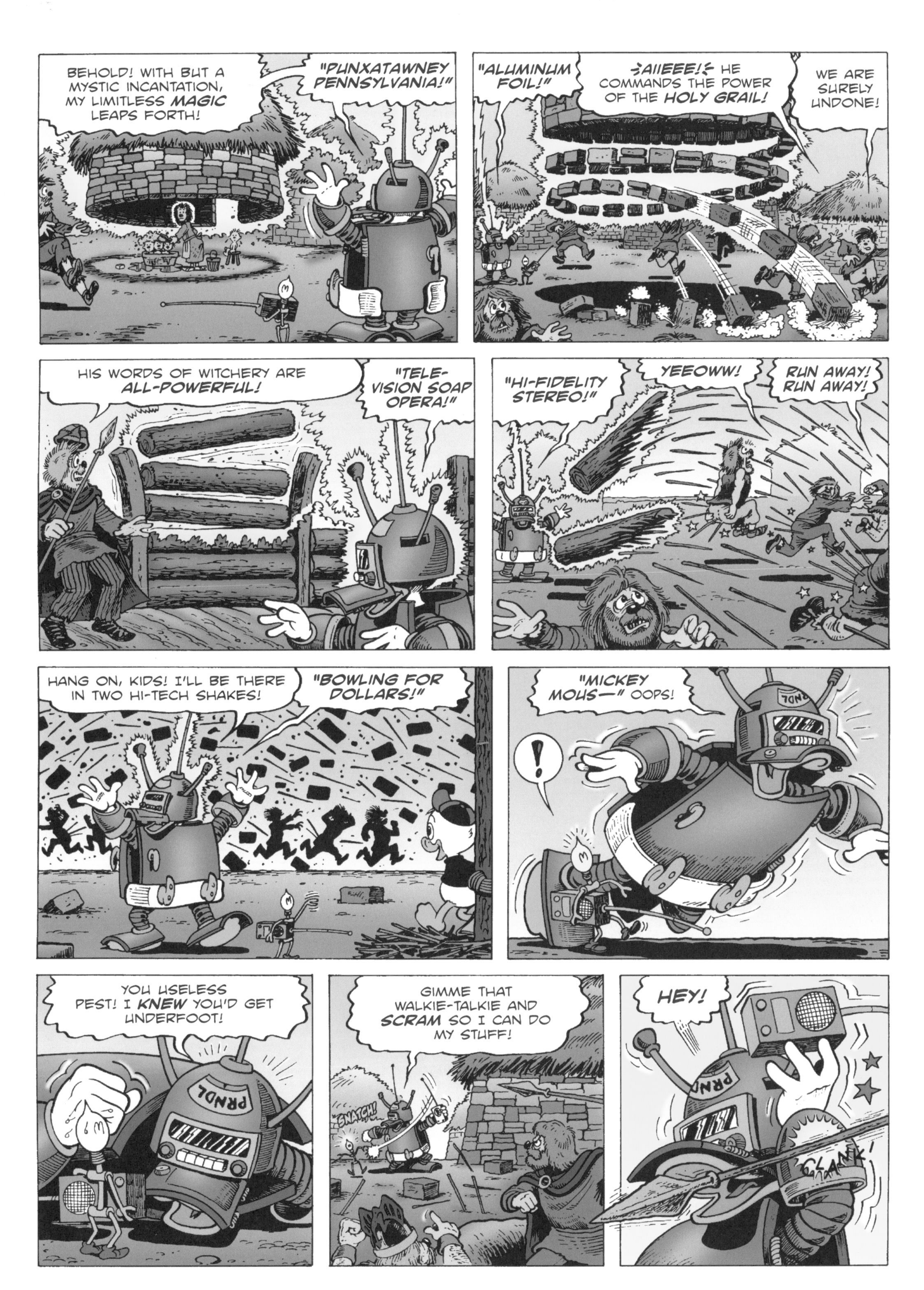
BEHOLD! WITH BUT A MYSTIC INCANTATION, MY LIMITLESS MAGIC LEAPS FORTH!
"PUNXATAWNEY PENNSYLVANIA!"
"ALUMINUM FOIL!"
AIIEEE! HE COMMANDS THE POWER OF THE HOLY GRAIL!
WE ARE SURELY UNDONE!
HIS WORDS OF WITCHERY ARE ALL-POWERFUL!
"TELE-VISION SOAP OPERA!"
"HI-FIDELITY STEREO!"
YEEOWW!
RUN AWAY! RUN AWAY!
HANG ON, KIDS! I'LL BE THERE IN TWO HI-TECH SHAKES!
"BOWLING FOR DOLLARS!"
"MICKEY MOUS—" OOPS!
!
YOU USELESS PEST! I KNEW YOU'D GET UNDERFOOT!
PRNDL
GIMME THAT WALKIE-TALKIE AND SCRAM SO I CAN DO MY STUFF!
SNATCH!
HEY!
PRNDL
CLANK!

M'LORD! THE ENCHANTER DROPPED SOMETHING!
IT LOOKS LIKE A MAGIC TALISMAN! PERHAPS I CAN TURN ITS POWER AGAINST ITS OWNER!
TEN THOUSAND GADZOOKS!
PTHZAK!
ZOUNDS! I FEEL MYSTIC POWER COURSING THROUGH MY VERY BONES! I SHALL TURN THE BATTLE!
BZZT!
OH, NO! THAT WALKIE-TALKIE IS INTERCEPTING PART OF UNCA DONALD'S POWER BEAM!
NOW THERE ARE TWO ATOMIC KNIGHTS!
HEY! HOW COME YOU CAN DO THAT?
REPENT, DAEMON! THE SAINTS FILL ME WITH THE POWER TO THWART YE!
CLANG!
CLANG!
CLANG!
BROTHER... THAT'S ACTION!

THE SPLIT BEAM IS GIVING THEM EQUAL POWER!
THIS COULD GO ON FOR DAYS!
DONALD! YOU HAVE ONLY ONE HOUR TO SUNSET! HURRY!
EGAD! AN EVIL FAERIE HAUNTS THIS TALISMAN!
I WILL SLAY THE EVIL MITE WITH MY SWORD CALIBURNE! HI-YAH!
PTHZAK!
THANK GOODNESS HE DESTROYED THE WALKIE-TALKIE! NOW HE HAS NO POWER SOURCE!
YOU'RE IN THE CLEAR, UNCA DONALD!
?
M'LORD! WHAT IS WRONG?
OOF! I KNOW NOT! I HAD THE POWER TO CLEAVE THIS ROCK, BUT NOW I AM AGAIN TOO WEAK TO WITHDRAW MY BLADE!
LET US FLEE, SIRE!
NAY! UNGH! CALIBURNE WAS HANDED DOWN FROM MY ANCESTOR, THE SARMATIAN NART OF THE ROMAN LEGION! I'LL NOT LEAVE IT!
DON'T WORRY, KIDS! WE HAVE JUST ENOUGH TIME TO GET BACK TO STONEHENGE! AND IF ANY OF THESE BOZOS TRY TO STOP US, I'LL SEND HIM FLYING HALFWAY TO SCOTLAND!
CLONG!
LOOK OUT!

UH-OH! THERE GOES MY POWER RECEIVER!
HURRY AND UNTIE US!
THE WIZARD'S POWER HAS FAILED HIM, SIRE! I HAVE HIM!
SORRY, KIDS... I ALMOST SAVED YOU!
COME, M'LORD ARTORIUS! WE HAVE THE SAXON DAEMON BOUND! COME LIGHT THE PYRE!
OOF!
UGH!
BUT...THIS IS THE ONLY SWORD IN DUMNONIA! I CANNOT LEAVE IT, FOR WHOEVER WIELDS IT WILL BE PENDRAGON OF THE REALM!
JUST LET ME GIVE IT ONE MORE GOOD PULL!
NAY, SIRE! THESE EVIL ONES ARE TOO DANGEROUS! WE MUST BURN THEM NOW!
UNCA DONALD—ISN'T THERE SOME OTHER WAY TO TAP INTO THAT POWER BEAM?
NO! YIPE! GYRO SAID I NEEDED SOME KIND OF ELECTRONIC DEVICE TO CONVERT THAT BEAM TO ENERGY! AND MY HELMET AND WALKIE-TALKIE ARE SHOT!
PTHZAK!

M'LORD! THE PYRE IS ABLAZE!
FINE! FINE! JUST STAND BACK AND GIVE ME ROOM TO PULL!
AHA! SUCCESS! ONLY THE MIGHTIEST HERO COULD HAVE PULLED THIS SWORD FREE!
RIP!
ZOW!
WHAT HO?
UH-OH!
NOW WHAT?
I AM UNCERTAIN! I FEAR IT IS THE DAEMON MOUSE I HEARD THE SAXON WIZARD SUMMON!
WHIIZZZZ
WE'RE FREE!
BUT IT'S NEARLY SUNSET! WE'LL NEVER REACH STONEHENGE IN TIME!
WHIIZZZZ!
SWISH!
SLASH!
CRUSH THE BEAST, M'LORD!
ARE YOU MAD? THAT'S THE MOST FOUL, CRUEL AND BAD-TEMPERED RODENT YOU EVER SET EYES ON!
ZOW!
LOOK! THERE'S STILL A CHANCE!
INTO THIS OXCART! HURRY!
OUTTA THE WAY, YOU STUMBLEBUMS! WE HAVE AN APPOINTMENT TO KEEP FIFTEEN HUNDRED YEARS FROM NOW, AND WE DON'T HAVE A SECOND TO SPARE!
ZOOM!
GADZOOKS! THAT'S SOME SPEEDY OXCART!

THEY ARE HEADED BACK TO THE ANCIENT STONE STABLE, SIRE!
AND THEY STILL HAVE CALIBURNE! I MUST HAVE IT BACK, MAGIC MICE OR NAY!
WE WILL TAKE THE SHORTER ROUTE THROUGH THE GLEN! WHO STILL STANDS WITH ME?
UH... NOBODY IS STANDING AT ALL, EXCEPT CAI AND TRYSTAN... AND ME, M'LORD!
OH, VERY WELL THEN! YOU THREE FOLLOW!
MEANWHILE, GYRO HASN'T BEEN WASTING TIME!
I'VE ADJUSTED THE TIME HELMET! I'M CONFIDENT IT CAN SEND US BACK TO THE FUTURE WHEN THE SETTING SUN TRIGGERS THE POWER SURGE!
BUT IT'S IMPOSSIBLE FOR DONALD AND THE KIDS TO GET HERE BY SUNSET! THERE'S ONLY ABOUT A MINUTE LEFT, AND THEY'RE NOWHERE IN SIGHT!
BUDDYUMP BUDDYUMP BUDDYUMP
WHAT THE— WHAT'S THAT?
YOU CAN SHUT OFF THE BEAM, GYRO! WE'RE BACK!
ER... YEAH... SO I SEE! AND YOU JUST MADE IT!
THE SUN IS SETTING! THE ENERGY GAUGE IS SOARING!
AND HERE COMES THAT SURLY KING ARTHUR AND HIS SHAGGY WARRIORS! LET'S HURRY!
THE GAUGE HAS HIT THE DANGER MARK! GATHER CLOSE— HERE WE GO! THREE...
...TWO...
...ONE...

...ZERO!
PTHZAK!
TH-THEY'RE GONE!
BUT HERE IS MY SWORD!
THE SAXON WIZARDS FLED BEFORE THE AWESOME MIGHT OF ARTORIUS, RESTITUTOR OF BRITAIN, ROYAL MONARCH OF ALL—
AND YOU ARE A ROYAL PAIN! I AM A MINOR WARLORD WHO WAS NEARLY WIPED OUT BY FOUR DUCKS AND A MOUSE! WHY DO YOU MOCK ME?
WE WILL SEE HOW WELL A BARD WITHOUT A HEAD CAN SING!
IF ONLY YOU'D UNDERSTAND, M'LORD! IT'S ALL A MATTER OF CREATING LEGENDS FROM NOTHING! I COULD MAKE THEE GREAT!
OH? PRAY TELL, HOW?
WHAT IF IT WERE YOU WHO WIELDED THE POWER OF THIS STONE STABLE? YOU WHO WORE THE METAL SUIT? YOU WHO PULLED THE SWORD FROM THE STONE?
BUT IT WAS NOT, FOOL!
SO WHAT? I WILL TRAVEL THE LAND AND SING OF SUCH FEATS, TILL THE SONGS BECOME LEGENDS AND THE LEGENDS BECOME FACT! SOON YOUR ENEMIES WILL COWER AT YOUR NAME!
FOR A NOMINAL FEE, OF COURSE!
HE'S RIGHT, SIRE! HIS SONGS COULD MAKE US ALL SOUND AS GREAT AS THE NART HEROES OF OUR SARMATIAN FOLKTALES!
I-I AM GETTING THE IDEA! YEA...
KING ARTORIUS AND HIS NARTS OF THE ROUND STABLE!
IF YOU PULL THIS HOAX OFF, MYRDDIN, YOU'RE A TRUE WIZARD!
THANK YOU, M'LORD! THAT IS A NICE TOUCH I CAN ADD!
AT NO EXTRA CHARGE!

MEANWHILE, 1500 YEARS LATER... UH... YOU KNOW WHAT I MEAN!
IT'S SUNSET, FOLKS! TIME TO CLOSE UP! PLEASE COME AGAIN!
?
PTHZAK!
YOU PEOPLE!? IT WAS BAD ENOUGH YOU TOOK OFF THIS MORNING AND LEFT THAT TRUCK FULL OF JUNK BEHIND, BUT NOW YOU'RE BACK TO PERFORM MORE SILLY EXPERIMENTS?!
!!!!!
NOT A CHANCE! I MUST ASK YOU TO LEAVE!
WELL, AT LEAST YOU'RE TAKING IT IN A CHEERFUL SPIRIT, I MUST SAY! GOOD SHOW!
WE'LL BE ON OUR WAY AS SOON AS WE SEND FOR SOME GAS! WE JUST RAN OUT!
YEAH ≷CHUCKLE!≶ ...AS OF JUST 1500 YEARS AGO!
VERY WELL!
DONALD—WE'LL PACK UP THE GEAR IF YOU POP INTO TOWN FOR SOME GAS!
ME? ALL THAT WAY? IN THE DARK?
GASOLINE
MY HELPER WILL LIGHT THE WAY FOR YOU!
OH, ALL RIGHT! BUT HE CARRIES THE CAN!
GASOLINE
MR. GUIDE—IS IT TRUE THAT KING ARTHUR PERFORMED HIS MIGHTIEST DEEDS NEAR HERE?
IT CERTAINLY IS, MADAM!
GASOLINE
WHY, JUST NEARBY ON CADBURY HILL YOU CAN SEE A CLEFT ROCK! THEY SAY IT'S THE VERY SITE WHERE THE NOBLEST HERO OF ALL TIME PULLED THE SWORD EXCALIBUR FROM THE STONE!
GASOLINE
!
GASOLINE
≷GRUMBLE!≶ OKAY, OKAY, MR. BIG SHOT—I'LL CARRY THE CAN!
End

Walt Disney's
UNCLE $CROOGE
INDIA! THE LAND OF ANCIENT MYSTERIES! BUT THERE'S A BRAND-NEW MYSTERY → WHY IS A MODERN-DAY TYCOON ON A VOYAGE UP AN INDUS RIVER TRIBUTARY INTO THE STEAMY RAINFOREST OF THE UNEXPLORED PUNJAB?
THE TREASURE OF THE TEN AVATARS
PUT IN TO THAT DOCK, LADS! IT'S IN THE HEART OF MY RECENT LAND PURCHASE!
THIS IS THE PROVINCE OF OLLIEYANSTAN! IT'S THE ONLY BIT OF LAND I DON'T OWN FOR HUNDREDS OF MILES!
THEY SAY IT'S ONE OF THE POOREST AREAS IN INDIA!
THAT WILL CHANGE NOW! ONCE I SCOUT THE JUNGLE FOR POTENTIAL RESOURCES, I'LL CREATE GOOD JOBS FOR ALL THESE PEOPLE — AND LOTS OF PROFIT FOR ME!
DONALD! HURRY UP WITH CHOW-DIRHEAD!
I'M COMING! I'M COMING!
YOU CAN HARDLY EARN YOUR THIRTY CENTS AN HOUR FOR DAWDLING!
OBVIOUSLY! I SHOULD EARN MORE THAN THAT JUST FOR BREATHING!
WHY DIDN'T YOU WAIT AND BUY AN ELEPHANT HERE?
Z.
CHUG CHUG

I COULDN'T PASS UP SUCH A MAGNIFICENT BEAST! THE MAN AT THE USED PACHYDERM LOT SAID CHOWDIRHEAD WAS ONLY USED BY AN AGED GURU ON HOLY DAYS!
?
PAT PAT
HE ALSO SAID HE'S BRAVE ENOUGH TO PROTECT US FROM A CHARGING RHINO!
ALL I REMEMBER IS THE PRICE WAS ONLY FIVE RUPEES!
!
EEEK!!
RIP!
SO HOW MUCH IS FIVE RUPEES IN DOLLARS?
HM... FOR ONE DOLLAR, UNCA SCROOGE COULD HAVE BOUGHT HALF A DOZEN CHOWDIRHEADS!
WHACK! WHACK! WHACK! WHACK!
DONALD! STOP TEASING CHOWDIRHEAD AND BRING HIM ASHORE!
HOW AM I SUPPOSED TO DO THAT? CARRY HIM?
WHY ARE WE STOPPING HERE, UNCA SCROOGE?
WE NEED TO BUY PROVISIONS AND EQUIPMENT TO OUTFIT AN EXPEDITION INTO THE JUNGLE! YOU KIDS CAN TAKE CARE OF THAT...
Z.
CRREEAAK!
UH-OH!
...WHILE I CALL ON THE LOCAL MAHARAJAH AND SEE IF HE CAN HELP ME RECRUIT SOME GOOD MEN!
SPLASH

SCROOGE IS SOON GRANTED AN AUDIENCE WITH THE MAHARAJAH...
YES, MR. McDUCK, I RECENTLY DEPOSED MY SOFT-HEARTED UNCLE BECAUSE I SAW HE WAS IGNORING MANY PROFITABLE OPPORTUNITIES FOR THIS POSITION! MY FIRST ACT WAS TO SELL OFF THAT USELESS JUNGLE!
I KNOW! I BOUGHT IT!
WHICH IS WHY I NEED TO RECRUIT SOME OF YOUR SUBJECTS TO HELP ME SEARCH FOR NATURAL RESOURCES!
ALAS... I AM SO SORRY TO FORBID THEM TO DO THAT!
WHAT?
YOU SEE, MR. McDUCK, MY BELOVED PEOPLE ARE MY NATURAL RESOURCE! I MUST KEEP THEM POOR!
GENEROUS COUNTRIES SEND MILLIONS IN FOREIGN AID TO MY POOR SUBJECTS! SADLY, I MUST SPEND IT ALL MYSELF... ON... ADMINISTRATIVE EXPENSES!
I SEE! IF THEY LOSE THEIR POVERTY YOU LOSE YOUR INCOME!
WELL, THE CABOOSE ON YOUR GRAVY TRAIN IS IN SIGHT! SCROOGE McDUCK FINDS BUSINESSES TO BUILD ANYWHERE HE LOOKS, EVEN IF HE HAS TO GO ON SAFARI ALONE!
UNCA SCROOGE!
COME QUICK! WE FOUND SOMETHING REALLY INTERESTING IN THE RIVERBED!
OH, SO?
LET'S HAVE A LOOK!
CURSE THIS McDUCK! I'VE HEARD OF HIM! HE IS SURE TO DISCOVER SOMETHING TO ENRICH HIMSELF AND MY PEOPLE... IF HE HASN'T ALREADY FOUND IT!

UNCA DONALD FOUND AN ANCIENT STONE COLUMN DEEP IN THE RIVER MUD!
HOW TYPICAL OF DONALD! PLAYING IN THE MUD ON MY TIME!
WE FIGURE THE COLUMN MUST HAVE ORIGINALLY STOOD UP THERE, ON THE KNOLL ABOVE THAT BUBBLING SPRING!
WHERE IS IT NOW?
UP HERE! WE HAD CHOWDIRHEAD ROLL IT ASHORE!
WHAT ARE THESE SILLY-LOOKING MARKS IN THE MUD?
Z
OH, UNCA DONALD SORTA SNAGGED HIS TIE ON IT— THAT'S HOW HE FOUND IT!
WELL, WHAT'S SO SPECIAL ABOUT THIS COLUMN?
JUST THAT IT'S NOT INDIAN! IT'S GREEK! MACEDONIAN GREEK FROM THE FOURTH CENTURY, B.C.!
DONALD! ARE YOU ALL RIGHT?
OH, YES, UNCLE SCROOGE! THANKS FOR ASKING!
WHAT'S IT DOING HERE?
IT'S A PROPERTY MARKER! IT SHOWS THE EASTERNMOST BOUNDARY OF LAND CLAIMED BY A CERTAIN MACEDONIAN GENERAL...
...NAMED ALEXANDER!
THE GREAT?
THE GREATEST! HISTORY RECORDS THAT ALEXANDER'S ELEVEN-YEAR MARCH OF CONQUEST TOOK HIM ACROSS EGYPT, PERSIA, BABYLONIA, AND THROUGH THE KHYBER PASS...
?
...INTO INDIA, WHICH HE REACHED IN 326 B.C.! HERE, SOMETHING SO TERRIFIED HIS TROOPS, THEY REFUSED TO GO ANY FARTHER!
THESE INSCRIPTIONS EXPLAIN THAT!

IT SAYS ALEXANDER LED HIS ARMY FROM THIS VALLEY UP THE SARASVATI RIVER TO PILLAGE SHAMBALA, THE RICHEST CITY IN ALL OF ANCIENT INDIA!
THE SARASVATI IS THE SACRED LOST RIVER OF HINDU LEGENDS!
SINCE THEY STARTED FROM HERE, WE BET THE SARASVATI ONCE FLOWED THROUGH THOSE HILLS, POINTING THE WAY TO THE CITY THAT HALTED ALEXANDER!
Z.
AND A TREASURE THAT ELUDED EVEN HIM!
MY, OH MY!
THERE'S NO GUARANTEE OF TREASURE, UNCA SCROOGE!
JUST FINDING A LOST CITY WOULD MEAN A TOURIST INDUSTRY! SOUVENIRS! SNACK STANDS! T-SHIRTS! ROAD CONTRACTS!
LET'S GO!
BUT WE HAVEN'T EVEN BOUGHT A HOWDAH SADDLE FOR CHOWDIRHEAD YET!
WHY WASTE MONEY WHEN WE HAVE THIS?
PREPARE MY FASTEST ELEPHANT! I LEAVE IMMEDIATELY ON A... A... NATURE STUDY!
I SHALL SUMMON THE ROYAL PORTERS, YOUR HIGHNESS!
FLOSS
NO!!! I WANT SOLITUDE!
MY SUBJECTS MUSTN'T SEE HOW I AM PLANNING TO KEEP THEM POOR AND OPPRESSED!
SOON, OUR HEROES ARE DEEP IN THE JUNGLE OF THE UPPER PUNJAB, SEARCHING FOR THE SACRED LOST RIVER OF THE ANCIENTS...
BOYS, WE'RE NOW BEYOND THE MOST REMOTE OUTPOST OF CIVILIZATION!
I'M SURPRISED THIS ELEPHANT GOT PAST THE MOST REMOTE COLA MACHINE OF CIVILIZATION!

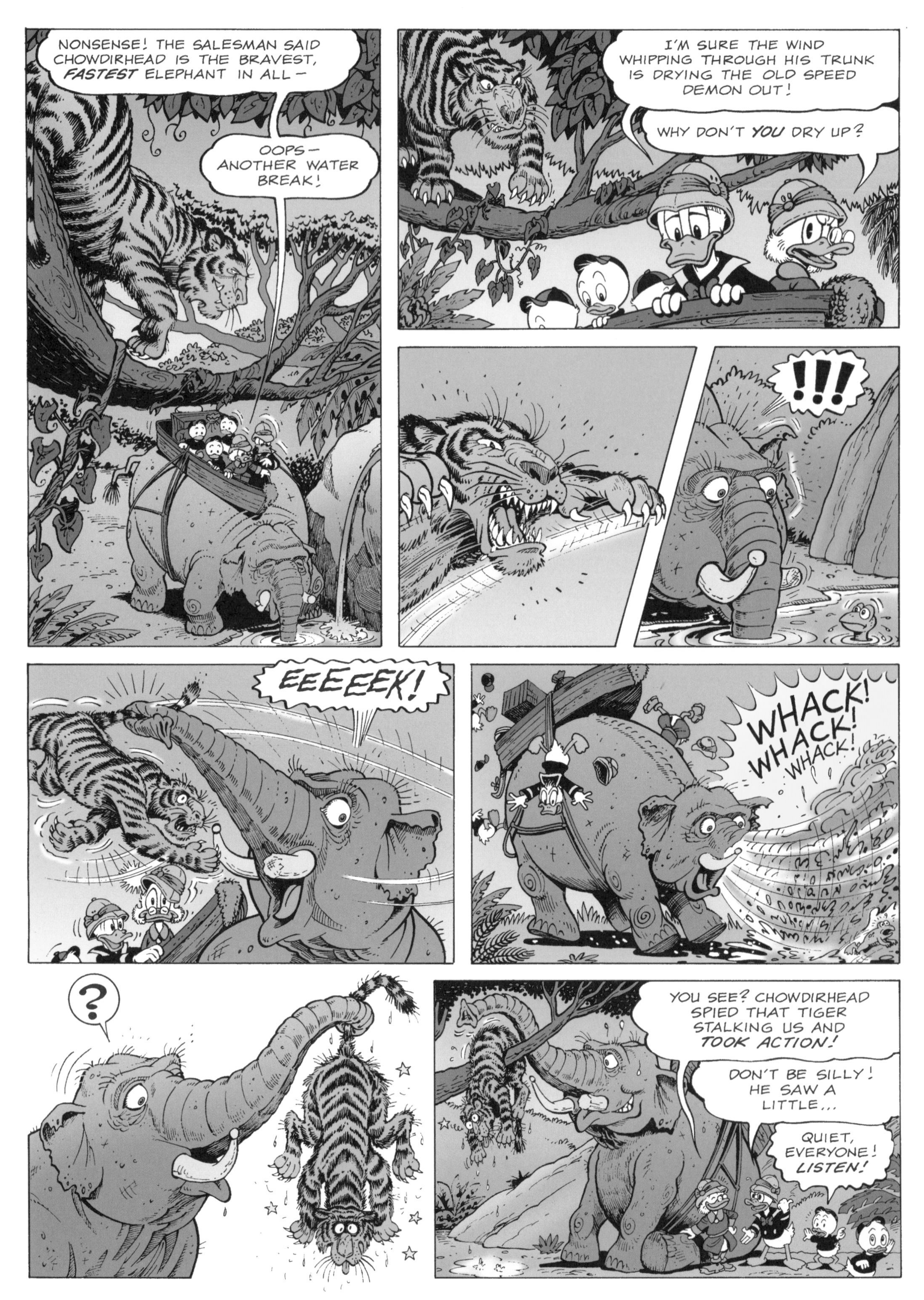
NONSENSE! THE SALESMAN SAID CHOWDIRHEAD IS THE BRAVEST, FASTEST ELEPHANT IN ALL—
OOPS— ANOTHER WATER BREAK!
I'M SURE THE WIND WHIPPING THROUGH HIS TRUNK IS DRYING THE OLD SPEED DEMON OUT!
WHY DON'T YOU DRY UP?
!!!
EEEEEEK!
WHACK! WHACK! WHACK!
?
YOU SEE? CHOWDIRHEAD SPIED THAT TIGER STALKING US AND TOOK ACTION!
DON'T BE SILLY! HE SAW A LITTLE...
QUIET, EVERYONE! LISTEN!

RUNNING WATER!
THE LOST SARASVATI RIVER RUNS UNDERGROUND!
HM! THAT'S A DARN GOOD WAY TO LOSE A RIVER, ALL RIGHT!
BUT IT MEANS WE'RE ON THE RIGHT TRACK!
LET'S KEEP MOVING!
HI YO, CHOW-DIRHEAD! AWAY!
?
SEVERAL DAYS LATER, THE DUCKS DECIDE TO CLIMB TO GET AN OVERVIEW OF THE MYSTERIOUS REALM WHERE HISTORY'S MIGHTIEST CONQUERER ONCE FEARED TO TREAD... OR WAS SORRY HE HAD!
ARE YOU TELLING ME THIS ELEPHANT ISN'T BRAVE TO BE DARING THESE HEIGHTS?
...I'M TELLING YOU THIS ELEPHANT IS SLEEPWALKING!
Z!
WHAT? I COULDN'T HEAR YOU! SOMEBODY IS SNORING! WHO — UH-OH!
Z!

Z.
BWOINGG!
WHEW!
Z.
PLOP!
SAY – I THINK I SEE EVIDENCE OF ANCIENT DWELLINGS!
GOOD BOY, CHOWDIRHEAD! SPOTTED THIS FROM WAY UP ON THAT LEDGE, EH? WHAT EYES!
Z.
WE MUST BE NEAR THE LOST CITY!
GOOD! I'M WALKING! IT'S SAFER DOWN WITH THE COBRAS THAN UP ON THAT DOZING DUMBO!
!
WAK!
CRUNCH!
GOOD JOB, UNCA DONALD! YOU FOUND AN ANCIENT DRAIN TUNNEL!
YES, I KNEW YOU'D LIKE IT!
OUT, PLEASE!
ANCIENT INDIAN CITIES HAD VERY SOPHISTICATED SEWERS AND STORM DRAINS.
SEWERS?
OUT! OUT!
OUTOUTOUTOUTOUT!
YOU MAKE THESE ANCIENT HINDUS SOUND PRETTY SHARP!
YOU BET! THEY DETERMINED THE EARTH IS ROUND EVEN BEFORE THE ALEXANDRIAN GREEKS!
!
THEY ALSO INVENTED THE NUMBER SYSTEM THAT NEARLY THE WHOLE WORLD USES NOW! WE SPEAK OF "ARABIC NUMERALS," BUT THE ARABS GOT THEM FROM THE HINDUS!
INDIAN MATHEMATICIANS EVEN INVENTED THE CONCEPT OF ZERO!
YOUR UNCLE DONALD WOULD APPRECIATE THAT! THE CONCEPT OF ZERO IS HIS LIFELONG CAREER GOAL!
NOW, JUST A DARN—
LOOK!

THAT MUST BE THE GATEWAY TO THE CITY OF SHAMBALA!
HEE HEE HEE! I LOVE IT WHEN MY PALMS ITCH!
I KNOW YOU YEARN FOR ACTION, CHOWDIRHEAD, BUT THIS IS AS FAR AS YOU CAN GO!
Z.
SH! YOU'LL WAKE HIM!
THERE'S ENOUGH WATER IN THE DRAIN TUNNEL TO LAST HIM TILL WE GET BACK!
THE LOST CITY SHOULD BE AT THE TOP OF THIS GRAND STAIRWAY!
WHAT A SIGHT THAT WILL BE! THE TOWN TOO TOUGH FOR EVEN ALEXANDER THE GREAT TO TAME!
HEY! WHAT'S THE GAG?
IT'S GONE? NOTHING AT ALL LEFT BUT AN EMPTY FIELD?
SHAMBALA MUST HAVE FALLEN INTO TOTAL RUIN!
IMPOSSIBLE! THE INDIANS HEWED THEIR MAIN STRUCTURES OUT OF SOLID ROCK!
WAIT! THIS ISN'T A FIELD OF SHRUBS! THE STAIRS GO DOWN NOW!
HOW'S THAT, UNCA SCROOGE?
I'D SAY IT'S A LITTLE MORE LIKE IT!

SHAMBALA! HACKED RIGHT INTO THE WALLS OF THIS HUGE ROCK BASIN!
AND THE RAIN FOREST HAS TAKEN ROOT! NO WONDER THIS PLACE HAS NEVER BEEN SPOTTED!
LET'S GET A MOVE ON! WE HAVE AN ENTIRE LOST CITY TO EXPLORE!
MEANWHILE, THE MAHARAJAH IS STILL FOLLOWING OUR HEROES...
THOSE CURSED DUCKS WENT ON FOOT FROM HERE! I'D BEST DO LIKEWISE!
?
LOOKS LIKE McDUCK FOUND HIS LOST CITY! I MAY BE OUT OF BUSINESS UNLESS I CAN THROW A MONKEY IN HIS PALM TREE!
AH — THERE THEY ARE!
WHO'S THIS GUY WITH THE FOUR FACES?
IT'S THE FIRST GOD OF THE HINDU TRINITY— BRAHMA, THE CREATOR!
DON'T TELL ME HE CREATED THE SWIMMING POOL?!
NO, THAT MUST BE ONE OF THE HUGE PUBLIC BATHS THE HINDUS ENJOYED!

GET A LOAD OF THE CHUBBY ELEPHANT-BOY!
THAT'S GANESHA, THE HINDU GOD OF SUCCESS!
THAT'S RIGHT, UNCA SCROOGE! HOW DID YOU KNOW THAT?
LADDIEBUCK, SUCCESS IS SOMETHING I KNOW ABOUT! SEE?
HMPH! A GANESHA KEY RING!
BRAHMA'S FOUR FACES LOOK AT THE "FOUR GOALS OF LIFE"! TOWARDS THE BATHS IS "KAMA," THE GOAL OF PLEASURE!
THAT WAY IS "DHARMA," OR WORK! PROBABLY SHOPS!
THEN COMES "MOKSHA," THE LOSS OF ALL DESIRES!
EASY FOR UNCLE SCROOGE! HE'S ONLY GOT ONE!
LAST IS "ARTHA," THE GOAL OF WEALTH!
NOW YOU'RE TALKIN'! C'MON!
WOW! THAT'S SOME GUARD AT THE ENTRANCE!
UM... THAT'S THE SECOND GOD OF THE TRINITY- VISHNU, THE PROTECTOR!
THAT FIGURES!
THAT LOOKS LIKE A CONTROL PANEL! WONDER WHAT THE BUTTONS DO?
WELL, THE SYMBOLS ARE THE TEN AVATARS, THE FORMS IN WHICH VISHNU APPEARED TO HELP THE WORTHY!
MAYBE THE BUTTONS ACTIVATE A HYDRAULIC SYSTEM POWERED BY THE UNDERGROUND RIVER!
HYDRAULIC, EH? THAT MEANS THERE MIGHT BE BOOBY TRAPS THAT ARE STILL WORKING!

YOU KIDS STAY HERE WITH A WALKIE-TALKIE AND MAN THE "CONTROL PANEL"— JUST IN CASE! DONALD AND I WILL ENTER THAT VAULT!
!

THE ANCIENT INDIANS DIDN'T FIGURE ON AN INVADER WITH A WALKIE-TALKIE! WE CAN TELL THE KIDS WHEN WE NEED THE HELP OF THOSE "AVATARS"!

HOW ABOUT IF I STAY AND HELP THOSE POOR LI'L KIDS WITH THOSE BIG, NASTY BUTTONS?
THEIR WOODCHUCK MANUAL IS ALL THE HELP THEY NEED! COME ALONG IF YOU WANT YOUR THIRTY CENTS AN HOUR!
UNCA SCROOGE - CAN YOU HEAR US?
YES! WE'VE JUST ENTERED THE FIRST CHAMBER AT THE END OF THE MAIN HALL!
WHAT'S THIS? DID THE INDIANS WEAR SUITS OF ARMOR?
IT'S GREEK! I THINK THIS IS ALL THAT'S LEFT OF SOME OF ALEXANDER'S HOPLITES!
WHAT WAS THAT?
SNARL!
YIKES! TIGERS!
WAIT! THEY'RE BEHIND BARS! THAT MUST BE THE BACK OF A CAVE THAT'S BEEN A TIGER DEN FOR THOUSANDS OF YEARS!
RAAWWRR!!

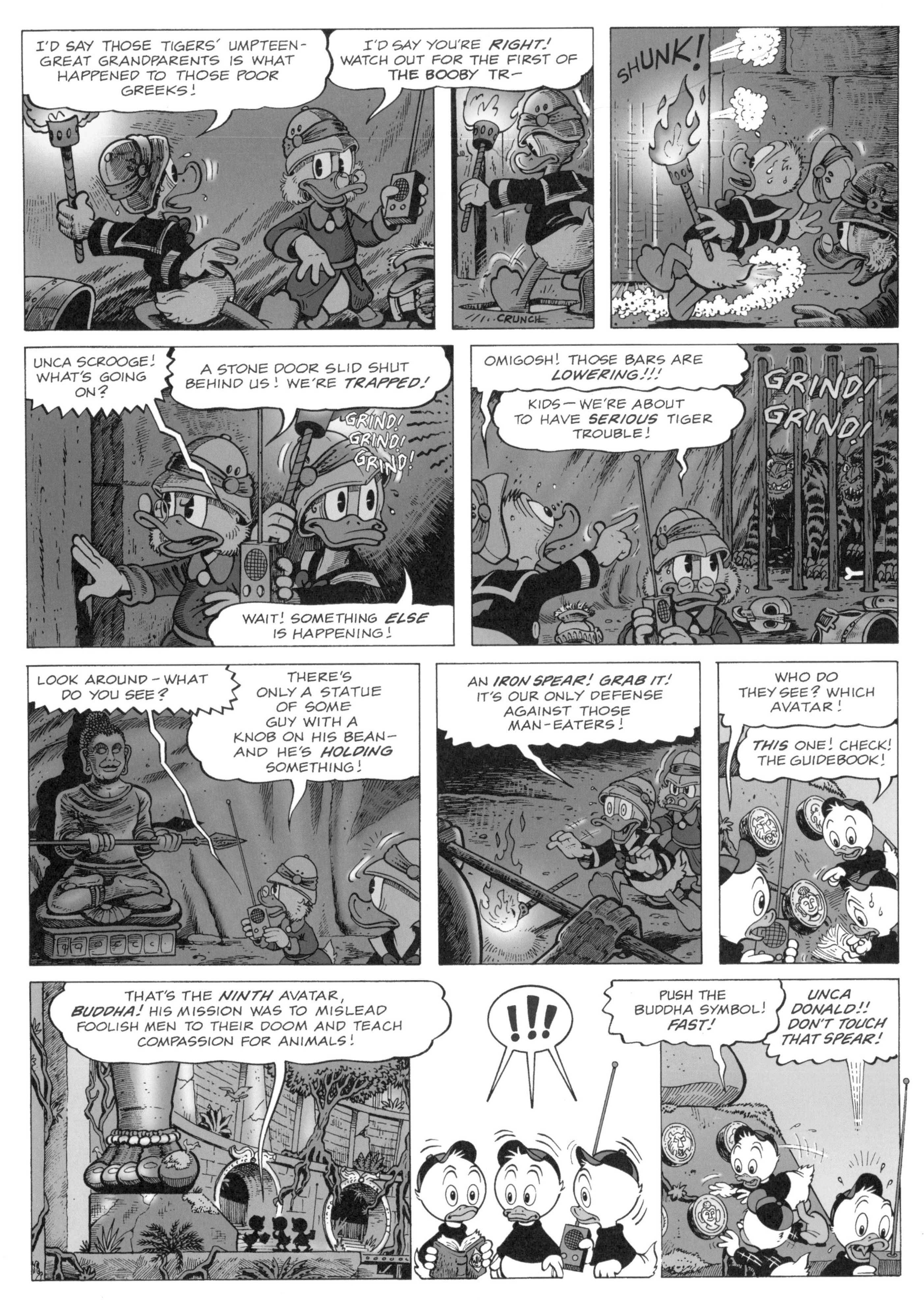

I'D SAY THOSE TIGERS' UMPTEEN-GREAT GRANDPARENTS IS WHAT HAPPENED TO THOSE POOR GREEKS!
I'D SAY YOU'RE RIGHT! WATCH OUT FOR THE FIRST OF THE BOOBY TR—
CRUNCH
SHUNK!
UNCA SCROOGE! WHAT'S GOING ON?
A STONE DOOR SLID SHUT BEHIND US! WE'RE TRAPPED!
GRIND! GRIND! GRIND!
WAIT! SOMETHING ELSE IS HAPPENING!
OMIGOSH! THOSE BARS ARE LOWERING!!!
KIDS—WE'RE ABOUT TO HAVE SERIOUS TIGER TROUBLE!
GRIND! GRIND!
LOOK AROUND - WHAT DO YOU SEE?
THERE'S ONLY A STATUE OF SOME GUY WITH A KNOB ON HIS BEAN—AND HE'S HOLDING SOMETHING!
AN IRON SPEAR! GRAB IT! IT'S OUR ONLY DEFENSE AGAINST THOSE MAN-EATERS!
WHO DO THEY SEE? WHICH AVATAR!
THIS ONE! CHECK! THE GUIDEBOOK!
THAT'S THE NINTH AVATAR, BUDDHA! HIS MISSION WAS TO MISLEAD FOOLISH MEN TO THEIR DOOM AND TEACH COMPASSION FOR ANIMALS!
!!!
PUSH THE BUDDHA SYMBOL! FAST!
UNCA DONALD!! DON'T TOUCH THAT SPEAR!

ARE THEY NUTS? THOSE TIGERS WILL EAT US ALIVE!
DO WHAT THEY SAY!
GRIND!
WHAT'S HAPPENING?
THE STATUE'S ARMS ARE RECEDING INTO ITS BODY!
AND IN ONE MORE MINUTE, WE'RE GOING TO BE RECEDING INTO THOSE TIGERS!
GRIND! GRIND! GRIND!
GRIND! GRIND!
CHUNK!
THE SPEAR KEPT THE ARMS FROM BEING PULLED ALL THE WAY IN!
GRIND! GRIND!
LOOK! THE IRON BARS ARE RAISING BACK UP TO PROTECT US FROM THE TIGERS!
AND THE SPEAR POINT WAS FAKE! IF I'D REMOVED THE SPEAR, WE'D BE CAT FOOD BY NOW!
ANOTHER DOOR IS OPENING! LET'S GO!
GRIND! GRIND! GRIND!
WE'VE ENTERED ANOTHER ROOM!
IS THERE A STATUE OR ANYTHING?
YES—THERE'S A DANDY ONE! A REAL GLAMOUR-BOY!
LOOK—MORE GREEK ARMOR!
AND IT'S GULP! PIERCED FULL OF HOLES!
I'M GETTIN' OUTTA HERE!
DON'T MOVE! YOU MIGHT—
SHUNK
CRUNCH!
GRIND! GRIND!
OH, NO! LOOK!
MOAN! I HOPE IT ISN'T SPIKES DESCENDING FROM THE CEILING!

KIDS! HELP! SPIKES ARE DESCENDING FROM THE CEILING!
GRIND! GRIND! GRIND!
I KNEW IT -SOB!- I JUST KNEW IT!
"GLAMOUR BOY" MUST BE THE EIGHTH AVATAR! KRISHNA! HE WAS SO ADORABLE THAT EVEN WISE MEN SOUGHT TO TOUCH HIM!
HERE'S HIS SYMBOL!
CRUNCH
UNCA SCROOGE! TOUCH THE STATUE!
NO CHANCE! THE SPIKES ARE LONGEST THERE!
GRIND! GRIND!
DO WHAT THEY SAY!
THERE MUST BE A HYDRAULIC LEVER HERE SOMEWHERE!
GRIND! GRIND!
CLICK
HIYA, PAL...
GRIND! GRIND! GRIND!
FWUMP
UNCA SCROOGE! ARE YOU GUYS OKAY?
YES! WE FELL INTO A LARGE DEAD-END CHAMBER! THERE ARE CARVINGS OF SOME SORT OF WARRIORS ON TWO OPPOSING WALLS!
WHAT'S THAT STUFF? IT'S TOO SMALL TO BE MORE ARMOR LEFT BY ALEXANDER'S UNFORTUNATE TROOPS!
THAT'S A RELIEF! I'LL LOOK!
ARMOR... MASHED FLAT...
CALL FOR HELP! NOW!
ER... GOOD IDEA!
TOO LATE!
KIDS! THE WALLS ARE CLOSING IN! WHAT DO WE DO?
GRIND! GRIND! GRIND!

THOSE CARVINGS ARE THE SIXTH AND SEVENTH AVATARS, RAMA AND PARASURAMA - WARRIORS SENT TO SAVE MEN FROM OPPRESSION!
CRUNCH
CRUNCH
PUSH BOTH SYMBOLS!
STAND BETWEEN THE CARVINGS!
I HOPE YOU BOYS ARE RIGHT! WE'RE ABOUT TO BE OPPRESSED SOMETHIN' AWFUL!
GRIND! GRIND!
GRIND! GRIND!
WAK!
FWUMP
WE KEEP FALLING DEEPER AND DEEPER INTO THE CITY! HOW WILL WE EVER GET OUT?
THUD!
JUST KEEP YOUR GRIP ON THAT TORCH!
WHERE ARE YOU NOW, UNCA SCROOGE?
ANOTHER ROOM...WITH A CUTE LITTLE STATUE! DID THEY HAVE GARDEN GNOMES IN ANCIENT INDIA?
UH-OH... MORE ARMOR! SHUDDER!
AH! THIS ARMOR IS UNDAMAGED! MAYBE THIS HOPLITE JUST GOT HOT AND TOOK IT OFF!
DON'T BET ON IT...
EEP!
HISSSS!
HALP! SNAKES! COBRAS! POURING OUT OF EVERY NOOK AND CRANNY!
HURRY! WHO'S THE SHORT AVATAR?
THE FIFTH-VAMANA, THE DWARF! HE SAVED MANKIND BY GROWING INTO A GIANT!
UNCA SCROOGE! RUN TO THAT "GARDEN GNOME"!
WE'RE WAY AHEAD OF YOU! PUSH THE DANG BUTTON!
CRUNCH
THE STATUE IS RISING!
ARE WE GONNA BE SMUSHED AGAINST THE CEILING?
GRIND! GRIND!
GRIND! GRIND!
NO! HERE'S A DOORWAY! C'MON!
GRIND! GRIND! GRIND!

WE'RE IN ANOTHER LARGE ROOM AND THERE'S AN OPEN DOOR ON THE OTHER SIDE! IT LOOKS TOO EASY!
IT'S GETTING HARDER TO PICK UP THEIR SIGNAL THE DEEPER THEY GO!
CRACKLE ANOTHER STATUE... SQUAWK MAN CRACK LION!
RIGHT! THE FOURTH AVATAR, NARASIMHA, THE MAN-LION!
THERE'S NO ARMOR— PIERCED, SQUASHED, SPINDLED OR MUTILATED! MAYBE WE'RE PAST THE BOOBY TRAPS!
OR NONE OF ALEXANDER'S MEN MADE IT THIS FAR! JUST BE CAREFUL...
YOW! PITFALL!
FWOOP!
I HAVE YOU! JUST DON'T DROP THE TORCH!
I...UH... FOUND THE ARMOR!
THE MAN-LION SAVED MANKIND FROM A DEMON WHO WAS INVINCIBLE IN BOTH DAY AND NIGHT!...
...BY SLAYING THE DEMON AT SUNSET!
HERE'S HOPING THAT MEANS SOMETHING!
CRUNCH
HOW ON EARTH CAN WE MANAGE TO GET ACROSS THIS ROOM?
GRIND!
GRIND!
GRIND!
LOOK— SOMETHING IS OPENING BEHIND THE LION-GUY!
IT'S A STONE BASIN WITH SOMETHING IN IT, BUT I CAN'T QUITE SEE—
FOOM

HM... OIL?
THAT'S MY GUESS!
≈CRACKLE≈ GO ≈SQUAWK≈ EDGE ≈CRACK≈ LIGHT ≈SQUEE≈ DARK...
DO WHICH?
LOOK AT THE SHADOW CAST BY THE STATUE! COULD IT SHOW THE SAFE PATH ACROSS THE ROOM?
ONLY ONE WAY TO FIND OUT...
...FOLLOW THE EDGE OF THE SHADOW! BUT HURRY!
THAT OIL WON'T BURN LONG!
ANOTHER DEAD END... AND ANOTHER STATUE...
I HOPE THE KIDS CAN STILL HEAR ME!
THAT'S ONE UGLY KISSER!
KIDS—THERE'S A STATUE HERE OF A HORNED FISH!
≈SQAWK≈ ≈SQUACK≈
SOUNDED LIKE HE SAID "FISH"!
LET'S SEE...
CHECK! MATSYA, THE FISH—HE WAS ONE OF THE FIRST THREE AVATARS WHO SAVED ALL OF MANKIND FROM EXTINCTION BY A GREAT FLOOD!
MATSYA WARNED OF THE COMING DANGER!
JEEPERS! THAT SOUNDS KINDA OMINOUS!
PUSH THE SYMBOL AND ≈GULP≈ HOPE!

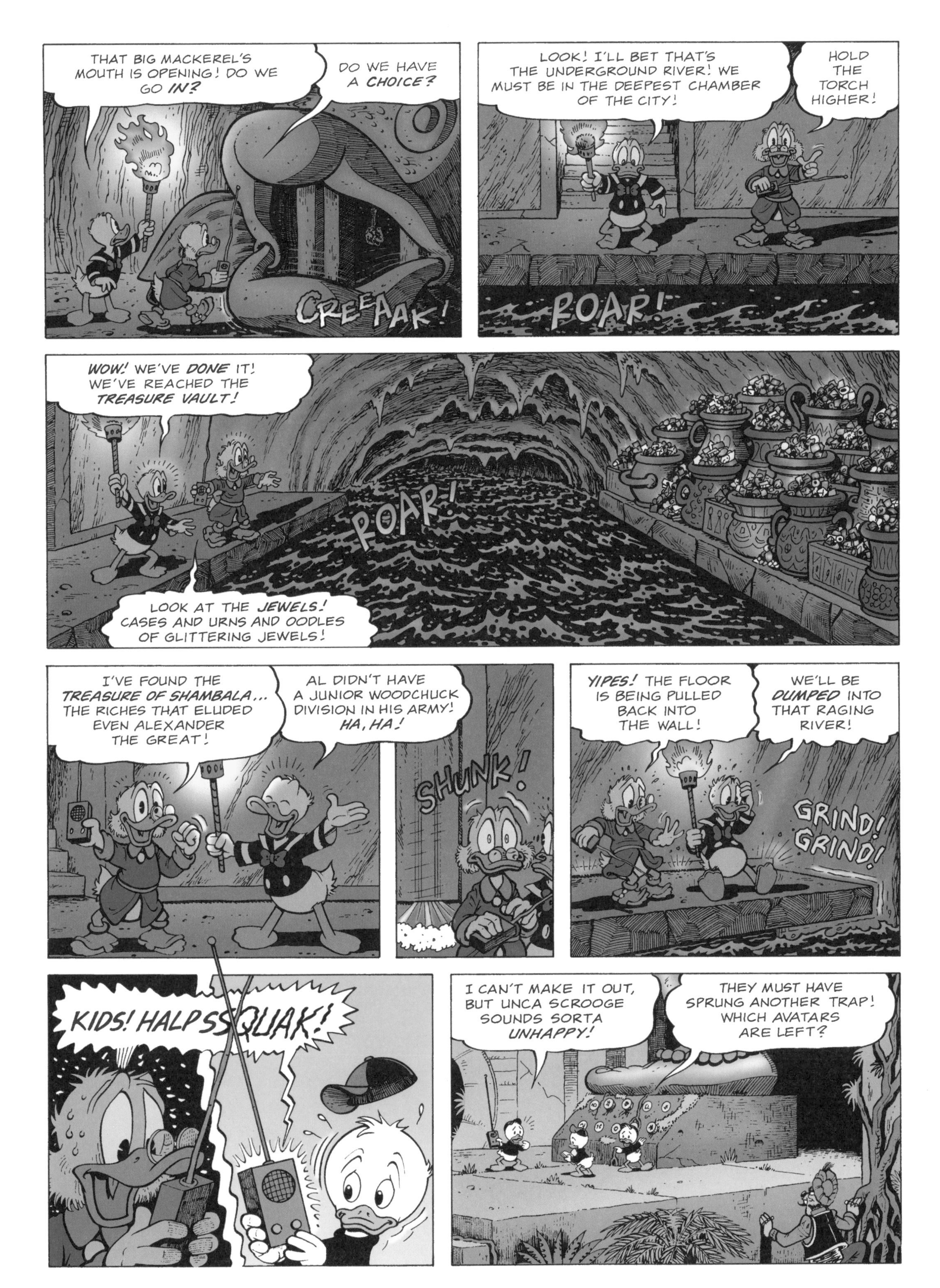
THAT BIG MACKEREL'S MOUTH IS OPENING! DO WE GO IN?
DO WE HAVE A CHOICE?
CREEAAK!
LOOK! I'LL BET THAT'S THE UNDERGROUND RIVER! WE MUST BE IN THE DEEPEST CHAMBER OF THE CITY!
HOLD THE TORCH HIGHER!
ROAR!
WOW! WE'VE DONE IT! WE'VE REACHED THE TREASURE VAULT!
ROAR!
LOOK AT THE JEWELS! CASES AND URNS AND OODLES OF GLITTERING JEWELS!
I'VE FOUND THE TREASURE OF SHAMBALA... THE RICHES THAT ELUDED EVEN ALEXANDER THE GREAT!
AL DIDN'T HAVE A JUNIOR WOODCHUCK DIVISION IN HIS ARMY! HA, HA!
SHUNK!
YIPES! THE FLOOR IS BEING PULLED BACK INTO THE WALL!
WE'LL BE DUMPED INTO THAT RAGING RIVER!
GRIND! GRIND!
KIDS! HALPSSQUAK!
I CAN'T MAKE IT OUT, BUT UNCA SCROOGE SOUNDS SORTA UNHAPPY!
THEY MUST HAVE SPRUNG ANOTHER TRAP! WHICH AVATARS ARE LEFT?

VARAHA THE BOAR RESTORED DRY LAND TO SAVE MANKIND FROM THE FLOOD!
SOUNDS GOOD! HIT IT!
CRUNCH
THEY CAN'T HEAR ME!
IF WE FALL INTO THAT TORRENT WE'LL BE SWEPT INTO THAT AIRLESS CAVE! WE'RE GONERS!
GRIND! GRIND! GRIND!
COURAGE, NEPHEW! I'VE GOTTEN OUT OF WORSE SPOTS THAN THIS... PROBABLY...
AIEEE!
GRIND! GRIND! GRIND!
SPLASH!
KONK!
HEY— THERE'S SOMETHING RISING UP OUT OF THE RIVER!
I TOLD YOU NOT TO WORRY! THE KIDS ARE STILL AT THE CONTROLS, AFTER ALL!
EW! A BIG PIG! THESE AVATARS ARE GETTIN' DARN UGLY!
WAIT A SECOND... THERE'S SOMETHING HAPPENING ON THE OTHER SIDE!
GREAT SCOTT! THE FLOOR HOLDING THE TREASURE IS ALSO BEING PULLED INTO THE WALL! ALL THOSE JEWELS WILL BE DUMPED INTO THE RIVER!
GRIND! GRIND!
GRIND! GRIND!
HEY! STOP!
SAVE WHAT YOU CAN! EVERY JEWEL FOR HIMSELF!
WHAT'S LEFT? WE'RE ALMOST FRESH OUT OF AVATARS!
KURMA THE TORTOISE! HE SAVED THE WORLD'S TREASURES FROM THE GREAT FLOOD!

THAT MEANS UNCA SCROOGE MUST BE IN THE TREASURE CHAMBER NOW!
PUSH THE KURMA SYMBOL AND OUR JOB IS DONE!
RIGHTO!
GLOM!
YIKES!
WHO ARE YOU?
I, LITTLE MONKEY, AM THE MAHARAJAH OF OLLIEYANSTAN!
THE DISCOVERY OF THIS LOST CITY WILL MEAN THE END OF MY LIFE OF LUXURY FROM FOREIGN AID,,, IF YOUR TYCOON UNCLE RETURNS TO TELL THE TALE!
WUMP!
WE'LL SEE HOW WELL HE FARES WITHOUT THE HELP OF THESE "AVATARS" OF MY FOOLISH ANCESTORS!
CHUCKLE!
MEANWHILE...
FORGET IT, UNCLE SCROOGE! SAVE YOURSELF BEFORE IT'S TOO LATE!
HERE! CATCH THIS RUBY! AND THIS EMERALD! AND THIS SAPPHIRE! AND —
WUH-OH!
GLOM!
SOB! THERE IT GOES! THE TREASURE OF ANCIENT INDIA! IT WAS SAFE IN THIS VAULT FOR TWENTY-FIVE CENTURIES, BUT WE SHOW UP AND IT'S GONE IN FIVE MINUTES! LOST FOREVER!
CHUNK!
plink
ROAR!
SPLASH

...LOST FOREVER! BECAUSE OF YOU OUR UNCLES MAY BE LOST FOREVER!
HMM... PERHAPS THERE IS STILL SOME TREASURE IN THIS MIGHTY CITY!
I MIGHT AS WELL BE RETURNING TO OLLIEYANSTAN WITH SOMETHING! AND YOU SEEM TO HAVE LEFT ONE OTHER BUTTON UNPUSHED!
YES! ONE CAN NEVER HAVE TOO MUCH TREASURE!
CRUNK
WHAT DID HE PUSH?
IT WAS THE TENTH AVATAR! THE HORSE-HEAD SYMBOL! QUICK! WHAT IS IT?
KALKIN – THE FINAL AVATAR... WHO HAS YET TO COME TO EARTH!
AHA! LISTEN! SOMETHING HAPPENS!
GRIND
KALKIN WILL PUNISH MANKIND FOR THE FOLLY OF GREED! HE'LL DESTROY THE EARTH WITH A SECOND GREAT FLOOD!
!
GRIND
MAYBE I SHOULD HAVE PAID MORE ATTENTION IN SCHOOL...
LOOK!
GRIND
GRIND
GRIND
GRIND
THOSE ENORMOUS STATUES ARE MOVING! WHO ARE THEY?
WHOA... THE NEWS GETS WORSE!

THEY'RE THE LAST OF THE HINDU TRINITY— SHIVA THE DESTROYER AND HIS WIFE, KALI THE KILLER!
CRUMBLE!
YOU KNOW, IT WOULD BE QUITE A DIFFICULT CHORE TO CARRY A TREASURE ALL THE WAY BACK TO OLLIEYANSTAN!
MAYBE I'LL PASS...
CURLY-TOED SHOES—DO YOUR STUFF!
CRASH!
GREAT BALLS OF FIRE! NOW WHAT?
CRASH!
WHY NOT AN EARTHQUAKE? WE'VE BEEN THROUGH EVERY OTHER MOVIE SERIAL CLICHÉ!
A...A HUGE STATUE CRASHED THROUGH INTO THE RIVER!
GRAB THAT TREE TRUNK OR WE'LL DROWN!
ROAR!
ROAR!
IS THIS HOW THOSE KIDS DECIDED TO GET US OUT OF HERE?
THEY DON'T MESS AROUND, BOY!

THAT DARN MAHARAJAH IS GETTING AWAY!
FORGET HIM! WE CAN'T LEAVE WITHOUT UNCA DONALD AND UNCA SCROOGE!
CRUMBLE!
CRUMBLE!
LOOK! IT'S THEM!
GURGLE
THEY'RE BEING WASHED UP BY THE UNDERGROUND RIVER!
YOU'RE SAFE!
WHAT THE BLUE BLAZES DID YOU KIDS DO, ANYWAY?
SPLASH
BONK!
WHEN THE JUNIOR WOODCHUCK ARCHAEOLOGICAL CLUB HEARS ABOUT THIS, YOU THREE WILL BE IN BIG TROUBLE!
NO TIME TO EXPLAIN IT ALL! WHAT CAN WE DO NOW?
CRUMBLE!
LET ME THINK! DON'T PANIC! DON'T PANIC!
WHY NOT? OUR LIVES ARE ABOUT TO GO DOWN THE DRAIN!
CRUMBLE!
NEPHEW – THAT'S IT! YOU'VE DONE IT AGAIN!
YEAH, I... UH... HUH?
CRUMBLE!
I HAVE AN IDEA! FOLLOW ME!
HURRY! THE WATER IS ON OUR HEELS!
CRUMBLE!
BUT... THIS IS THE WAY TO THE PUBLIC BATH!
YES – AND DIDN'T YOU KIDS BRAG ABOUT THE MUNICIPAL DRAINAGE SYSTEM OF THE ANCIENT INDIANS?
YES, BUT... DO WE HAVE TIME TO FIND IT?
CRUMBLE!
LOOK!

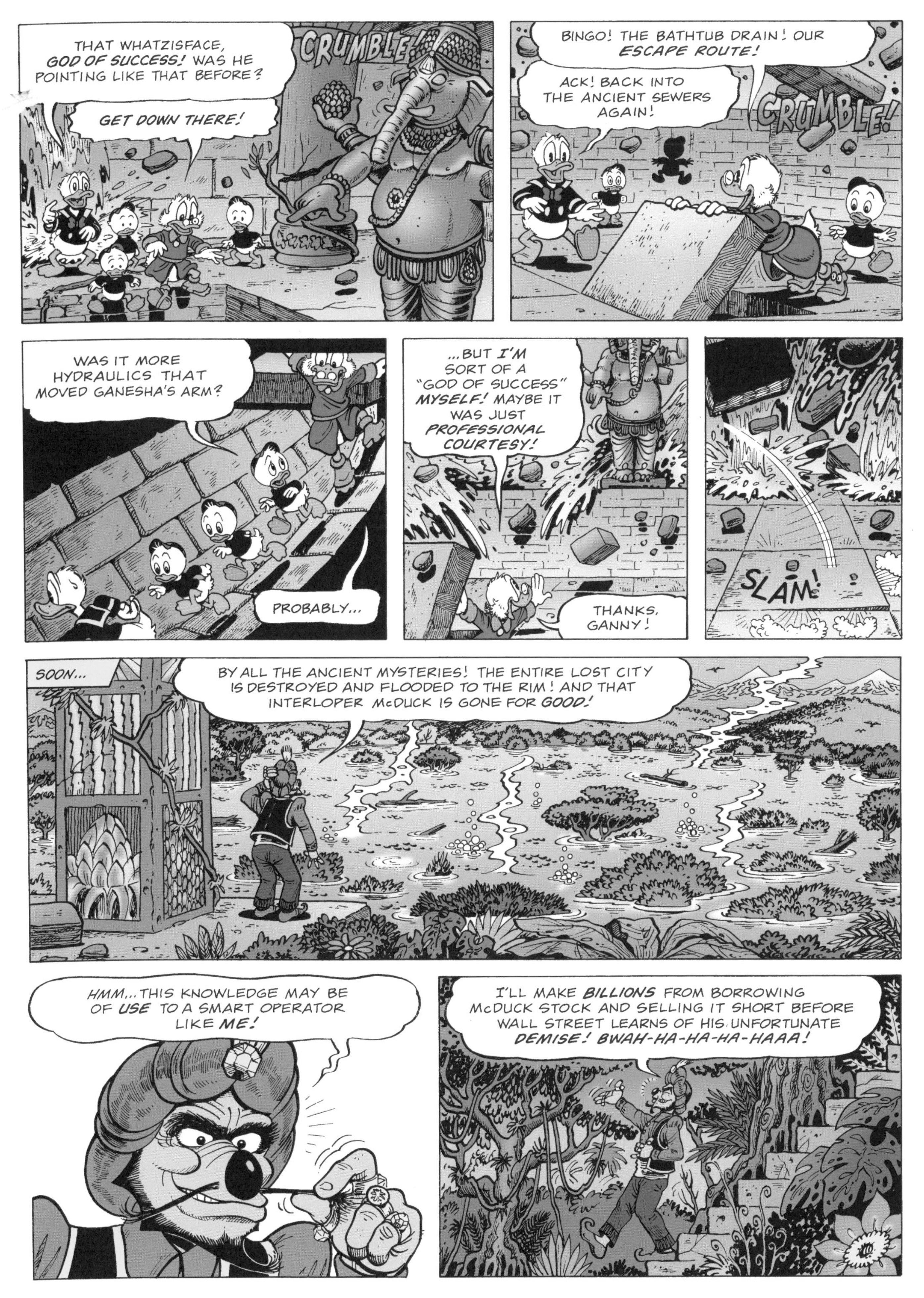
THAT WHATZISFACE, GOD OF SUCCESS! WAS HE POINTING LIKE THAT BEFORE?
CRUMBLE!
GET DOWN THERE!
BINGO! THE BATHTUB DRAIN! OUR ESCAPE ROUTE!
ACK! BACK INTO THE ANCIENT SEWERS AGAIN!
CRUMBLE!
WAS IT MORE HYDRAULICS THAT MOVED GANESHA'S ARM?
PROBABLY...
...BUT I'M SORT OF A "GOD OF SUCCESS" MYSELF! MAYBE IT WAS JUST PROFESSIONAL COURTESY!
THANKS, GANNY!
SLAM!
SOON...
BY ALL THE ANCIENT MYSTERIES! THE ENTIRE LOST CITY IS DESTROYED AND FLOODED TO THE RIM! AND THAT INTERLOPER McDUCK IS GONE FOR GOOD!
HMM... THIS KNOWLEDGE MAY BE OF USE TO A SMART OPERATOR LIKE ME!
I'LL MAKE BILLIONS FROM BORROWING McDUCK STOCK AND SELLING IT SHORT BEFORE WALL STREET LEARNS OF HIS UNFORTUNATE DEMISE! BWAH-HA-HA-HA-HAAA!

AS FOR THE FORTUNATELY NOT-QUITE-YET-LOST McDUCK AND COMPANY...
OUCH! MY NOGGIN! IT'S HARD TO RUN IN THIS LOW TUNNEL IN THE DARK!
BONK!
LUCKY THERE ARE NO WRONG TURNS TO MAKE!
WHUP! WATER! THIS IS AS FAR AS WE GO!
NO! SEE THE LIGHT! THAT MEAN THERE'S AN EXTERIOR OPENING A SHORT WAY AHEAD! WE CAN SWIM THAT FAR!
AND THE MAHARAJAH...
BACK TO OLLIEYANSTAN, RAVANA! I FEEL A TAX-COLLECTION COMING ON!
Z.
!!!
SPLISH
EEEK!!
UH-OH! DUCK!
WHACK! WHACK! WHACK! WHACK! WHACK!
?
THUD!
?
DON'T WORRY! IT WAS JUST OUR BRAVE ELEPHANT! HE SEEMS TO HAVE CALMED DOWN NOW!

IT'S THAT CROOKED MAHARAJAH! NO DOUBT HE FOLLOWED US TO SEE IF MY SEARCH WAS SUCCESSFUL, THE RAT!
SEE HERE, YOU'RE TRESPASSING–SAY... WHAT HAPPENED TO YOU?
...STRANGEST THING...I...I'M NOT REALLY QUITE SURE...
MAYBE A HIT-AND-RUN RHINO?
UNCA SCROOGE! HE'S THE GUY WHO... WHO...
HM? WHO WHAT?
ER...NEVER MIND! IT DOESN'T MATTER ANY MORE!
GULP!
SOMETIMES YOU DARN KIDS ARE MORE MYSTERIOUS THAN ALL INDIA!
?
SEVERAL DAYS LATER, SOME DEJECTED DUCKS AND A BATTERED BUT TRIUMPHANT MAHARAJAH MAKE THEIR WAY BACK TO OLLIEYANSTAN.
...OR MAYBE A...A BERSERK FRUIT BAT PLOWED INTO YOU!
SILENCE, DUCK!
WHAT'S ALL THE COMMOTION? LOOKS LIKE EVERYBODY'S MOVING OUT!
WHAT? IMPOSSIBLE!
WHAT'S GOING ON?
JEWELS, SAHIB! THOUSANDS OF GEMS OF EVERY TYPE!
THEY CAME SPEWING FROM THE MOUTH OF THE PUBLIC SPRING!
GASP! THE TREASURE OF SHAMBALA!
LET ME SEE!

TOO LATE, FORMER SIRE! NOT A ZIRCON LEFT! EVERYONE IN OLLIEYANSTAN NOW HAS ENOUGH WEALTH TO MOVE AWAY AND START UP A NEW LIFE!
PSST! HIS HIGHNESS NEEDS A NEW TAILOR!
WELL, GOOD FOR YOU! I'LL BE DOWNRIVER TO TALK TO ANY OF YOU WHO STILL NEED OR WANT JOBS!
YOU VERY MUCH BETCHA, SAHIB!
FUNNY HOW THIS WORKED OUT! THESE PEOPLE ARE SURELY THE DESCENDANTS OF THE ANCIENT INDIAN INHABITANTS OF THE LOST CITY!
YES!
MAYBE VISHNU WAS HOLDING THE TREASURE FOR THEM UNTIL THE RIGHT TIME!
MYTHS AND FABLES!
THERE GOES YOUR "NATURAL RESOURCE," MAHA!
SOB! WHAT WILL HAPPEN WHEN THE PAYMENTS COME DUE ON MY PALACE AND CARS AND CRICKET BATS AND TURBANS... AND... AND...
DON'T FRET! YOU'RE STILL LEFT WITH A LIMITLESS SUPPLY OF THE MOST IMPORTANT CREATION FROM THE ANCIENT HINDU CULTURE!
HAH? WHAZAT? HAH?
THE CONCEPT OF ZERO!
USE IT WISELY!
EEK!!
GR!

Walt Disney's
Uncle Scrooge
DOGGONNIT, UNCLE SCROOGE! IF YOU WANT ME TO CLEAN THESE COBWEBS OFF THE CEILING, CAN'T YOU GET ME A BETTER LADDER?
THAT LADDER WAS IN PERFECT CONDITION THE LAST TIME I USED IT TO CHANGE LIGHT FIXTURES!
I.B.M.
N.Y.S.E.
D.U.C.K.
COINS
SILVER FILINGS
GOLD DUST
DIRT
1954
BILL COLLECTORS BEWARE!
SC
%@#@
A MATTER OF SOME GRAVITY
HMPH! JUDGING BY THE "LIGHT FIXTURE" I FOUND STUCK TO IT, THAT WAS BACK IN YOUR KLONDIKE DAYS!
GRIPING! GRIPING! ALWAYS GRIPING!
WELL, HOW CAN I— WHOOPS!
CRACK!
CRASH!
RECEPTIONIST
BY THE WAY, MISS QUACKFASTER STEPPED OUT FOR A MOMENT, SO WHY DON'T YOU FILL IN FOR HER AS LONG AS YOU'RE RESTING?
...A PLEASURE...
RECEPTIONIST

COME IN...
KNOCK KNOCK
GREAT CIRCE! WHAT SECRETARIAL SCHOOL DID YOU GRADUATE FROM?
RECEPTIONIST
DON'T WORRY— I'M ONLY A TEMP!
CAN I HELP YOU?
RECEPTIONIST
JUST TELL MR. McDUCK I'M HERE!
CERTAINLY— GO RIGHT IN!
ECEPTIONIST
UNCLE SCROOGE... MAGICA DE SPELL TO SEE YOU...
CLIK
!!!
WAIT! YOU CAN'T—
BUON GIORNO, SCROOGE!
WHAT THE—?! IS THIS SOMEBODY'S IDEA OF A JOKE?
YOU MUST KNOW BY NOW THAT YOU CAN'T JUST WALTZ IN HERE AND HOPE TO SNATCH MY NUMBER ONE DIME!
NO DISGUISE... IN BROAD DAYLIGHT... YOU DON'T HAVE A CHANCE!
AH, BUT I HAVE A NEW SPELL IN MY BAG OF TRICKS! A NEW MAGIC WAND!
YIPES! LOOK OUT, UNCLE SCROOGE!
GRAVITATUS HORIZONTUS!
ZAP!
OOG! WHA... WHAT'D SHE DO TO US?
CHECK YOURSELF! DO WE STILL HAVE THE RIGHT NUMBER OF ARMS AND LEGS? DID WE GROW MONKEY TAILS OR ANYTHING?
HA! HER NEW WAND DIDN'T WORK!
NOW... WHERE'D SHE RUN OFF TO?
I HAVEN'T BUDGED AN INCH, McDUCK!

BUT I SEE THIS WAND IS WORTH WHAT I PAID FOR IT AT THE SORCERERS' CONVENTION IN LUCCA!
YOU'RE WALKING ON THE WALL? NICE TRICK— BUT SO WHAT?
LOOK AGAIN, McDUCK! YOU'RE THE ONES DOING THE WALL-WALKING!
WHAT THE SAM HILL—
I'VE REDIRECTED YOUR PERSONAL GRAVITY HORIZONTALLY! AND WHILE YOU'RE HUNG UP, I'LL JUST HELP MYSELF TO THIS LOVELY COIN!
DON'T JUST STAND THERE! GRAB HER!
HOW CAN I GRAB HER WHEN SHE'S WAY UP THERE? ER... I MEAN OVER THERE... ER... UH...
YES, IT'S ALL IN HOW YOU LOOK AT IT! THE WORLD IS NOW SIDEWAYS TO YOU— BUT TO ME, EVERYTHING IS QUITE NORMAL!
CIAO!
SHE WALKED THROUGH THAT HOLE IN THE CEILING! ER... I MEAN THE OFFICE DOOR!
DO SOMETHING! CLIMB UP THERE!
I CAN'T! THIS FURNITURE ONLY LOOKS LIKE IT'S NAILED DOWN! I'M TOO HEAVY FOR IT!
SQUEEK

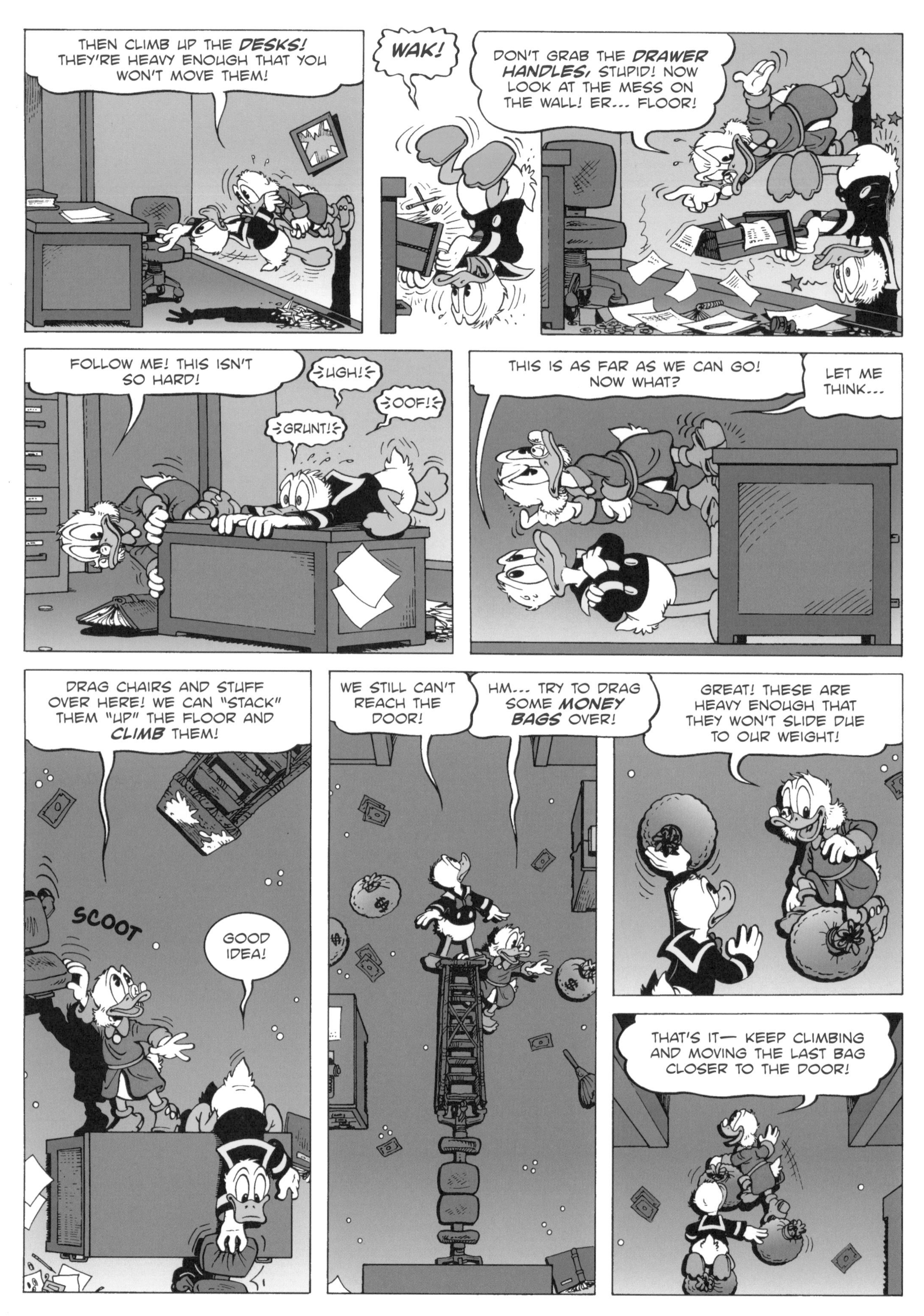

THEN CLIMB UP THE DESKS! THEY'RE HEAVY ENOUGH THAT YOU WON'T MOVE THEM!
WAK!
DON'T GRAB THE DRAWER HANDLES, STUPID! NOW LOOK AT THE MESS ON THE WALL! ER... FLOOR!
FOLLOW ME! THIS ISN'T SO HARD!
UGH!
OOF!
GRUNT!
THIS IS AS FAR AS WE CAN GO! NOW WHAT?
LET ME THINK...
DRAG CHAIRS AND STUFF OVER HERE! WE CAN "STACK" THEM "UP" THE FLOOR AND CLIMB THEM!
SCOOT
GOOD IDEA!
WE STILL CAN'T REACH THE DOOR!
HM... TRY TO DRAG SOME MONEY BAGS OVER!
GREAT! THESE ARE HEAVY ENOUGH THAT THEY WON'T SLIDE DUE TO OUR WEIGHT!
THAT'S IT— KEEP CLIMBING AND MOVING THE LAST BAG CLOSER TO THE DOOR!

THE NEXT PART IS EASY! THE STAIRS WORK THE SAME SIDEWAYS AS RIGHT-SIDE UP!
AH— MISS QUACKFASTER! YOU'LL NEED TO WATCH THE OFFICE FOR A WHILE!
!
I'M HAVING A SLIGHT PROBLEM THAT I, ER... CAN'T EXPLAIN RIGHT NOW!
HURRY, DONALD! WE CAN RACE UP THESE STAIRS THAT GO DOWN!
ER... 'SCUSE ME, MISS Q!
SIGH!
SOMETIMES I WONDER IF OTHER SECRETARIES' JOBS ARE QUITE THIS "INTERESTING"!
HEY! YOUR MONEY BIN USED TO BE AT THE TOP OF THIS HILL... NOT THE BOTTOM!
OH... I FORGOT! EVERYTHING IS SIDEWAYS TO US NOW!
GO AWAY!
DANGER
SCRAM!
JUST KEEP CLIMBING! MAGICA IS WAY AHEAD OF US!
GULP! THE SIDEWALK IS LIKE A GIANT WALL! WHAT DO WE DO NOW?
?
NO SALESMEN
ONE THING NOT TO DO IS LOOK BEHIND YOU!
WAK!!! U-U-UNCLE SCROOGE! IF WE FALL FROM HERE, WE'LL... WE'LL...
JUST DON'T THINK ABOUT IT! FIGURE OUT HOW WE CAN CATCH MAGICA!
HANDS OFF!

YIPES!
CRACK
NO SALESMEN
WE'RE SLIDING OFF THE SIDE OF THE HILL! WE'LL FALL FOREVER!
WHAT'S THAT AHEAD?
OOF!
WHACK!
EMPLOYEE PARKING 5¢
NEPHEW! THERE'S NO NICKEL IN THIS PARKING METER!
UNCLE SCROOGE! WE CAN USE MY CAR TO CHASE MAGICA!
I'VE NEVER HAD MUCH REASON TO DRIVE IN THIS POSITION BEFORE, BUT I GUESS IT'S POSSIBLE!
I'LL WORK THE PEDALS! LET'S GO!
NO LOITERI
ZOOM!
WHACK!
CRASH!
WHAM!
BOINK!
HALT! HALT!
ER... SORRY, OFFICER! I SEEM TO BE HAVING SOME TROUBLE WITH MY CAR!
I CAN SEE THAT! PERHAPS YOU SHOULD WALK AND I'LL CALL A TOW TRUCK!

DONALD! THERE GOES MAGICA! C'MON!
GROCERY
THANK YOU, OFFICER! G'BYE!
WOW! THIS IS LIKE RUNNING AN OBSTACLE COURSE!
WATCH OUT FOR THAT DISPLAY WINDOW!
SALE MELONS
WAK!
CRASH!
RIPE MELONS
SPLAT!
LOOK WHAT YOU'VE DONE! WHAT'S THE MATTER WITH YOU?!
WELL... UH... I'M A BIT GRAVITATIONALLY CHALLENGED AT THE MOMENT!
GET OUT! OUT!
HEY! STOP GETTING FOOTPRINTS ALL OVER MY WALLS!
THERE SHE GOES, DONALD! GRAB HER!
TAKE THIS!
WHAT THE—?!
BOOT
YIPES!
SIR, IF YOU'VE INJURED MY EMPLOYEE BY MAKING HIM FALL HORIZONTALLY DOWN THE STREET, YOU'LL HEAR FROM MY LAWYER!
I'M COMING, NEPHEW!

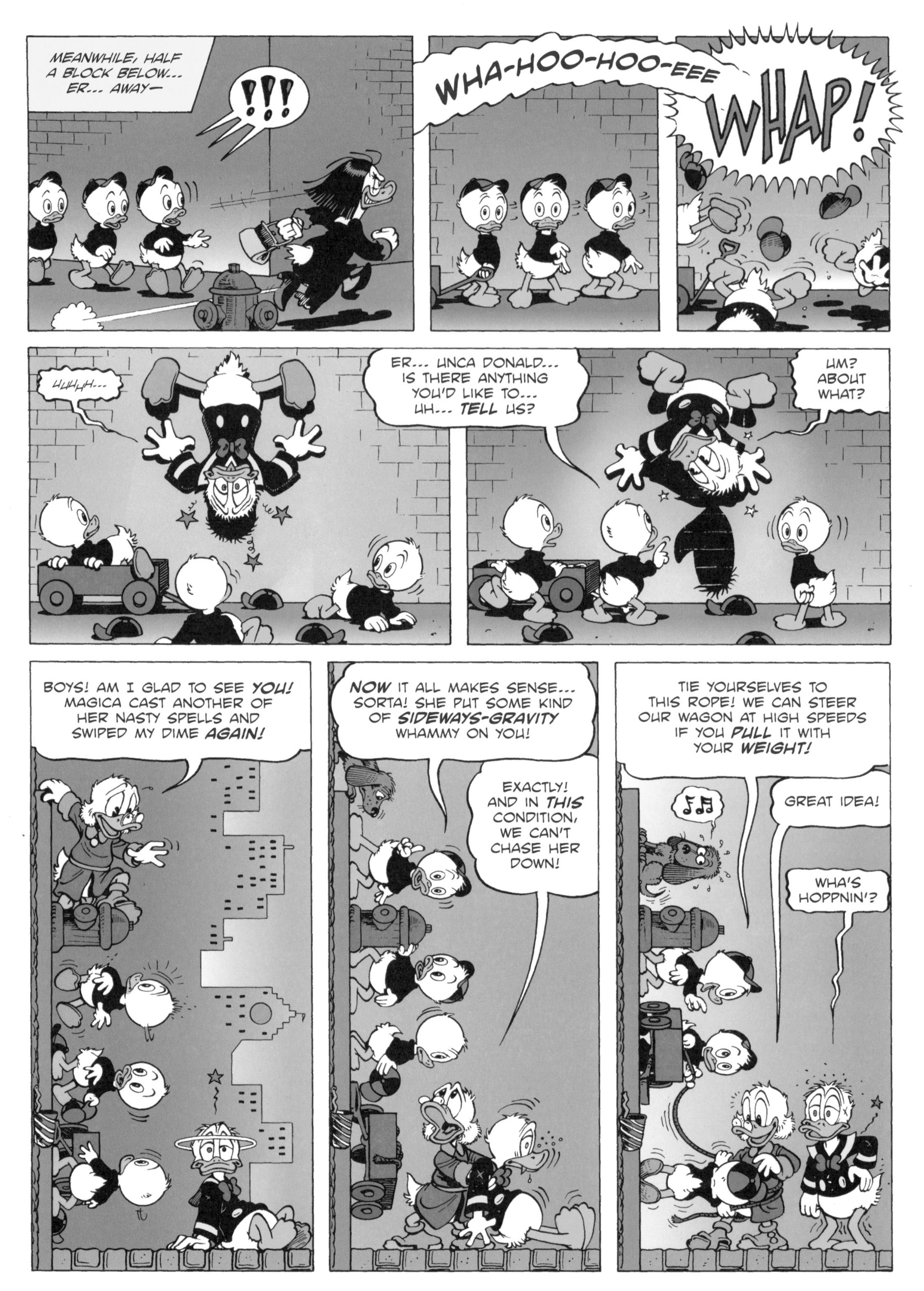
MEANWHILE, HALF A BLOCK BELOW... ER... AWAY—
!!!
WHA-HOO-HOO-EEE
WHAP!
UUUHH...
ER... UNCA DONALD... IS THERE ANYTHING YOU'D LIKE TO... UH... TELL US?
UM? ABOUT WHAT?
BOYS! AM I GLAD TO SEE YOU! MAGICA CAST ANOTHER OF HER NASTY SPELLS AND SWIPED MY DIME AGAIN!
NOW IT ALL MAKES SENSE... SORTA! SHE PUT SOME KIND OF SIDEWAYS-GRAVITY WHAMMY ON YOU!
EXACTLY! AND IN THIS CONDITION, WE CAN'T CHASE HER DOWN!
TIE YOURSELVES TO THIS ROPE! WE CAN STEER OUR WAGON AT HIGH SPEEDS IF YOU PULL IT WITH YOUR WEIGHT!
GREAT IDEA!
WHA'S HOPPNIN'?

OKAY— WE'RE READY! JUMP!
HERE WE GO!
SAY... WATCH OUT FOR THE EDGE OF—
WAK!
ZOW!
TWANG!
THERE'S MAGICA!
YES! SHE'S GETTING INTO A CAB! SHE'S PROBABLY HEADING OUT TO THE AIRPORT!
-SOB!- IF SHE GETS ON A PLANE BACK TO ITALY, MY DIME IS LOST!
LOOK OUT FOR THAT POTHOLE!
CRASH!
YOW!!!
CORNELIUS COOT PARK
HALP!
OUCH!
YOWTCH!
COURAGE, NEPHEW! WE'LL SNAG A TREE WITH THIS ROPE!
HONK!
?

RATS! THERE GOES MAGICA'S CAB AROUND THE LAKE, BUT WE'RE STRANDED HERE!
NO, WE'RE NOT! I HAVE AN IDEA!
JUMP INTO THE LAKE! THE WATER WILL CONTROL OUR FALLING!
SNIF SNIF
WHOOPEE! I CAN USE MY FEET LIKE A RUDDER! WE'RE ON OUR WAY AGAIN!
UH-OH! I DIDN'T GET ALL THE WAY INTO THE WATER!
BROTHER— THAT'S WHAT I CALL A POWERFUL SWIMMER!
ZOW!
ACK! THE BEACH! OOF!
THUD!
EXCUSE ME! MAY I BORROW YOUR UMBRELLA?
UH... SURE!
ULP! THE UMBRELLA'S STARTING TO COLLAPSE!
AIM FOR THAT SIGNPOST!
BUS STOP
PERFECT! THIS IS THE PICKUP SPOT FOR THE AIRPORT BUS!
AND HERE IT COMES!
SCREECH!
BUS STOP

ER... GOING OUR WAY?
UH-OH! WHY DO I GET ALL THE WISE GUYS ON MY ROUTE?!
SIR— YOU'RE NOT ALLOWED TO STAND ON THE FLOOR BEFORE THAT YELLOW LINE!
WHO'S ON THE FLOOR? I'M STANDING ON THE WINDSHIELD! GET GOING!!!
THERE'S MAGICA! SHE JUST GOT OUT OF HER CAB AND WENT INTO THE AIRPORT TERMINAL!
FASTER! FASTER!
DON'T RUSH ME, SIR! I NEED TO MAKE A U-TURN TO REACH THE BUS STOP!
COOT INTERNATIONAL AIRPORT
SCREEE...
A U-TURN? NO— WAIT!
PLEASE LEAVE THROUGH THE FRONT EXIT!
-SIGH- NO COOPERATION WHAT-SO-EVER!
WAK!
CRASH!
WHOMP!
GANGWAY!
WHAP!
ONE SIDE!
BONK!
THUD!
COMIN' THROUGH!
-OOF!-
-EEK!-
STOP SHOVIN'!
HEY!
WAIT YER TURN!
WATCH IT!
OW!
-WUF!-

WHAT DO YOU MEAN THERE'S NO PLANE TO ITALY? I'M IN A HURRY!
EVERYONE'S IN A HURRY! WHY, JUST LOOK AT THOSE GENTLEMEN BEHIND YOU!
FLIGHT DESTINATION TIME
109 GOOSEVILLE 11:02
315 FARAWAYSTAN 11:37
757 COSTA LOTTA 11:56
714 PUERTO POORO 12:14
666 LOUISVILLE LATE
WATCH IT!
HEY!
SPLAT!
YOU?! HOW COULD YOU POSSIBLY HAVE GOTTEN HERE IN YOUR CONDITION?!
FIE ON YOU, MADAM! IT TAKES MORE THAN THE DISRUPTION OF THE BASIC LAWS OF PHYSICS TO THWART SCROOGE McDUCK!
I THINK YOU HAVEN'T HAD ENOUGH GRAVITY REDIRECTION YET!
OH, I BELIEVE I HAVE! NO SENSE IN BEING A PIG, I ALWAYS SAY!
GRAVITATUS OPPONERE!
ZAP!
BONK!
DON'T LOOK NOW, BUT WE'RE SITTING ON THE CEILING!
YES... IT'S VERY NICE... NO LITTER... PLENTY OF SPACE...
IF THERE'S NO SCHEDULED FLIGHT BACK TO ITALY, I'LL TAKE AN UNSCHEDULED FLIGHT!
TO PLANES
!!!
YOU WILL FLY ME TO ITALY NOW!
GOSH-YOU'RE-RIGHT-I-SUDDENLY-HAVE-AN-UNCONTROLLABLE-URGE-TO-DO-JUST-THAT.
FOOF!

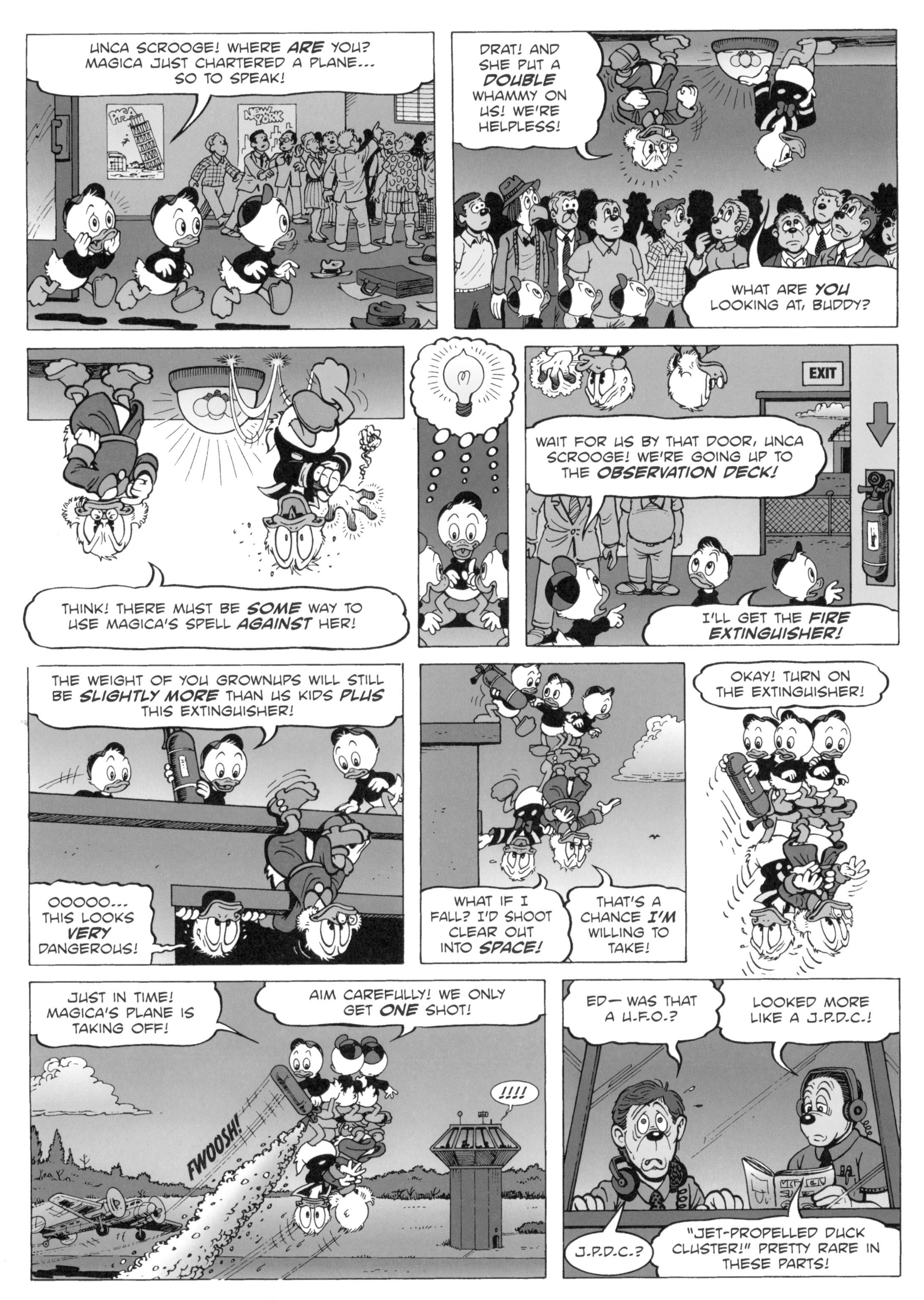
UNCA SCROOGE! WHERE ARE YOU? MAGICA JUST CHARTERED A PLANE... SO TO SPEAK!
DRAT! AND SHE PUT A DOUBLE WHAMMY ON US! WE'RE HELPLESS!
WHAT ARE YOU LOOKING AT, BUDDY?
THINK! THERE MUST BE SOME WAY TO USE MAGICA'S SPELL AGAINST HER!
EXIT
WAIT FOR US BY THAT DOOR, UNCA SCROOGE! WE'RE GOING UP TO THE OBSERVATION DECK!
I'LL GET THE FIRE EXTINGUISHER!
THE WEIGHT OF YOU GROWNUPS WILL STILL BE SLIGHTLY MORE THAN US KIDS PLUS THIS EXTINGUISHER!
OOOOO... THIS LOOKS VERY DANGEROUS!
WHAT IF I FALL? I'D SHOOT CLEAR OUT INTO SPACE!
THAT'S A CHANCE I'M WILLING TO TAKE!
OKAY! TURN ON THE EXTINGUISHER!
JUST IN TIME! MAGICA'S PLANE IS TAKING OFF!
AIM CAREFULLY! WE ONLY GET ONE SHOT!
FWOOSH!
!!!!
ED— WAS THAT A U.F.O.?
LOOKED MORE LIKE A J.P.D.C.!
J.P.D.C.?
"JET-PROPELLED DUCK CLUSTER!" PRETTY RARE IN THESE PARTS!

WHOOPS! THE EXTINGUISHER IS EMPTY!!
SPUTTER!
IF WE MISS THE PLANE, IT'S OUTER SPACE FOR ALL OF US!
MADE IT!
I'LL HAVE TO KICK OPEN THE CARGO BAY BEFORE WE GET BLOWN OFF!
BAM! BAM!
WHAT WAS THAT?
I-AM-MESMERIZED-AND-BEYOND-CARING.
CRASH!
STOWAWAYS! I'LL MAKE YOU PLENTY SORRY YOU DARED TO—
GLOM!
?!
HAND OVER MY DIME, WITCH!
NO! AND IF YOU TOUCH ME, I'LL LEAVE YOU UPSIDE-DOWN FOREVER!
ZAP!
JOIN US, THEN! I REMEMBER THAT INCANTATION!
GRAVITATUS OPPONERE!
YOW!
YOU STUPID PILOT! CAN'T YOU CONTROL THIS PLANE?
WE-ARE-IN-A-SPIN. I-WILL-CORRECT-IT.
THAT'S BETTER!
SEE, McDUCK? THAT WAND ONLY WORKS FOR A SORCERESS SUPREME!
HA HA HA HA HA— HUH?!!

EEK! WHAT'S THE GROUND DOING UP THERE?!!
CAN'T YOU GUESS, MAGICA? WE'RE ALL IN REVERSE GRAVITY, INCLUDING THE PLANE!
NOW WILL YOU TELL ME THE INCANTATION THAT WILL LIFT THE SPELL?
NO, CURSE YOU!!!
FLY AS CLOSE AS YOU CAN TO THAT GROUND ABOVE US, MR. PILOT!
YESSIR-BUT-GOSH-AM-I-GLAD-I'M-MESMERIZED-OR-I'D-BE-SCARED-SILLY.
EEEK!!!
LET'S HAVE THE INCANTATION, WITCH, OR WE MIGHT BREAK A PROPELLER AND FALL TO THE MOON!
⇶SOB!⇷ YOU WIN! IT'S "GRAVITATUS NORMALIS"!
SO BE IT! GRAVITATUS NORMALIS!
ZAP!
!!!
SCREEEEEEEECH!
ED! DID YOU SEE THAT?!!
RELAX! IT'S PROBABLY JUST ONE O' THOSE SILLY MOVIE STUNTS!
MODERN SOMNABULIST

NOW! GIVE ME MY DIME!
NOT UNTIL YOU GIVE ME BACK MY WAND! TRUST ME!
WH-WHERE AM I?
HA! I'M NOT AN IDIOT! TAKE THIS, WITCH!
GRAVITATUS HORIZONTUS!
HA! LOUSY AIM, McDUCK!
ZAP!
ERK!
PLOP
UNFORTUNATELY, I'M VERY CLUMSY WITH WANDS!
OOPS! YOU SEE? BUTTER-FINGERS ME DROPPED IT!
SMASH!
YOU SILLY SORCERESS! WON'T YOU EVER LEARN NOT TO MATCH WITS WITH US DUCKS?
THERE'S JUST ENOUGH JUICE IN THIS BUSTED WAND TO ANSWER THAT!
SNAP!
ZAP!
WAK!
GRAB HIM! GRAB HIM!
AND SO...
QUIT WHINING! MAGICA CONFESSED THAT THE GRAVITY SPELLS ARE ONLY TEMPORARY!
THE WHAMMY WILL SOON WEAR OFF MY DIME— AND YOU! AND IN THE MEANTIME, IT'LL BE MUCH EASIER TO CLEAN THOSE COBWEBS OFF THE CEILING!
OH, SURE...
...BUT NOW I NEED A DANG LADDER TO SWEEP THE FLOOR!
GRIPING! GRIPING! ALWAYS GRIPING!
End

WALT DISNEY'S
UNCLE $CROOGE
"The VIGILANTE of PIZEN BLUFF"
ONCE AGAIN UNCLE $CROOGE HAS UNEARTHED (OR UNCOINED) HIS OLD TRUNK OF MEMORIES OF HIS EARLY LIFE AND TIMES WHEN HE WANDERED THE FRONTIERS OF THE WORLD, SEEKING HIS FORTUNE...
DEPTH GAUGE
100
99
CAIRO
CAPE TOWN
BUTTE
JOHANNESBURG
DAWSON
LONDON
POINT BARROW
PARIS
OSLO
NEW ORLEANS
LOUISVILLE
ARIZONA - 1890
SIGH! THIS WILD WEST SHOW HANDBILL CERTAINLY BRINGS BACK MEMORIES, BOYS! I GOT IT FROM AN OLD PROSPECTOR PAL IN... GOSH, WHERE WAS IT? TOMBSTONE? PRESCOTT? NO...
"PIZEN BLUFF, ARIZONA! JUST ANOTHER OF THE GHOST TOWNS LYING IN THE COOLING EMBERS OF A DYING ERA OF HISTORY... AND WHERE, ON A COOL NIGHT IN OCTOBER 1890, I MET A FELLOW ARGONAUT..."
HARDWARE
NUGGET CAFE
WHO?
HOLD YER HOSSES, JACOB! IT'S ONLY ME-- DOWN FROM MY DIGGIN'S IN RAWHIDE! I'M HEADIN' INTO PHOENIX FOR SUPPLIES!
ACH! SCROOGE! YOU SCARED ME! THE DALTON BOYS WERE SEEN IN THESE PARTS!
CAN YOU SPARE A CUP OF COFFEE FOR A FELLOW PROSPECTOR?
I WISH I WAS A YOUNG PROSPECTOR LIKE YOU, BUT I'VE DECIDED I'VE GOTTEN TOO OLD! THIS IS MY LAST TRIP INTO THESE MOUNTAINS!
BAH! I'LL NEVER BE TOO OLD TO GO TREASURE HUNTIN'!

I BELIEVE YOU WON'T, SCROOGE! MAYBE... MAYBE IT'S FOR YOU THAT I'VE BEEN DRAWIN' THESE MAPS ON SCRAP PAPER!
MAPS?
CAMPIN' IN THIS OLD GHOST TOWN TONIGHT GOT ME TO THINKIN'! I FIGURED I SHOULD MAKE MAPS TO MY GOLD CACHES BEFORE I'M AS DEAD AS IT IS!
GOLD CACHES! chuckle! DO TELL!
THIS MAP SHOWS WHERE I HID TWO SADDLEBAGS OF NUGGETS FROM THE PEGLEG MINE WHEN I WAS IN CALIFORNY!
YOU NEVER WENT BACK FOR THE GOLD?
NOT AFTER I FOUND THIS-- THE LOST PERALTA MINE! BUT APACHES MADE IT TOO DANGEROUS TO VISIT VERY OFTEN! I NEVER TOOK MUCH GOLD OUT!
WELL, THANKS FOR THE MAPS, JACOB! WISH I COULD STICK AROUND AND SWAP STORIES, BUT I WANNA GET TO PHOENIX BY MORNING!
FAREWELL, SCROOGE!
"PEGLEG" MINE, EH? THESE "LOST MINES" ARE LIKE DREAMS TO OLD PROSPECTORS LIKE JACOB! THEIR VERSION OF "THE ONE THAT GOT AWAY"!
AND THE "PERALTA" MINE! SAY, WHAT'S THIS HANDBILL HE DREW HIS MAP ON THE BACK OF?
ULP!
UNCLE ANGUS!!!
PHOENIX FAIRGROUNDS
P. T. BARNUM PROUDLY PRESENTS
BUFFALO BILL'S
WILD WEST
WILD EAST
featuring POTHOLE McDUCK: MASTER of the MISSISSIPPI
BANG!
BANG!
POW!
BAM!

DON'T WORRY, FOLKS -- THOSE ARE ONLY BLANKS OUR GUNS ARE SHOOTING!
SO, JUST SIT BACK AND ENJOY BUFFALO BILL CODY'S WILD WEST-WILD EAST EXTRAVAGANZA!
BANG!
POW!
BAM!
BANG!
POW!
BANG!
BANG!
POW!
176-167
176-617
176-716
THE GREAT PHINEAS T. BARNUM ASKED ME TO PUT ON A SPECIAL SHOW TO CELEBRATE THE CHOICE OF PHOENIX AS THE NEW CAPITAL OF THE TERRITORY-- SO I'M PUTTING ON A WILD EAST SHOW FOR YOU WESTERNERS!
AND OUR STAR IS THE AUTHOR AND HERO OF THOSE FAMOUS DIME-NOVELS, THE MASTER OF THE MISSISSIPPI HIMSELF--POTHOLE McDUCK!
BANG!
OH, SAVE ME, UNCLE POTHOLE! SAVE ME!
LEAVE MY POOR, STUPID NEPHEW SCROOGE ALONE, YOU COWARDLY BEAGLE BOYS, OR I'LL BLOW YOU TO SMITHEREENS!
BANG!
POW!
176-716
WHOOF!
HEY, WHO THE HECK ARE YOU, WISE GUY?
OH, JUST WAIT TILL I TELL YOU!

YOU LOOK LIKE THAT GUY! ARE YOU HIS UNDERSTUDY?
ACTUALLY, IT'S MORE LIKE HE'S MINE!
STUPID, AM I?
AWK!
CRUNCH!
YOU HOPE TO FIND A JOB HERE, LIKE ME?
BUT--YOU'RE AN APACHE! I THOUGHT THE ARMY SENT YOU ALL TO A RESERVATION IN FLORIDA!

I SLIPPED AWAY TO SEEK JOBS FOR MY PEOPLE! THESE WILD WEST SHOWS ARE GOOD WORK--AND WE MIGHT EVEN SHOW WHITE PEOPLE WHAT OUR CULTURE WAS LIKE!
MAYBE I CAN HELP! I ... uh ... KNOW ONE OF THE STARS!
HEY! YOU!

YOU'RE SUPPOSED TO BE PLAYING A BANK ROBBER NOW! TAKE OFF THAT DUMB LOOKIN' MASK AND GET OUT THERE!

ULP! SCROOGE! IT'S YOU! FOR REAL!
Y'S, UN'CL PT'HL! LEGGO UVMA F'CE!

HEH! NOW DON'T GET RILED, NEPHEW! THIS IS JUST SHOWBIZ! IT'S A NEW IDEA YOU'RE JUST NOT FLAMBOYANT ENOUGH TO UNDERSTAND!
OH, SO?
GRR.

I'M ONLY WORKING IN IT TO RAISE CASH TO FINANCE A SECRET PROJECT--AN EVEN NEWER FORM OF ENTERTAINMENT! BUT HERE COMES MY OLD PAL, BUFFALO BILL, SO SHHHH! AND TRY NOT TO MAKE A FOOL OF YOURSELF!
I'LL TRY!
BILL, HE'S NOT MUCH TO LOOK AT, BUT THIS IS MY NEPH--
BUCK! BUCK McDUCK! YOU YOUNG SCALLYWAG! WOTTA TREAT FOR THESE OLD EYES!
?

POTHOLE, IT WAS BUCK HERE WHO GAVE ME THE IDEA OF DOIN' WILD WEST SHOWS!
IT WAS IN NORTH PLATTE BACK IN '82, RIGHT, BUCK?
I WAS PASSIN' THROUGH ON A CATTLE DRIVE!
WHY, I'VE EVEN TOURED EUROPE WITH THE SHOW, BUCK! BUT WHAT HAVE YOU BEEN UP TO?
OH, PROSPECTIN' IN MONTANO, LION WRANGLIN' IN AFRICA, TRADIN' COCONUTS IN THE SOUTH SEAS ...IN OTHER WORDS...
...NOT MUCH!
@#%@!
HM! THAT SOUNDS LIKE SIOUX! DO YOU TALK APACHE, TOO?
BUCK, LET'S GO IN AND TALK TO MR. BARNUM! I KNOW HE'LL WANT YOU TO JOIN THE SHOW!
THAT'S NOT MY STYLE, BILL! BUT MY NEW FRIEND HERE NEEDS JOBS FOR HIS PEOPLE! HOW ABOUT IT?
IT'S A DEAL! C'MON -- I'LL INTRODUCE YOU TO LITTLE SURE SHOT!
PHINEAS T. BARNUM PRODUCTIONS
OFFICE
176-716
OH, GODFREY DANIEL! WHO CAN THAT BE?!
COME IN!
KNOCK KNOCK
FORK OVER THE CASH, PAL!
YOU "BEAGLE BOYS" KNOW THIS ISN'T PAYDAY! SO GET BACK TO WORK OR YOU'RE FIRED!
176-716
176-617
SURPRISE, FATSO! WE AIN'T MAKE-BELIEVE OUTLAWS! WE'RE THE FER-REAL DALTONS!
THESE DISGUISES WERE JUST TO GET US BACK STAGE!
WHAT'S THE COMBINATION TO THIS SAFE?
HAVE YOU NO SENSE OF SHOWMANSHIP? BLOWING IT UP WOULD BE MUCH MORE DRAMATIC!
YOU GOT IT, ACE!
BANG! BANG!
WHAT'S THAT?
DON'T WORRY...IT'S JUST TARGET PRACTICE.

YESSIR, BUCK--ANNIE OAKLEY'S THE BEST TRICK-SHOT ARTIST IN THE WEST!
SO I SEE!
BANG! BANG!
NICE TO MEETCHA, BUCK! TRY YOUR AIM?
OH, I DON'T HOLD MUCH WITH GUNS, MA'AM! I TRY TO AVOID 'EM WHEN I CAN!
NEPHEW, DON'T BE SUCH A SISSY! YOU CAN'T BE AN AMERICAN IF YOU DON'T LOVE GUNS!
'SCUZE ME! MIND IF I PICK A TARGET?
NO, I--
BANG! BANG! BANG!
ZING
ZING
ZING
THREE SHOTS AND HE NEVER HIT THE BOTTLE ONCE! I'M SO EMBARRASSED!
I WASN'T AIMIN' AT THE BOTTLE, UNCLE POT-HOLE!
I WAS AIMIN' AT THE BLOW-FLIES BUZZIN' AROUND IT!
THREE OF 'EM, DEAD AS BUFFALO CHIPS!
PLEASE, BUCK! LET'S GO SEE MR. BARNUM! YOU COULD BE HIS BIGGEST STAR SINCE JUMBO!
@£#$%&*!
HM... THAT SOUNDS MORE LIKE COMANCHE!
WANT A FLY?
BOOM!
STOP, THIEVES! HELP!
ONE SIDE, BUDDY!
176-167
BUMF!
THEY DYNAMITED THE SAFE!
AND A TURKEY?
HEY! THOSE WERE THE DALTON BOYS!

THEY STOLE ALL OUR CASH!
OH, NO! THAT'S WHERE I WAS KEEPING THE MONEY I RAISED FOR MY SECRET PROJECT! IF IT'S GONE, I'M BROKE!!
CALL THE MARSHAL! CALL WYATT EARP! CALL THE PINKERTONS!
WAIT A MINUTE! I'M GETTING ONE OF MY COLOSSAL, SEN-SATIONAL EXTRAORDINARY IDEAS!
WE'LL FORM AN ALL-STAR POSSE AND GO AFTER THOSE DALTONS OURSELVES! JUST THINK OF IT-- THE PUBLICITY WILL MAKE THE SHOW BIGGER THAN EVER!
IT'S STUPENDOUS! IT'S FABULOUS!
IT'S NUTS! I'M NO COWBOY!
SOUNDS LIKE YOU'LL HAVE A REAL AD-VENTURE TO WRITE ABOUT, UNCLE POTHOLE! GOOD LUCK!
NEPHEW--YOU DON'T UNDERSTAND! I BORROWED MOST OF THAT MONEY...USING MY FAMILY OWNERSHIP IN CASTLE McDUCK AS COLLATERAL!
WHAT! YOU DID WHAT?!
IF WE DON'T GET THAT MONEY BACK, YOUR PARENTS AND SISTERS WILL BE HOMELESS!
OKAY! OKAY! I'LL HELP!
BILL! I'M COMIN' WITH YA!
TROUBLE IS, THEY HEADED INTO THE MOUNTAINS! THAT'S SACRED APACHE LAND AND I DON'T KNOW IT!
I KNOW THOSE MOUNTAINS... AND I WOULD LIKE TO HELP GET BAD MEN OUT OF OUR THUNDER GOD'S LANDS!
THEN YOU'RE HIRED AS OUR GUIDE! A CLASSIC TOUCH! THE NOBLE RED WARRIOR VANQUISHES THE WHITE RENEGADES AND EXPELS THEM FROM HIS SACRED MOUNTAINS! I LOVE IT!
QUICK! CALL MY PHOTOGRAPHER!

FLASH!
OKAY! PACK THAT CAMERA UP AND HITCH IT TO MY SADDLE! NEWSPAPERS AROUND THE WORLD WILL FIGHT TO GET PHOTOS OF THIS ADVENTURE!
OH!
OH!
OH!
?
IT'S NO USE, NEPHEW! I'VE NEVER EVEN BEEN ON A HORSE! I'D BETTER STAY BEHIND!
PLOP!
NONSENSE! THE FAMOUS MASTER OF THE MISSISSIPPI MUST BE ON THIS EXPLOIT!
I WILL HELP THE OLD DUCK! HE CAN RIDE IN HERE!
WHAT? LIKE A PAPOOSE?
THANKS,,, ER,,, JUST WHAT IS YOUR NAME, FRIEND?
I AM GOKHLAYEH! IT IS APACHE MEANING "ONE-WHO-YAWNS"!
GOKHLAYEH? YOU'RE GOKHLAYEH?
YES. BUT PLEASE SAY NOTHING AND LET ME HELP CATCH THE BADMEN BEFORE I RETURN TO MY RESERVATION!
GRR,,, I'M THE PAPOOSE OF THE YAWNING INDIAN! @#$%£&*!
NOW HE SPEAKS ARAPAHO, TOO! THE OLD DUCK MUST BE A GREAT DIPLOMAT OF RED NATIONS!
TIME'S A-WASTING! LET'S GET MOVING! THE MAGNIFICENT SEVEN RIDE!!
BUT,,, THERE'S ONLY SIX OF US!
SONNY, I'M PHINEAS T. BARNUM! I COUNT MYSELF TWICE!

HYiii! WHAT IS THAT BEAST?
COMING SOON!
P.T. BARNUM'S
GREATEST SHOW ON EARTH!!!!
THAT, ONE-WHO-YAWNS, IS AN INDIAN ELEPHANT!
HMPH -- THE APACHES HAVE NOTHING THAT UGLY!
NO, NOT AMERICAN INDIAN! THE REAL INDIANS! IN INDIA!
THE OLD DUCK TALKS GIBBERISH!
STOP YAWNING AND LISTEN! WHEN WE DISCOVERED YOUR LAND, WE THOUGHT IT WAS INDIA, WHICH IS ACTUALLY 11,000 MILES AWAY!
!
HMPH! IT'S EASY TO SEE WHY YOU NEED ME TO GUIDE YOU!
MEANWHILE, HIGH UP IN THE MOUNTAINS...
LOOKIT THIS, EMMETT! THAT WILD WEST SHOW SAFE HELD MORE THAN JUST THEIR BOX OFFICE TAKE!
176-70
WOW! SOME SUCKER MUST'VE USED IT FOR A BANK! WE'RE RICH!
HEY, YOU GUYS! WE'RE BEIN' FOLLERED BY A POSSE!
I DIDN'T THINK ANYONE WOULD FOLLOW US INTO THESE HAUNTED MOUNTAINS!
OR TRACK US OVER THESE ROCKS!
WHO ARE THOSE GUYS?
BOB, WHEN WE GET TO CORONADO MESA, YOU DROP BACK AND PICK 'EM OFF AS THEY COME OVER THE RIDGE!
SURE THING, GRATTON!

SOME HOURS LATER--
GREAT HONK, BUT THESE MOUNTAINS ARE RUGGED! HOW CAN WE HOPE TO FOLLOW ANYONE THROUGH THIS TERRAIN?
REMEMBER, P.T., POTHOLE McDUCK HAS TRACKED THE DASTARDLY BEAGLE BOYS FROM THE EVERGLADES TO THE DEPTHS OF MAMMOTH CAVE!
THAT WAS IN YOUR DIME NOVELS, UNCLE POTHOLE!
THAT'S RIGHT! JUST TAKE THE WAY I TRACKED BLACKHEART BEAGLE THROUGH THE OKEFENOKEE SWAMP IN ISSUE No. 237 BY FOLLOWING TINY BROKEN TREE TWIGS!
THOSE DALTON BOYS WOULD HAFTA BE MIGHTY CLUMSY TO RUN INTO THE ONLY TREE WITHIN 30 MILES!
IT COULD HAPPEN!
LET'S TAKE A LOOK, ONE-WHO-YAWNS!
AHA! ONE OF THESE CACTUS THORNS HAS BEEN BLUNTED!
AND HERE--THIS GRAIN OF SAND HAS CLEARLY BEEN DISLODGED!
BUT THIS CLINCHES IT! THIS SHADOW HAS BEEN BRUISED ON THE NORTH EDGE!
BAH! I DON'T HAVE TO LISTEN TO SARCASM!
BOOMF!
SEE? WHAT'D I TELL YOU?
BILL, THIS WOULD MAKE A GOOD SPOT FOR A PUBLICITY PHOTO! YOU AND ANNIE AND POTHOLE STRIKE A POSE ON THAT ROCK!
PERFECT! DON'T MOVE!
ARE THEIR WIG-WAMS EMPTY?
NAH! IT'S JUST SHOWBIZ!
BANG!
THOK

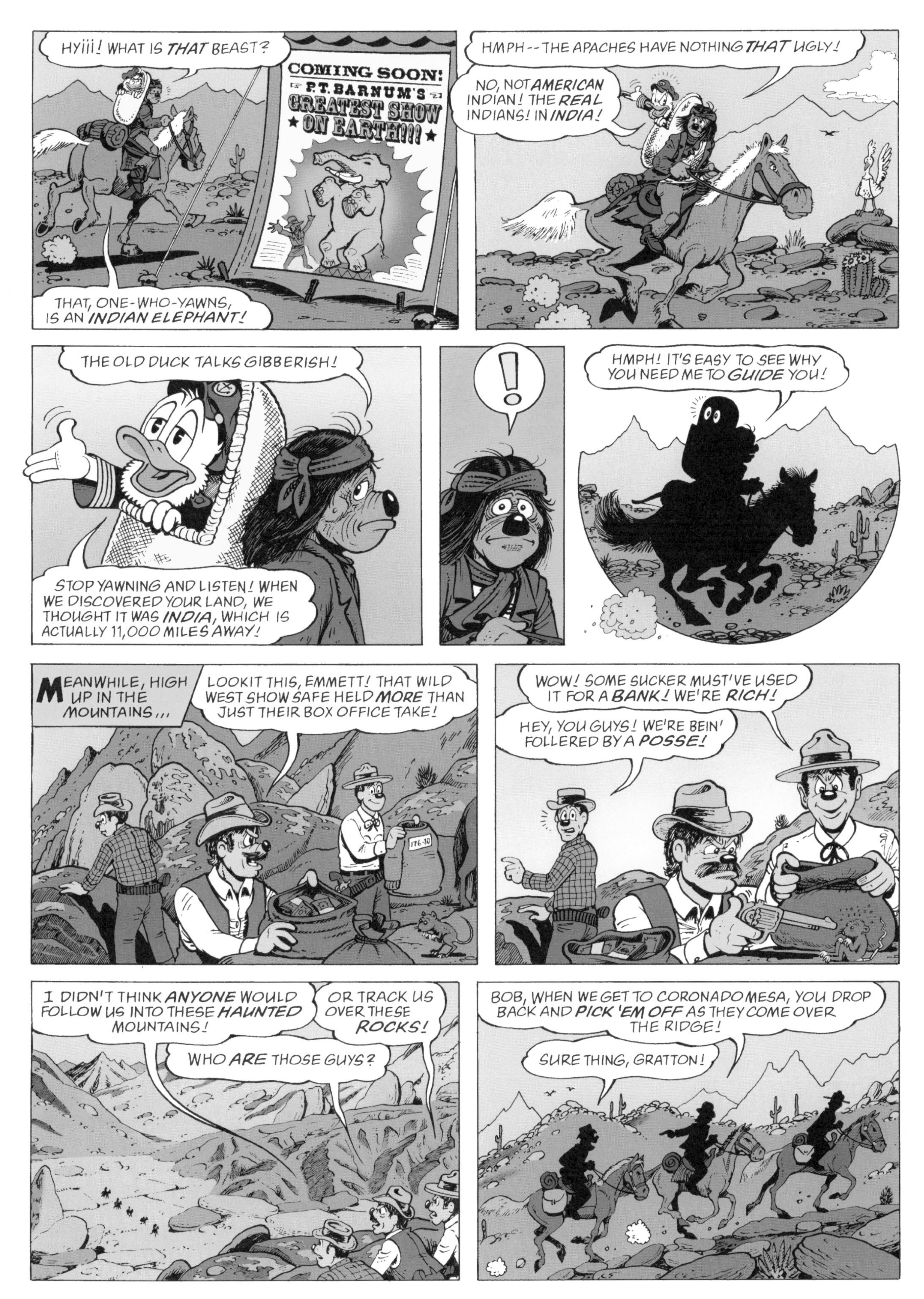

SAY, WHERE DID POTHOLE GO? HE MOVED OUT OF THE PICTURE!
BANG!
TWEEEOOO!
I ... er ... JUST WANTED TO CHECK THE COMPOSITION OF YOUR SCENE!
TAKE COVER!
ONE OF THE DALTONS IS TAKING POTSHOTS AT US FROM THAT BOULDER! WE'RE PINNED DOWN UNLESS WE DISARM HIM!
I THINK I CAN HIT HIS GUN HAND!
GIVE ME THAT BOW, ONE-WHO-YAWNS! I PUT FLESH WOUNDS IN A ROW OF BEAGLE BOYS WITH JUST ONE ARROW IN ISSUE Nº 199!
CAREFUL! THAT THING IS LOADED!
GET THIS SHOT, P.T.! THE MASTER OF THE MISSISSIPPI BATTLES WESTERN OUTLAWS NATIVE STYLE!
SENSATIONAL! HOLD IT!
FLASH!
TWANG!
OUCH!
WAIT! HOLD IT, P.T.! THERE'S SOMETHING WRONG WITH THIS INFERNAL CONTRAPTION!
BAH! WHOEVER INVENTED THIS THING SHOULD HAVE HIS HEAD EXAMINED!
ANNIE, CAN YOU GET A BEAD ON HIM?
SURE.
KPOW!
HE'S DISARMED! IF WE COULD ONLY CATCH HIM BEFORE HE REJOINS HIS BROTHERS!
LEAVE IT TO ME!
HI-YO, HORTENSE! AWAY!!!

DADBLAME IT! YER S'POSED TO RIDE HOSS BACK, NOT HOSS HAID! THIS IS PLUMB UNFAIR!
GIT AWAY, YOU! THIS HERE'S A PRIVATE HOSS! NO TRESPASSIN'!
CHOMP!
DON'T MAKE ME GET ROUGH WITH YOU, DALTON!
WOULD SOMEBODY COME AN' GIT THIS CRAZY DUCK? HE'S PUTTIN' A CREASE IN MUH FAV'RIT HAT!
PUT UP YER DUKES, VARMINT!
!
SOB! AH CAIN'T HAVE A PROPER FISTFIGHT ON A DANG HOSS! AH NEEDS A BARROOM WITH TABLES AND CHAIRS TO BUST UP! SOB!
RATS! I CAN'T HIT A MAN WHO WON'T DEFEND HIMSELF! BUT IF I CAN'T STOP YOU...
SNATCH!
...I'LL STOP YER HOSS!
WHA-HOO-HOO-EEEEE!!

PLEASE CUT THAT DALTON DOWN, ONE-WHO-YAWNS! WE CAN'T JUST LEAVE HIM THERE WHILE WE GO AFTER HIS BROTHERS!
AAAAHHHHH!
RIGHT!
BUCK, THAT WAS THE FINEST DISPLAY OF TRICK RIDING I EVER WITNESSED!
RIDIN' HORSES IS A CINCH AFTER RIDIN' LIONS!
THEIR MANES ARE ALWAYS SO FULL OF FLEAS! UGH!
DUCK-WHO-SEEKS-GOLD! I CUT DOWN THE CACTUS, BUT THE BAD MAN RAN AWAY!
AAAAAHHHH!
WELL, HE'LL BE EASY ENOUGH TO TRACK NOW!
SHORTLY...
...AND I BARELY ESCAPED! MOSTLY THE POSSE'S JUST A BUNCH O' OLD MEN AND A GIRL--BUT THERE'S A YOUNG WADDIE WHO'S DYNAMITE!
WE'D BETTER GET MOVING ON TO THE HIDEOUT!
HOP ON, BOB--BUT FIRST GET SHET OF THAT THING, OR YOU'LL MAKE US AN EASY TARGET!
OH, RIGHT!
BAD MEN'S TRAIL IS HEADING FOR AN OLD TOWN IN MESQUITE FLATS!
YEAH--I KNOW THAT PLACE!
THAT'S PIZEN BLUFF! I WAS A PROSPECTOR THERE UNTIL THEY STRUCK GOLD IN RAWHIDE LAST YEAR, AND THE WHOLE TOWN PACKED UP AND MOVED NORTH! I DON'T KNOW WHAT'S HOLDIN' THOSE RAMSHACKLE BUILDINGS UP!
SEEMS LIKE THEY OUGHTTA BLOW AWAY IN THE WIND!
HOTEL
NUGGET CAFE

LET US SNEAK IN ON FOOT!
GOOD IDEA, ONE-WHO-YAWNS! WE'LL DO IT INDIAN-STYLE, WITHOUT MAKING A SOUND EVEN ON DRY LEAVES!
SUPERB IDEA! DON'T MOVE UNTIL I GET A CAMERA SET-UP, THEN BILL AND POTHOLE AND ANNIE CAN MARCH DOWN THE STREET!
EXCELLENT!
THEY ARE ALL GOING TO GET SHOT, EH, DUCK-WHO-SEEKS-GOLD?
I'M AFRAID SO! WE'LL HAVE TO FIND THOSE DALTONS BEFORE THIS WILD WEST SHOW DIES ON THE ROAD!
AND NOT MAKE IT TO BROADWAY? BAD MEDICINE!
THIS IS JUST LIKE "SHOWDOWN IN CINCINNATI" IN ISSUE Nº 417... EXCEPT... I'M NOT WEARING SPURS!
OKAY! I'M READY!
SALOON
CHING! CHING! CHING!
CHING! CHING! CHING!
CHING! CHING! CHING!
CHING! CHING!
EVERYBODY GIT OFF'N THE STREET! THAR'S A'GONNA BE TROUBLE! JESSE JAMES AIMS TA BUY MAM'SELLE'S PARFUME DE PAREE SO'S HE CAN SMELL AS FEMININE AS--
OOPS! SORRY! THE PAGES GOT STUCK TOGETHER!
LOOKIT CH'ERE, GRATTON! WE'RE IN THE MIDDLE OF A DANG PHOTO ESSAY!
OH, BOY! DON'T START SHOOTIN' 'EM DOWN LIKE DOGS TILL I GIT PURTIED UP!
REMEMBER NOW, BOYS, KILL THE PHOTOGRAPHER LAST!
LOOK AT THAT OLD DUCK WITH HIS PUSS BURIED IN A MAGAZINE! IF HE DON'T WATCH OUT, HE'LL--

BOOMF!
THUNDERATION! WHERE DO ALL THESE TREES KEEP LEAPIN' OUT FROM?
PUT YER MAGAZINES AWAY AND LETS GIT DOWN TO BUSINESS, POTHOLE!
THE CACTUS NEEDLES LEAD TOWARD THAT OLD SALOON! THE DALTONS MUST BE HOLED UP IN THERE!
ONE MAN'S PIZEN SALOON
WE'LL KICK DOWN THE DOOR AND ORDER THEM TO SURRENDER!
Gulp! BUT BILL! THEY HAVE GUNS! SHOULDN'T WE DRAW OURS?!
DON'T WORRY! THEY WON'T DARE RESIST BOTH THE GREAT SCOUT OF THE PLAINS AND THE MASTER OF THE MISSISSIPPI!
WE HOPE!
ANNIE! YOU HANG BACK WITH P.T.! THIS AIN'T WOMAN'S WORK!
POW!
I...I THINK I RILED HER!
NAH! WHEN SHE REALLY GETS MAD, SHE'LL AIM AT THE OTHER END OF YOUR PIPE!
DUCK-WHO-SEEKS-GOLD! I SAW THE DALTON TRIBE HIDING IN THE SALOON!
GOOD WORK! ARE THE OTHERS SAFELY OUT OF OUR WAY SO WE CAN TAKE 'EM?
NO! THEY'RE GOING THROUGH THE FRONT DOOR! NOT LONG TO LIVE!
HEP HEP HEP
YIPES! WE GOTTA MOVE FAST!!!

HURRY! WE'LL HAVE TO REALLY DO IT INDIAN STYLE NOW! SNEAK AROUND BACK AND JUMP THE DALTONS WITHOUT A SOUND!
HMPH! WE FELL IN A DRY WELL! TRAPPED LIKE PRAIRIE CHICKENS!
YES, BUT, BY THUNDER, WE DID IT WITHOUT A SOUND! CONGRATULATIONS!
THOSE TWO OLD COOTS ARE COMIN' RIGHT IN THE FRONT DOOR!
THIS IS TOO EASY! QUICK-- GET OUTA' SIGHT!
CRASH!
HM... THIS IS BAD! VERY BAD! THERE'S NOBODY HERE! THEY'VE FLED LIKE RATS FROM A SINKIN' RIVERBOAT!
WHAT'S SO BAD? THEY LEFT THE MONEY!
BUT IF WE DON'T HAVE AN EXCITING CLIMAX TO THIS CHASE, P.T.'S PUBLICITY SCHEME WILL BE WORTHLESS!
BLAZING BOILERS! YOU'RE RIGHT!
WHAT DO WE DO NOW? WHAT WILL HAPPEN NEXT?
IF THIS WERE ONE OF MY DIME NOVELS, THIS IS WHERE I'D WRITE "CONTINUED NEXT WEEK" TO GIVE ME TIME TO THINK!

HOW ABOUT THIS? THE DALTONS SUDDENLY SPRING ON US FROM THE DARKNESS!
YES! THE DASTARDS HAVE NO SENSE OF FAIR PLAY!
I BUST A BOTTLE ACROSS A DALTON HEAD!
MEANWHILE, I SO DAZZLE ANOTHER DALTON WITH FANCY GUNPLAY THAT HE SWOONS!
THEN I BREAK A CHAIR ACROSS THE NEXT DALTON'S BACK!
AND I PIN TWO MORE TO THE WALL WITH BOWIE KNIVES!
NEXT I BUST A TABLE ACROSS A ROW OF DALTONS!
?
?
?
THEN I BUST MY HOSS ACROSS A--
POTHOLE! WHAT'S WRONG? WHY DID YOU STOP?
BECAUSE MY GOLDURN PENCIL BROKE JUST AS--
!
HANDS UP, YOU OLD GEEZERS!
ZOUNDS! THE DALTONS REALLY WERE LAYING IN AMBUSH, LIKE WE JUST WROTE!
LIFE IMITATES ART! DONE IN BY OUR OWN SHOWMANSHIP!
LOOKIT WHAT WE GET AS A BONUS, BOYS! SOME HIGH-CLASS, CHAMPEEN SHOOTIN' IRONS!
NOW, WHATCHA GOT IN HERE, DUCK?
HUH? THERE AIN'T NUTHIN' BUT SOME DANG DIME NOVELS!
HEY! THAT'S A COLLECTOR'S EDITION! PUT IT BACK IN ITS OIL-SKIN SLEEVE BEFORE YOU BEND IT!!
I'LL GUARD THESE TWO COOTS! YOU GUYS GO OUT AND TELL THEIR BUDDIES TO GIVE UP!

MEANWHILE, P.T. BARNUM AND ANNIE OAKLEY HAVE FINALLY LOCATED $CROOGE AND ONE-WHO-YAWNS IN THE OLD WELL...
BUT THEY'RE SITTING THERE IN TOTAL SILENCE!
STILL PRACTICING INDIAN STYLE, EH? WELL, DROP THEM A ROPE!
WAIT! DON'T CLIMB OUT TILL I GET THE CAMERA READY!
FORGET THAT! UNCLE POTHOLE WAS IN DANGER THE LAST TIME I WAS AT THIS ALTITUDE!
HE AND BILL WENT INTO THAT SALOON! WE THINK THE DALTONS GOT 'EM!
I WAS AFRAID OF THAT!
HEY, YOU! POSSE PEOPLE!
CAFÉ
THERE'S ONE OF THE DALTON RATS NOW! ANNIE, LEND ME YOUR RIFLE!
CAFÉ
BANG!
HA! MISSED ME!
WHOP!
OUCH!
GOLDURN! WHAT A RUDE POSSE YOU ARE! YOU WENT AND BROKE MY POOR BROTHER'S NOSE!
TOUGH BEANS! WHAT HAVE YOU DONE WITH OUR FRIENDS?
OH, THAT'S RIGHT! I ALMOST FORGOT! YOU'RE TA THROW DOWN YOUR GUNS OR IT'S CURTAINS FOR 'EM BOTH!
CURTAIDS VOR DA BLAYAGDORS! HA! THAD'S A GOOD WUD, EBBETT!
OW! BY DOZE!
WHAT NOW, DUCK-WHO-SEEKS-GOLD? WE CAN'T GET PAST THEM! THERE'S NO COVER OUT ON THE STREET!
YOU'RE RIGHT, BUT I GOTTA SAVE UNCLE POTHOLE AND THAT MONEY SOMEHOW!
ONE MAN'S PIZEN SALOON

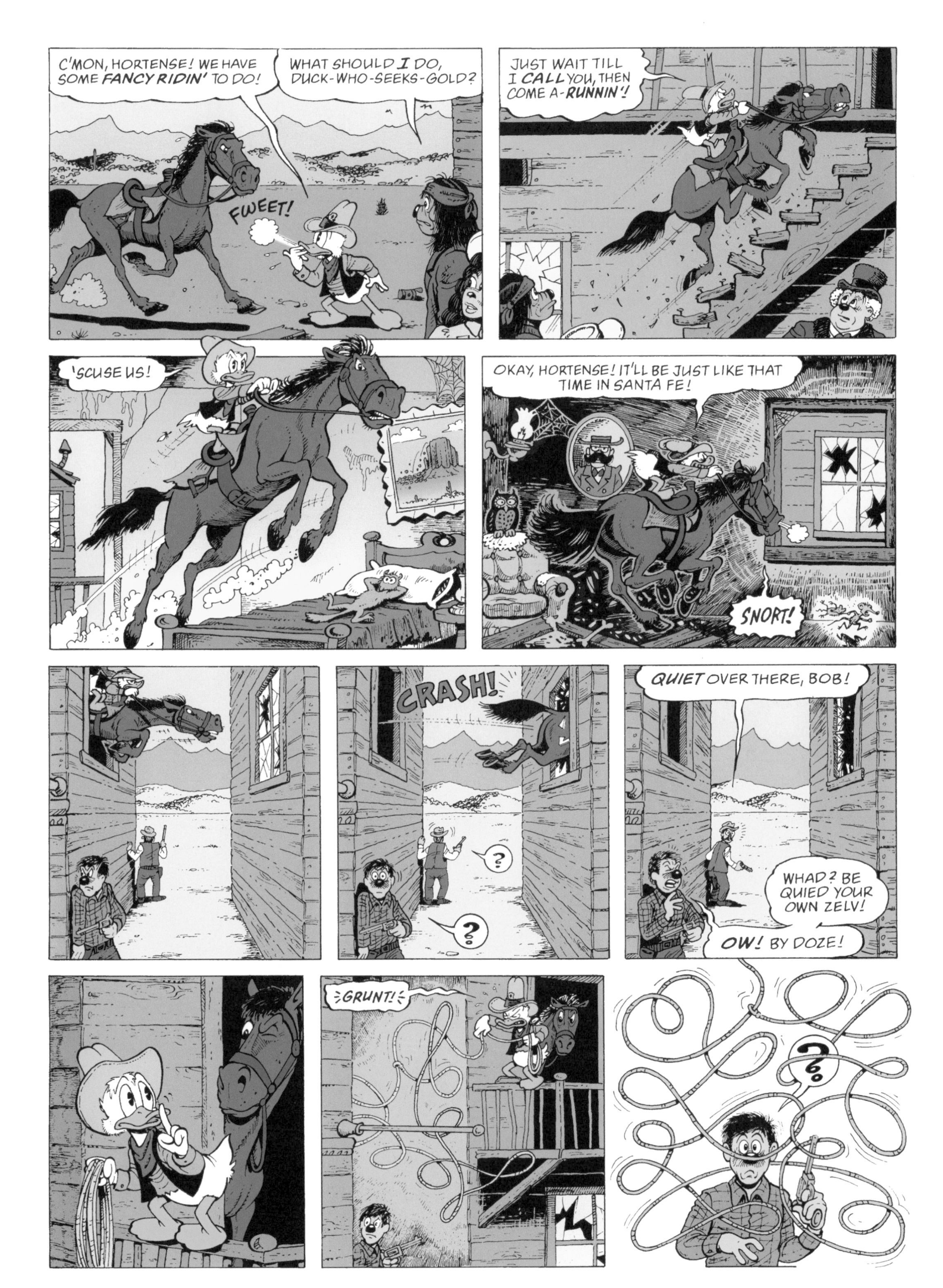
C'MON, HORTENSE! WE HAVE SOME FANCY RIDIN' TO DO!
WHAT SHOULD I DO, DUCK-WHO-SEEKS-GOLD?
FWEET!
JUST WAIT TILL I CALL YOU, THEN COME A-RUNNIN'!
'SCUSE US!
OKAY, HORTENSE! IT'LL BE JUST LIKE THAT TIME IN SANTA FE!
SNORT!
CRASH!
?
?
QUIET OVER THERE, BOB!
WHAD? BE QUIED YOUR OWN ZELV!
OW! BY DOZE!
GRUNT!
?

JERK
AGH! EBBETT! HELB!
?
WHAT THE--HOGTIED AND COVERED BY YOUR OWN GUN?
PATHEDIG, EH?
OW! BY DOZE!
I BETTER WARN GRATTON THAT SOMEBODY'S UP TA SOMETHIN'!
OGAY! I'LL,,, uh,,, WAID RIDE 'ERE!
DRAT! WE LOST THE ELEMENT OF SURPRISE, HORTENSE! WE'LL HAVE TO TRY SOMETHING DESPERATE!
GIDDYAP! HERE'S HOPING THESE BUILDINGS ARE AS DRY-ROTTED AS THEY LOOK!
GERONIMOOOOO!!
CRASH!

HANDS UP, DUCK! OR WE'LL FILL YA FULLA LEAD!
LISTEN TO HIM, BUCK! THEY HAVE OUR GUNS!
YOUR GUNS?!
THAT'S RIGHT, NEPHEW! GET 'EM!
I INTEND TO DO JUST THAT, UNCLE POTHOLE!
BANG! POW! BLAM! BWANG! BOOM!
KCHOW! BAM! POW! BLAM!
POW!
BANG! KCHOW!
GREAT FALLS, MONTANA! BUCK BROKE A CHAIR ACROSS THAT DALTON'S HEAD!
SOK!
BOP!
KRASH!
ZOW!
I TAUGHT THE LAD ALL HE KNOWS!
THERE GOES THE TABLE ACROSS THE OTHER ONE!
THAT BOY HAS THE BLOOD OF THE FIGHTIN' CLAN McDUCK!
BIFF!
BASH!
I JUST HOPE HE KEEPS IT ON THE INSIDE!
BRAVO! DID YOU SEE THE PUNCH HE JUST THREW?!
I'LL HAFTA REMEMBER TO USE THAT IN MY NEXT ISSUE!
PAF!
CRACK!
GONG!
HOO-BOY! I BET THAT HURT! THAT POOR DALTON!
CRUNCH!
RATTLE!
WHOA, NELLIE! THAT WOULD NEVER GET PAST THE CENSOR!
I HEARD YOU CALL, DUCK-WHO-SEEKS-GOLD, BUT I COULD SEE YOU NEEDED NO HELP!
HAH! ONE-WHO-YAWNS WAS PROBABLY NAPPING!

WHAT KINDA GUY ARE YOU THAT BULLETS DON'T BOTHER YA?
YOU FORGET-- YOU HAD BILL AND UNCLE POTHOLE'S GUNS! FROM THE WILD WEST SHOW!
BLANKS!
CAREFUL! THIS DOESN'T SHOOT BLANKS!
COLOSSAL! WE'LL PUT THAT WHOLE SCENE INTO THE NEXT SHOW!
I DON'T KNOW WHY BUCK YELLED "GERONIMO" WHEN HE JUMPED INTO THE AIR, BUT I'LL MAKE THAT SHOUT FAMOUS!
WHY DID YOU YELL THAT, NEPHEW?
AT THAT MOMENT, IT SEEMED EASIER THAN "GOKHLAYEH" OR "ONE-WHO-YAWNS"! I JUST USED HIS SPANISH NAME!
Gasp! Y-YOU'RE GERONIMO?!!
ER... I-I HOPE YOU DIDN'T TAKE ANY OF MY COMMENTS PERSONALLY, MR. GERONIMO!
DON'T WORRY! I'M NOT IN A SCALPING MOOD TODAY, DUCK-FULL-OF-HOT-AIR!
BESIDES, OLD BRAVES LIKE US MUST STICK TOGETHER THESE DAYS!
THAT'S TRUE! OUR GLORY DAYS ARE QUICKLY COMING TO AN END!
Z
THE GREAT INDIAN TRIBES ARE ALL ON RESERVATIONS AND WE AGING FRONTIERSMEN ARE IN SILLY WILD WEST SHOWS! WE'RE AS OBSOLETE AS THIS GHOST TOWN!
THIS YEAR'S CENSUS SHOWS THAT THE FRONTIER HAS NOW DISAPPEARED, PROMPTING THE PRESIDENT TO PROCLAIM THAT THE FIRST ERA OF AMERICAN HISTORY HAS ENDED! WE'RE OFFICIALLY RELICS OF A BYGONE AGE!
TRULY, THE SPIRIT WE REPRESENT IS DYING AWAY!

WELL, MAYBE OUR ADVENTUROUS SPIRIT WILL BE PASSED DOWN TO FUTURE GENERATIONS BY YOUNGSTERS LIKE BUCK HERE!
NO! IT'LL BE PASSED DOWN BY ME AND MY SECRET PROJECT!
MY IDEA FOR A NEW KIND OF MAGAZINE CAN'T FAIL! IMAGINE THIS--MY ADVENTURES TOLD IN A SERIES OF DRAWINGS, AND THE DIALOGUE WRITTEN INTO SOME KINDA BUBBLES!
MASTER of the MISSISSIPPI
YESSIR--SOMEDAY GREAT ADVENTURE STORIES WILL BE TOLD IN JUST SUCH A WAY AND SOLD EVERYWHERE! THE WORLD WON'T SOON FORGET THE NAME McDUCK!
AND SO...
REMEMBER, UNCLE POTHOLE--TAKE THAT MONEY AND GET CASTLE McDUCK OUT OF HOCK!
ALL RIGHT, NEPHEW, BUT HOW ABOUT IF YOU HELP ME FINANCE MY NEW MAGAZINE! IN RETURN, I'D AGREE TO MAKE YOU THE TITLE CHARACTER!
NOT A CHANCE! NOT ONLY DO I NOT HAVE THE MONEY, NO ONE WOULD BE INTERESTED IN READING A MAGAZINE ABOUT A NOBODY NAMED SCROOGE McDUCK. YOU'D BETTER DROP THAT IDEA!
Sigh!
PLOP!
YOUR LOSS, NEPHEW, BUT I COULD HAVE MADE YOU A STAR! WHY, I CAN ALMOST SEE YOUR FIRST ISSUE NOW!
THEN AGAIN, MAYBE NOT!
NEPHEW SCROOGE
PICTURE STORIES
The CHEAPEST GUN IN THE WEST!
DRAW? ARE YOU NUTS? DO YOU KNOW WHAT BULLETS COST NOWADAYS?
10¢
NO. 386
WELL, THERE THEY GO! THE WILD WEST ITSELF RIDING (AND PARTLY RUNNING) OFF INTO ITS LAST SUNSET!
BUT I'LL KEEP HUNTING FOR NEW FRONTIERS! AND I'LL NEVER FORGET THOSE WHOSE SPIRIT LEADS ME ON!
PIZEN BLUFF
PHOENIX
SUPERSTITION MOUNTAINS
AND I NEVER DID!!!

THAT WAS A SWELL STORY, UNCA SCROOGE!
YES, IT WAS ANOTHER ENCOUNTER THAT INSPIRED ME ONWARD TO EVENTUALLY MAKE MY FORTUNE!
AS A MEMENTO, I HAD BUFFALO BILL, ANNIE OAKLEY, GERONIMO AND UNCLE POTHOLE... AND THAT GREAT MONEYMAKER, P.T. BARNUM... ALL SIGN MY WILD WEST SHOW HANDBILL THAT LAUNCHED THE ADVENTURE!
"AND ON THE BACK OF THE HANDBILL ARE THE SCRIBBLES OF ANOTHER ONE OF MY IDOLS--A GOLD PROSPECTOR!"
ON THE BACK OF THIS HAND-BILL IS THE MAP TO A LOST MINE IN THE SUPERSTITION MOUNTAINS?!
HA HA! I KNOW WHAT YOU'RE THINKING...
...BUT JACOB WASN'T A DUTCHMAN--HE WAS GERMAN! HIS WASN'T THE "LOST DUTCHMAN MINE"--JUST HIS IMAGINATION!
OTHERWISE I SURE WOULDN'T HAVE LET MY SISTER MATILDA GLUE THE HANDBILL INTO THIS SCRAPBOOK!
UH... UNCA SCROOGE...
IT SAYS IN OUR GUIDE-BOOK THAT THE OLD PROS-PECTOR PEOPLE CALLED THE DUTCHMAN WAS ACTUALLY A GERMAN NAMED JACOB WALZ!
DRAT THAT SISTER OF MINE! I ALWAYS TOLD HER NOT TO BUY THE EXPENSIVE GLUE!!!
GOLLY! MAYBE UNCA SCROOGE'S STORY HAS A PART TWO SOME-WHERE IN THE FUTURE!
AND MAYBE WE'LL GET TO BE INVOLVED FIRST HAND IN IT!
JUST MAYBE...
DEPTH GAUGE
100
99
End

Walt Disney's
UNCLE SCROOGE
in "A LITTLE SOMETHING SPECIAL"
MISS QUACKFASTER, I'M GOING DOWNTOWN TO CHECK THE LATEST STOCK QUOTES. KEEP EVERYONE BUSY ON THE ANNUAL CORPORATE RECONFIGURATION!
YESSIR! WE ALL KNOW THE PROFITS FROM YOUR WORLDWIDE BUSINESS EMPIRE WILL STOP FLOWING UNTIL WE FINISH THE JOB!
WORK!
D96325
EXACTLY! NOT MY FAVORITE TIME OF YEAR!
NO, SIR! IT'S CERTAINLY NOT AS HAPPY AN OCCASION AS YOUR GOLDEN JUBILEE NEXT WEEK!
!
MY WHAT? I DON'T KNOW WHAT THAT IS, BUT THE "GOLDEN" PART SOUNDS NICE!
WHY, YOU KNOW, SIR – THE 50TH ANNIVERSARY OF YOUR ARRIVAL IN DUCKBURG!
OH, SO? HOW ON EARTH DID YOU KNOW ABOUT THAT?
THE DUCKBURG TIMES IS FULL OF IT TODAY! AND THERE ARE BIG ADS ABOUT THE CONTEST!
Duckburg Times
SCROOGE McDUCK FIFTY YEARS IN DUCKBURG
BAH! NEWSPAPERS ARE FULL OF SUCH HOGWASH! THAT'S ONE REASON I DON'T BUY THEM!
YESSIR. THE MAIN REASON IS THEY COST TEN CENTS!

WHO COULD POSSIBLY KNOW THE DAY I ARRIVED? SO FEW PEOPLE LIVED HERE THEN!
AND WHAT MALLET-HEAD IS SPREADING IT ALL OVER THE FRONT PAGE?
SCRAM
GO!
Salesmen will be EATEN!!
NOBODY IN TOWN REALLY CARES THAT MUCH ABOUT ME! THEY RESENT THAT I OWN 99.9% OF THE LAND AND BUSINESSES! ALL THEY WANT FROM ME IS PAYCHECKS AND TAXES!
BAH!
Grrr!
OH, THEY FALL ALL OVER THEMSELVES HONORING THE CITY'S FOUNDER — CORNELIUS COOT! BUT THIS TOWN WAS A FLY-SPECK UNTIL I SHOWED UP!
SNORT!
Snort!
NOW IT'S A THRIVING METROPOLIS, FILLED WITH PEOPLE WHO WANT TO KNOW WHAT SCROOGE McDUCK WILL DO FOR THEM TODAY!
HMPH! AND HERE COMES MOOCHER PAR EXCELLENCE, DONALD!
SALE
HI, UNCLE SCROOGE! I HAVE AN IMPORTANT QUESTION FOR YOU!
AND I HAVE AN IMPORTANT ANSWER FOR YOU: NO! I WON'T LEND YOU A NICKEL FOR A SODA! GO AWAY!
HUH? OH, I DON'T WANT YOU TO GIVE ME ANYTHING! I WANT TO KNOW WHAT I CAN GIVE YOU!
IT'S CRUEL TO PLAY PRACTICAL JOKES ON AN OLD MAN, NEPHEW! I COULD DROP DEAD!
IT'S NO JOKE, UNCLE SCROOGE! DIDN'T YOU SEE TODAY'S PAPER?
THAT NEWS-PAPER AGAIN? LET ME SEE!
GASP!
SNATCH!
SCROOGE McDUCK'S GOLDEN JUBILEE!
To commemorate our beloved patriarch's fifty years in Duckburg, there will be a contest! Make the best suggestion for a gift of something special for the duck who has everything, and win $1,000,000!!!

THIS IS ABSOLUTE MADNESS!
THE WINNER WILL BE ANNOUNCED AT A GIANT FREE PARTY NEXT WEEK!
MR. McDUCK! HOW ABOUT FREE WHISKER TRIMS FOR LIFE?!
I'LL BET I KNOW YOUR SECRET DESIRE— A LIFETIME SUPPLY OF NUTMEG TEA!
HAH? WHAT?
WHAT IF I COVER YOUR BIN WITH PORTRAITS OF YOUR SMILING FACE?!
SO IT BEGINS!
ACK! ONE SIDE!
HOW ABOUT A COLOGNE THAT REPELS CON MEN?
HOW ABOUT A SIGNED, NUMBERED, COLLECTIBLE, LIMITED-EDITION FIGURINE OF CORNELIUS COOT?
YUCK! WHAT'S THAT STENCH?!
HOW ABOUT MY FULL SET OF *SUPER SNOOPER* COMIC BOOKS?!
AN AUTOGRAPHED PICTURE OF MICKEY MOUSE?
WHAT ABOUT...
KEEP OUT!
AT THAT MOMENT, NOT FAR AWAY...
GYRO GEARLOOSE INVENTOR OF ANYTHING
HALF-FINISHED THOUGHTS CHEAP!
YOU WANT IT, I'LL INVENT IT (IN FIVE MINUTES!)
DRAT! THIS IS A BAD IDEA! I'LL HAVE TO START OVER AND...
KNOCK KNOCK!
COME IN!
MR. GYRO GEARLOOSE, INVENTOR-FOR-HIRE?
GREAT QUASARS! THE BEAGLE BOYS!
176-176
ONE MORE STEP AND I'LL FILL YOU FULL OF... EH... LIGHT!
RELAX! WE'RE HERE ON LEGITIMATE BUSINESS!
YES! WE'VE COMPLETELY REFORMED!
AND PIGS CAN FLY!
ER... I MEAN, WITHOUT MY PIG-ROCKET (PATENT NO. 3721)!
NO, IT'S TRUE! WE'VE GONE INTO BUSINESS, AND WE HAVE UNLIMITED FUNDS AT OUR DISPOSAL!
#3721

SEE? AND WE CAN GET MORE IF YOU SAY WE NEED IT! OBVIOUSLY, WE NO LONGER NEED TO BE CROOKS!
176-761
-GASP!- WHERE'D YOU GET THAT MUCH MONEY?
WE HAVE A SPONSOR WHO IS CONVINCED OF OUR HONESTY!
THEN WHY DID HE SAY WE'D BE WATCHED EVERY SECOND?
176-176
176-671
176-761
IX-NAY!
A SPONSOR, EH? HM... WHAT DO THE INITIALS ON YOUR MONEY BAGS MEAN?
THEY STAND FOR ...UH... FEDERAL GOVERNMENT! YEAH—WE HAVE A FEDERAL GRANT!
F.G.
OH? WELL THAT'S GOOD ENOUGH FOR ME! WHAT DO YOU NEED INVENTED?
HERE'S THE GENERAL IDEA—A GIANT SUCTION DEVICE FOR ...UM...UH... HARVESTING ORANGES!
176-176
YEAH! WE BOUGHT FLORIDA!
DON'T OVERDO IT!
IT WILL TAKE A WEEK TO BUILD AND WILL COST YOU $17,000,050 IN MATERIALS AND LABOR!
YES, I'M SURE YOUR LABOR DOESN'T COME CHEAP!
DARN RIGHT! THAT'S THE $50!
I'LL DROP MY PROJECT TO INVENT A GIFT FOR MR. McDUCK AND GET RIGHT ON IT! A MACHINE TO TURN LAWN CLIPPINGS INTO GOLD WAS A BAD IDEA ANYWAY! YOU CAN ERASE IT!
WOULDN'T WORK, EH?
HM? OH, SURE IT'D WORK GREAT! BUT I REALIZED MR. McDUCK WOULD HATE IT, SINCE IT WOULD DESTROY THE GOLD MARKET!
ARRGH!
FORGET IT! WE WON'T NEED A GOLD-MAKING MACHINE WITH THIS MASTER PLAN!
SPEAKING OF THE MASTER PLAN—I ALMOST FORGOT...
MR. GEARLOOSE, WE ALSO WANT ONE BIKE-SAUCER!
GYRO GEARLOOSE INVENTOR OF ANYTHING
HALF-FINISHED THOUGHTS CHEAP!
FOR SALE
BIKE-SAUCERS
$4.95

AS THE WEEK PASSES, DUCKBURG'S FRENZY OVER THE "SOME-THING SPECIAL" CONTEST GROWS!
WHAT ABOUT A HEN AND ROOSTER FROM PLAIN AWFUL?
HEY, McDUCK! HOW ABOUT A SUBSCRIPTION TO MODERN TIGHTWAD?
GET THEE HENCE!
A MODEL OF YOUR MONEY BIN MADE OUT OF MATCHSTICKS?! 1:1 SCALE!
WOW! WE BARELY GOT THROUGH THAT CROWD!
THANK HEAVENS YOU'RE HERE! POOR MR. McDUCK IS ABOUT TO HAVE A BREAKDOWN!
WHO'S THAT?
DONALD! HELP ME! THE ENTIRE CITY HAS GONE CRAZY OVER THIS CONTEST! THE OUTPUT OF MY FACTORIES IS DOWN 90% AND I CAN'T GET MY STAFF TO WORK ON THE ANNUAL RESTRUCTURING!
MR. McDUCK! HOW ABOUT A PLATINUM-PLATED VEEBLEFRAM?
NO... A CONDO IN TRALLA LA!
GET BACK TO WORK!
DONALD! YOU MUST FIND OUT WHO'S BEHIND THIS INSANE CONTEST AND STOP HIM!
THAT'S A BIG SECRET, UNCLE SCROOGE. BUT THEY SAY IT'LL BE REVEALED AT THE GIANT FESTIVAL TOMORROW!
GOLLY! WE'RE ASHAMED TO SAY EVEN WE WERE TRYING TO WIN THAT PRIZE FOR THE JUNIOR WOOD-CHUCKS, UNCA SCROOGE!
OH? WHAT WAS YOUR IDEA?
ALL THE INFOR-MATION ON LOST TREASURE FROM THE WOODCHUCK GUIDEBOOK!
TOO BAD IT'S NOT POSSIBLE. THE GUIDEBOOK IS FOR WOODCHUCKS ONLY!
NICE TRY! THAT MIGHT BE MY SECOND CHOICE FOR AN IMPOSSIBLE "SOME-THING"...
SO THERE IS SOMETHING SPECIAL YOU WANT! WHAT IS IT?...
TELL ME! TELL ME!! TELL ME!!!
NO!

MEANWHILE, AT THE SORCERERS' BAZAAR IN AN ANCIENT BACK ALLEY IN CAIRO...
MAGICA DeSPELL! ARE YOU STILL TRYING TO BUY A MAGIC SPELL TO HELP YOU STEAL THAT AMERICAN TYCOON'S COIN?
Marcus, Neiman & Abdul ~FINE MAGICKS~ Wands · Potions · Spells
YOU SHOULD KNOW BY NOW THAT DECENT MAGIC POTIONS AND CHARMS COST MONEY, AND THAT'S ONE THING YOU DON'T HAVE! NOW WHAT DO YOU WANT HERE?
I WANT ONE PROJECTO-GEM, ONE TRANSMUTATION WAND AND ONE BAG OF GLOBAL-TRANSPORT DUST!
HAH! MY VERY BEST MERCHANDISE! HOW DO YOU PLAN TO PAY FOR ALL THAT?
WITH THIS! AND THE TEN MORE CAMEL-LOADS OF IT I HAVE OUT BACK! SEND YOUR HELPER TO TAKE CHARGE OF IT!
PLOP!
F.G.
CHOKE YES MA'AM!
HERE, MISS DeSPELL – THAT'S THE BEST MAGIC YOU EVER BOUGHT! BUT... WHERE DID YOU GET ALL THAT MONEY?
OH, MAYBE I JUST CONJURED IT UP!
POOH! YOU COULD NEVER AFFORD A WEALTH SPELL!
HEY! WHOSE INITIALS ARE ON THESE MONEY BAGS?
F.G.
I CAST A SPELL ON MY FAIRY GODMOTHER AND MADE HER GIVE IT TO ME! NOW STOP ASKING QUESTIONS!
STAND BACK! I'M IN A HURRY!
COOT'S EMPORIUM! DUCKBURG... CALISOTA!
ER... DON'T USE THAT TRANSPORT DUST INDOORS! IT'S FAR TOO...
NO SANDALS NO BURNOOSE NO SERVICE!
FOOM
...POWERFUL...

COOT'S EMPORIUM
WELL, BOYS, OUR "ORANGE-SUCKING MACHINE" IS FINISHED! HAR!
GREAT! I PROPOSE A TOAST TO THE MASTER PLAN!
BROTHERS MINE - RAISE YOUR MUGS!
HERE'S TO... AWK!
FOOM
WHAT? IT'S THAT EYE-TALIAN WITCH!
I'M A SORCERESS, YOU LOUT!
DANG! THIS PRUNE JUICE STAIN WILL NEVER COME OUT!
PHOOEY! YOU'RE A WITCH! YOU DON'T JUST WEIGH AS MUCH AS A DUCK—YOU ARE A DUCK!
CAREFUL! SHE'LL TURN YOU INTO A NEWT!
I CAN DO MUCH WORSE WITH THE MAGIC ALL THAT MONEY BOUGHT!
STOP FIGHTIN'! SHE'S RIGHT! ALL THAT DOUGH FINALLY BOUGHT US SURE-FIRE EQUIPMENT FOR KNOCKIN' OVER McDUCK'S MONEY BIN! THANKS TO OUR NEW SPONSOR! A TOAST TO...
...FLINTHEART GLOMGOLD!
THANK YOU, GENTLEMEN AND SIGÑORINA WE SHOULD HAVE FORMED THIS TEAM YEARS AGO!
YES! OUR OBJECTIVES DO NOT OVER-LAP! I DON'T WANT McDUCK'S MONEY! ALL I NEED TO MAKE MYSELF FANTAS-TICALLY RICH IS HIS FIRST DIME!
SPEAK FOR YERSELF! WE DO WANT HIS MONEY! AND HOW!
AND I WANT NOTHING McDUCK HAS! I ONLY WANT TO SEE HIM RUINED—SO I WILL BECOME THE RICHEST DUCK ON EARTH... BY DEFAULT!

WHAT ABOUT THE MAN WHO THOUGHT UP THIS MASTER PLAN?
YEAH! THE GUY WHO GETS HALF OUR SHARE!
HE'S OUT TEST-FLYIN' HIS SKY-SCOOTER FOR SOME REASON.
176-176
176-167
PROBABLY THE SAME REASON I'M SAVING SOME TRANSPORT DUST...
PROBABLY THE SAME REASON I HAVE A JET STANDING BY...
...FOR A GETAWAY WHEN ONE OF THESE IDIOTS BOTCHES THE PLAN!
WELL, HE'D BETTER GET BACK SOON! WE NEED TO MAKE SURE WE'RE READY FOR ZERO HOUR!
YES! THE VERY INSTANT I STAND BEFORE ALL DUCK-BURG AND PROCLAIM...
PZAK!
WELCOME TO SCROOGE McDUCK'S GOLDEN JUBILEE!
YES, PEOPLE OF DUCKBURG, I AM THE MYSTERY SPONSOR OF THIS GALA CELEBRATION HONORING OUR MOST ILLUSTRIOUS CITIZEN! I WILL ANNOUNCE THE WINNER OF THE CONTEST TO CHOOSE THE "SOMETHING SPECIAL" TO BE GIVEN TO THE DUCK-WHO-HAS-EVERY-THING—AS SOON AS OUR MAYOR ESCORTS HIM FROM HIS BIN!
50 YEARS in DUCKBURG
$CROOGE McDUCK
EVEN AS I SPEAK, I CAN ENVISION THE EX-PRESSION OF DELIGHT ON DEAR MR. McDUCK'S FACE!
YAAAAAH!!

ER... HOW'S THAT AGAIN?
WHAT NINCOMPOOP THINKS I WOULD TAKE ANY PART IN THAT INFERNAL JUBILEE IDIOCY?
PLEASE, UNCA SCROOGE! YOUR BLOOD PRESSURE!

LOOK AT THE TROUBLE AND MONEY IT'S COST ME! ALL MY FACTORIES IN TOWN ARE CLOSED BECAUSE THE ENTIRE POPULATION IS AT THAT FREE PICNIC — WAITING TO SEE WHO WON A MILLION BUCKS!

AND MY OFFICE STAFF HAS STOPPED MY ANNUAL CORPORATE REVIEW, SO ALL MY BUSINESSES ARE SHUT DOWN WORLD-WIDE! I'M LOSING BILLIONS EVERY SECOND!
I'LL KICK YOU OUT ON YOUR...
SAY, UNCLE SCROOGE! MAYBE IF YOU WENT DOWN THERE, THEY'D GET ON WITH THE FESTIVAL AND GET IT OVER WITH!
THAT'S A GOOD IDEA! YOU'RE RARELY SO INSPIRED, DONALD!
TUT!
WELL, ARE YOU COMING OR NOT, MAYOR? DON'T DAWDLE!
HUH? WHAT? TO THE FESTIVAL? YES SIR!!!
DONALD, YOU STAY HERE WITH MISS QUACKFASTER. DON'T LET ANYONE INTO THE BIN!
ME? BUT I WANT TO SEE IF I... ER... WON THE MILLION BUCKS WITH... UH... MY IDEA OF A LIFETIME TAX EXEMPTION!
SO, THAT'S WHY YOU WERE SO INSPIRED, EH? OKAY, I'LL SAVE YOU THE TRIP...
≈BUZZZ≈ SORRY, YOU LOSE! THAT WOULD BE WRONG IF I WERE GOING TO SAY WHAT MY SECRET DESIRE REALLY IS — WHICH I'M NOT!
NOW LET'S GO!
*#%@!
ALL RIGHT YOU HOARDS OF MOOCHERS! LET'S GET THIS FARCE OVER WITH!
HEH! WOTTA KIDDER! THAT'S WHY WE... EH... LOVE HIM SO!

IT IS MY PRIVILEGE TO WELCOME OUR GUEST OF HONOR, THE FIRST CITIZEN OF DUCKBURG, THE DUCK WHO... (ETC. ETC.)!
MOAN! KEEP YOUR EYES ON MY BIN, BOYS! THIS WILL TAKE HOURS!
MEANWHILE, BACK AT THE MONEY BIN...
WE'LL JUST SIT TIGHT UNTIL UNCLE SCROOGE GETS BACK, MISS QUACK-FASTER! I WON'T LET ANYBODY IN THE DOOR!
RIGHT!
NOT EVEN US?
?!
WE'RE HERE TO SET UP A SPECIAL SURPRISE PARTY FOR SCROOGE AS PART OF THE JUBILEE!
WELL, THAT'S DIFFERENT! SURE, C'MON IN!
WE DON'T WANT NO TROUBLE FROM YOU, DUCK! HIT THE ROAD OR I'LL HAFTA GET TOUGH!
WHAAAT?
YOU IMBECILE! THAT'S NOT HOW CUTE LI'L DUCKS TALK!
OKAY, SMART GUY! YOU TRY IT!
WE SOWWY WE TALK NAUGHTY, UNCA DUCKY! OO GIVE-UM BIG HUG?
SAAAY... DID SOMEBODY SLIP THESE KIDS SOME SPIKED PUNCH DOWN AT THAT PARTY?
NAH, BUT LISSEN UP, PAL, HERE'S THE DEAL! McDUCK SENT US UP TO FETCH HIS NUMBER ONE DIME SO HE CAN DISPLAY IT AT THE CELEBRATION!
YOU, UH, GOT A PROBLEM WITH THAT?
HOMINA... HOMINA...
THAT DANG DUCK WILL SCREW UP THE WHOLE PLAN!
NAH, IT'S THE OLD SECRETARY WHO CONTROLS THE BIN'S DEFENSE SYSTEM! YOU DISTRACT AND COLDCOCK HIM WHILE I DEAL WITH HER!
!!!

SO WHAT'LL IT BE, BUDDY? DO I GET THE DIME, OR...
DIME? OH... SURE GRANDMA, SURE... WHATEVER UNCLE SCROOGE WANTS!
WHY ARE DAISY AND GLADSTONE SO SECRETIVE? IS HE TRYING TO STEAL MY GIRL AGAIN? I'D BETTER DO SOMETHING!
MEANWHILE, BACK AT THE FESTIVAL...
...THE MASTER OF THE MISSISSIPPI, THE TERROR OF THE TRANSVAAL, THE LAIRD OF THE CLAN McDUCK, THE KING OF THE KLONDIKE, THE...
THAT NUT HASN'T EVEN FINISHED MY INTRODUCTION YET!
!
?
...THAT DUCK AMONG DUCKS, THE ⸗GROAN⸗ RICHEST DUCK IN THE WORLD, THE TYCOON'S TYCOON, THE (ETC. ETC.)!
IT'S A TRICK! BACK TO THE BIN! FAST!
NO! NOT YET! IT'S TOO SOON! SOMEBODY STOP HIM!
DO SOMETHING, YOU MORONS! DON'T JUST SIT THERE! SHOOT HIM! SHOOT HIM!
SHOOT THE GUEST OF HONOR? IN THE BACK?
ER... WOULDN'T THAT PUT A DAMPER ON THE FESTIVITIES?

MEANWHILE...
WHAT'S THE IDEA, DAISY? WHY ARE YOU SO COZY WITH GLADSTONE?
WITH WHO? OH, HIM! MAYBE I GOT SOME BIZNIZ WIT' HIM! WHAT'S IT TO YA?
JUST THAT MAYBE I HAVE A LI'L "BIZNIZ" WITH YOU MY OWNSELF... EH, TOOTS?
YOU WACKY DUCK! WHAT ARE YOU...
HMMMF!
SMOO--
AND RIGHT OUTSIDE...
THERE'S UNCA DONALD! EVERYTHING LOOKS OK!
MAYBE... BUT I'LL CHECK INSIDE!
BEAT IT!
ONE SIDE, NEPHEW!
!!!
GASP! IT'S A FALSE IMAGE!
CAST BY MAGICA DeSPELL!
OOF!
BEAT IT!
WHUMP!
YIPES! A GIANT MACHINE POISED TO TEAR INTO UNCA SCROOGE'S MONEY VAULT!
WHY WOULD MAGICA WANT TO DO THAT?
TALK! JUST WHAT ARE YOU UP TO?
EEK! YOU'VE CRACKED THIS EXPENSIVE TRANS-MUTATION WAND! I'LL SUE!
BUT BEFORE LITIGATION CAN COMMENCE...
--OOCH!

@#%☆@
SPIT! GAG! SPIT!
HEY! WHAT HAPPENED?
LOOK AT YOU! HAR HAR!
CHECK A MIRROR AND YOU'LL LAUGH OUTTA THE OTHER SIDE OF YER BEAK!
176-671
WHOOOOAAA... I CAN'T STAND UP!
176-176
THIS PLAN HAS REALLY TAKEN AN UGLY TURN!
AND IN MISS QUACKFASTER'S OFFICE...
I DON'T CARE WHAT YOU CLAIM MR. McDUCK TOLD YOU, MR. GANDER, I WON'T TURN OFF THE DEFENSES!
LISTEN LADY, EITHER YOU... UH, OH... I FEEL FUNNY!....
EEEK!
PLOP!
OOPS! HOW EMBARRASSING! SORRY, LADY!
FORGET HER! SHE DROPPED THIS! IT MUST BE THE MASTER KEY TO THE ENTIRE SECURITY GRID!
176-
CLICK!
I DID IT! THE WHOLE SYSTEM'S SHUT DOWN!
GO! GO! GO!

AWK! THAT BUZZ-SAW THING IS TEARING INTO MY BIN! STOP THE— YIPES! COUGH!
SUCK!
ZAZZNZZZ
YOU CAN'T BEAT GOOD, CHEAP FOOF BOMBS WHEN THE CHIPS ARE DOWN! EAT FOOF, McDUCK!
FOOF!
INSIDE...
GOT HIM! THAT WAS AS DISTRACTED AS I EVER SAW A GUY!
I KNOW JUST HOW HE FELT! GAG!
176-671
HEY, FELLAS! LOOKIT!
OUR MACHINE IS SUCKING THE BIN DRY!
HOO-HAH! LET'S HURRY DOWN AND GET THE ESCAPE POD READY!
SUCK!
HURRY? THAT'S EASY FOR YOU TO SAY!
OH, HERE! I'LL HELP YOU, FER CRYIN' OUT LOUD!
176-176
CAN'T YOU DO SOME-THING? THIS IS VERY IRRITATING!
OH, YES! I'LL SWITCH OFF THIS BROKEN WAND!
CLIK
TAP! TAP!
THE CROWD BELOW IS TOO CONFUSED TO DO ANYTHING!
THE PLAN IS A COMPLETE SUCCESS! HERE YOU GO, MISS MAGI CASTA SPELLICA!
THE NUMBER ONE DIME! GRAZIE!
176-617
WHAT HAPPENED TO McDUCK?
DON'T WORRY! I FOOFED THEM ALL BLIND!
C'MON! THE ESCAPE CAPSULE IS READY!
176-176

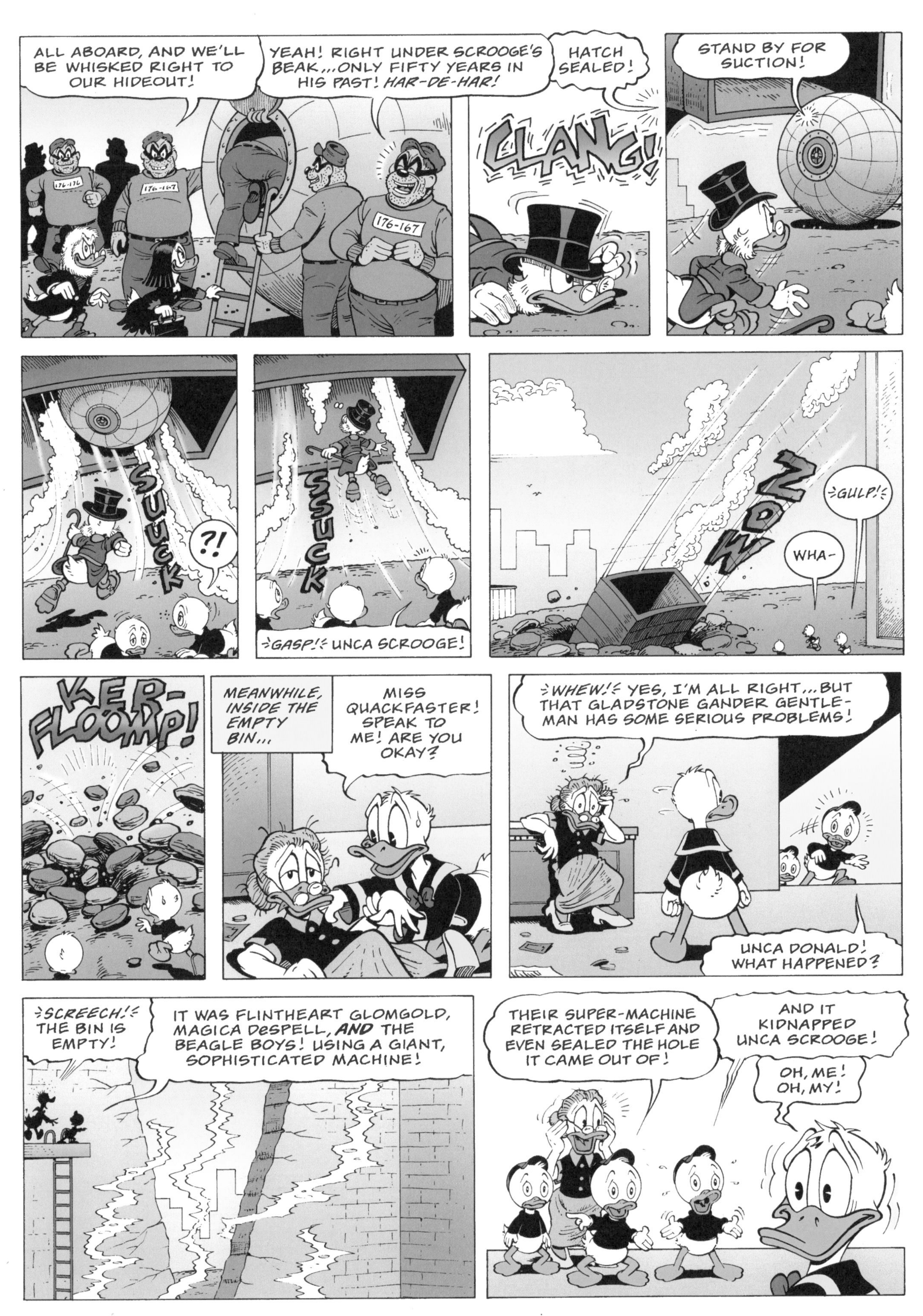
ALL ABOARD, AND WE'LL BE WHISKED RIGHT TO OUR HIDEOUT!
YEAH! RIGHT UNDER SCROOGE'S BEAK,..ONLY FIFTY YEARS IN HIS PAST! HAR-DE-HAR!
176-176
176-167
176-167
HATCH SEALED!
CLANG!
STAND BY FOR SUCTION!
SUUCK
?!
SSUCK
GASP! UNCA SCROOGE!
ZOW
GULP!
WHA-
KER-FLOOMP!
MEANWHILE, INSIDE THE EMPTY BIN...
MISS QUACKFASTER! SPEAK TO ME! ARE YOU OKAY?
WHEW! YES, I'M ALL RIGHT... BUT THAT GLADSTONE GANDER GENTLE-MAN HAS SOME SERIOUS PROBLEMS!
UNCA DONALD! WHAT HAPPENED?
SCREECH! THE BIN IS EMPTY!
IT WAS FLINTHEART GLOMGOLD, MAGICA DeSPELL, AND THE BEAGLE BOYS! USING A GIANT, SOPHISTICATED MACHINE!
THEIR SUPER-MACHINE RETRACTED ITSELF AND EVEN SEALED THE HOLE IT CAME OUT OF!
AND IT KIDNAPPED UNCA SCROOGE!
OH, ME! OH, MY!

LATER, SOMEWHERE BELOW THE STREETS OF DUCKBURG...
OHH... WHERE AM I?
I'D BETTER GET OUT OF THIS GIANT VACUUM CLEANER BEFORE SOMEBODY TURNS IT BACK ON!
I'LL HEAD FOR THE LIGHT SOURCE.
I'M UNDERGROUND SOMEWHERE! THERE'S MY MONEY!
BUT WHERE'S THAT LIGHT COMING FROM?
HUH? BUILDINGS! OLD, CRUMBLING, BOARDED-UP BUILDINGS!
DUCKBURG DRYGOODS
HARDWARE
WHY, IT'S DUCKBURG! THE ORIGINAL DUCKBURG! OR WHAT'S LEFT OF IT! JUST THE WAY IT LOOKED ON THE DAY I ARRIVED, FIFTY YEARS AGO!
OVER THE YEARS, NEW CONSTRUCTION SLOWLY ROSE ABOVE THE ORIGINAL STREET LEVEL—BUT THE OLD CITY IS STILL PART OF THE FOUNDATION OF THE CITY ABOVE!
WELL, HERE'S WHERE THE LIGHT IS COMING FROM!
YIPPEE! WE DID IT! WE FINALLY DID IT!
YEAH! THANKS TO GLOMGOLD'S MONEY!
BUT MAINLY, THANKS TO THE MASTER PLAN GIVEN TO ME BY THE TRUE ARCHITECT OF OUR SUCCESS!
THANK YOU!
176-716
YES, I'VE HAD MANY DECADES OF EXPERIENCE WITH TEAMWORK, AND I'M THE ONLY GUY LEFT WHO'S BEEN IN DUCKBURG LONGER THAN McDUCK!
HIM!
CRASH

YOU!!! BLACKHEART BEAGLE! MY OLDEST ENEMY!
GAH! I REALLY WISH PEOPLE WOULD MAKE MORE RESTRAINED ENTRANCES IN THIS JOINT!
YEAH! NOW I HAVE MATCHING PRUNE JUICE STAINS!
VERY STYLISH!
WELL, IF IT ISN'T "YOUNG" SCROOGE! WHAT AN UNEXPECTED BONUS!
SEE IF HE'S ALONE!
NOBODY IN SIGHT!
DID YOU PLAN TO LICK THE LOT OF US SINGLEHANDEDLY? YES, YOU PROBABLY DID! SAME OL' SCROOGE!
I THOUGHT YOU'D RETIRED, BLACKHEART!
I DID! BUT YOUR JUBILEE SEEMED LIKE THE PERFECT TIME TO JOIN MY INEPT GRANDSONS AND TAKE A LAST STAB AT YOU!
YOU KNOW—FOR OLD TIME'S SAKE!
HOW SWEET! BUT HOW DO YOU FIGURE ON GETTING MY MONEY OUT OF TOWN? WAIT! I THINK I KNOW!
YOU'D REMEMBER MY ABANDONED SUBWAY TUNNELS AND THE OLD LOCOMOTIVES THERE!
COOT'S EMPORIUM
VERY GOOD, SCROOGE!
BUT YOU CAN'T HIDE A TRAINLOAD THAT BIG! MY NEPHEWS WILL ALREADY BE SEALING OFF EVERY WAY OUT OF TOWN!
OH, LET ME TELL YOU THE BEST PART!
I SPENT YEARS HAULING STOLEN DYNAMITE DOWN INTO THESE TUNNELS! WHEN I DETONATE IT BEHIND US, THIS TOWN WILL BE TOO BUSY TO WORRY ABOUT US!
GASP! THAT'LL BLOW THE FOUNDATIONS OUT FROM UNDER DOWNTOWN DUCKBURG!
SAY! YOU NEVER TOLD US ABOUT THAT PART OF YOUR PLAN!
YEAH? SO WHAT?

YOU JUST WATCH OUR GUEST WHILE WE LOAD UP THE TRAIN!
CAREFUL WHO YOU ORDER AROUND, GRAMPS!
GULP! WHAT'LL I DO? MY NEPHEWS WILL NEVER FIND ME DOWN HERE!
WHAT'S THIS? LOOKS LIKE THE UNDERGROUND TELEPHONE LINES MY COMPANY INSTALLED 47 YEARS AGO!
THE WIRES LOOK PRETTY FRAYED, BUT I THINK I'M GLAD I NEVER SPENT ANY MONEY TO UPGRADE, THE SYSTEM! I WONDER IF...
OH, WOE! OH, ANGUISH!
?
SOB! I'M FINALLY BEATEN! AND ON MY 50TH ANNIVERSARY, TOO! I'M REDUCED TO POVERTY!
WAIL!
KICK! KICK! KICK!
FOR CRYING OUT LOUD! PULL YOURSELF TOGETHER!
MEANWHILE, AT THE FESTIVAL SITE...
SPREAD OUT! THEY SUCKED UNCLE SCROOGE UNDERGROUND! WE GOTTA FIND HIM!
BAH! THE WHOLE CITY'S ALREADY BEEN USED IN THIS JUBILEE HOAX!
YEAH! IT TURNS OUT TO BE JUST ANOTHER OF THE ANNOYANCES McDUCK CAUSES EVERY OTHER AFTERNOON!
HE'S YOUR UNCLE! YOU FIND HIM!
YOU INGRATE OF A MAYOR! MY UNCLE OWNS 99.9% OF THIS TOWN, BUT HAS HE EVER TRIED TO TELL YOU HOW TO DO YOUR JOB?
WELL, NO, BUT...
IF NOT FOR HIM, THIS TOWN WOULD STILL BE A FEW SHACKS AROUND AN OLD FORT ON KILLMOTOR HILL! IT'S IMPOSSIBLE TO IMAGINE WHAT EFFECT HE'S HAD ON ALL OUR JOBS! OR EVEN OUR LIVES!
MY UNCLE IS DUCKBURG! I DON'T KNOW ABOUT YOU, BUT MY LIFE WOULD BE A LOT EMPTIER WITHOUT SCROOGE McDUCK!
OKAY, DUCK! I'M WITH YOU!
ME TOO!
CALL HEADQUARTERS AND ASK EVERY WOODCHUCK IN THE STATE TO HURRY HERE AND JOIN THE SEARCH!

HEY! THE PHONES AREN'T WORKING!
WAIT! THAT SOUNDS LIKE MORSE CODE!
CLIK, CLIK, CLIK.
WHAT'S IT SAY?
"COOT'S EMPORIUM... S.O.S.... COOT'S EMPORIUM"!
COOT'S EMPORIUM!?
WHY, THAT WAS MY FATHER'S GENERAL STORE! BUT IT WAS TORN DOWN DECADES AGO, WASN'T IT?
WHERE WAS IT, GRANDMA?

I RECALL WHEN I STOOD ON THE FRONT STEP, MOUNT DEMONTOOTH WAS TO THE RIGHT, THE BAY WAS TO THE LEFT, KILLMULE HILL WAS DUE NORTH...
HARDWARE
THAT'D BE THIS WAY!
C'MON EVERYONE!
NOT SO FAR AWAY...
STOP CRYING, YOU OLD WRETCH!
SOB! IT'S JUST THAT I FEEL SO SORRY FOR MYSELF! AND FOR YOU!
KICK! KICK! KICK!

SORRY FOR ME? WHEN I FINALLY HAVE THE FIRST COIN EARNED BY THE WORLD'S MOST SUCCESSFUL MAN? WHEN I CAN USE IT IN A MAGIC SPELL TO MAKE MYSELF INFINITELY WEALTHY? HEEHEEHEE!
BUT NOW I'M PENNILESS! SOB! A COMPLETE FAILURE!
A GULP! PENNILESS FAILURE?
YES, AND I FEEL AWFUL ABOUT IT! AFTER ALL YOUR YEARS OF EFFORT, MY DIME IS NOW WORTHLESS FOR YOUR MAGIC CHARM! SOB!
GREAT CIRCE! YOU'RE RIGHT! IF MY SPELL DEPENDS ON THIS COIN'S OWNER BEING THE RICHEST MAN ON EARTH-IT'S WORTHLESS TO ME NOW!
HOW CAN I GET MY SPELL TO EVER WORK?
SOB THE LEAST I CAN DO IS GIVE YOU A SUGGESTION... SOB... FOR A PRICE...
HEY SCROOGE! THE TRAIN'S ALL LOADED! TIME TO SAY OUR FINAL FAREWELLS!

YOU'VE HAD QUITE A HALF-CENTURY IN DUCKBURG, *EH,* SCROOGE? THIS OLD TOWN WON'T SEE THE LIKES OF EITHER OF US AGAIN!
I GRANT YOU THAT!

I KNOW JUST THE THING TO TOAST THE OCCASION! A LAST GLASS OF SARSAPARILLA FROM COOT'S SODA FOUNTAIN! YOU KNOW,...FOR OLD TIMES!
WHY NOT? I'M NOTHING IF NOT A SENTIMENTAL SLOB!
Moxie

ME, TOO! WHY, I CAN ALMOST SEE OL' CLINTON COOT THERE BEHIND THE COUNTER, SERVIN' UP THOSE BIG...*UH*...

...ICE CREAM CONES...HE... *UH*...?

WOMP!

HALP! I'M A-SWARMIN' IN DUCKS!
HOLD HIM DOWN, BOYS, WHILE I STOP THAT TRAIN!

BLACKHEART IS THE ONLY ONE WHO KNOWS THE WAY THROUGH THIS LABYRINTH! IF THE KIDS CAN HOLD HIM, I'VE WON THE DAY!

WOW! FIFTY COAL-CARS FILLED WITH *CASH!*
ALL ABOARD! NEXT STOP, ***EASY STREET!***
HOP ABOARD, MISS DeSPELL. WE'RE READY TO GO!
176-671

WHAT'S KEEPING GRANDPA?
GREAT SCOTT, LOOK!
YOU'RE LICKED! YOU'LL NEVER FIND YOUR WAY OUT OF HERE WITHOUT BLACKHEART! I'LL RUN YOU FULL-STEAM INTO A DEAD END!
GRANDPA! WHADDA WE DO?
PUT 'EM ON THE RIGHT TRACK, SCROOGE, OR I'LL BLOW THE BOTTOM OUTTA DUCKBURG!
186-802
CLANK
SO LONG, McDUCK! WE'RE ON OUR WAY TO BUY A PRIVATE ISLAND IN THE PACIFIC!
YEAH, HAWAII!
BYE, PAUPER! HAHAHA!
NOTHIN' CAN STOP THEM NOW! THAT TUNNEL LEADS TO THE MAIN TRACK OUTTA TOWN!
I KNOW... I BUILT IT 48 YEARS AGO... AND CONDEMNED IT 46 YEARS AGO!
YEAH, I... HUH? YOU CONDEMNED IT?
YES, WHEN I DETERMINED IT WASN'T STRONG ENOUGH TO SUPPORT A LOADED TRAIN!
186-802
ER... WHAT WILL IT FALL TO?
THE DUCKBURG MAIN SEWER... THAT I PUT IN 47 YEARS AGO!
I SUGGEST WE TAKE COVER!
GET A WHIFF OF THAT FREE AIR! THE "SWEET SMELL OF SUCCESS"! HOO-HAH!
I SMELL SOMETHING, ALL RIGHT, BUT WHATEVER IT IS, I'D SAY IT'S MORE DISTASTEFUL THAN ANY "SUCCESS" I'VE EXPERIENCED!
CHUG! CHUG! CHUG!
YAAAH!
CRUMBLE!

CRASH!
YOU'LL REGRET THAT, SCROOGE!
GRAB HIM!
186-802
I'LL HANDLE BLACKHEART! DONALD, THERE'S HIS RADIO-CONTROLLED DETONATOR! DISARM IT!
WHO? ME?!
OH, NO! HE HAS ONE OF GYRO'S BIKE SAUCERS!
TRY AND CATCH ME NOW, SCROOGE! BWAH-HAHAH!
ZOOM!
SNAG!
UH, OH! THAT'S THE MANHOLE COVER WE CAME DOWN!
QUIET! I NEED TO CONCENTRATE ON STAYING IN ONE PIECE!
I'M WORRIED! IT'S BEEN TOO LONG SINCE THOSE DUCKS WENT DOWN BELOW!
WAIT! I HEAR SOMEONE COMING!
LOOK OUT!
ZOOM
DADGUMMIT! LEGGO MY GABARDINES, YOU OLD FOOL! YOU'LL KILL US BOTH!

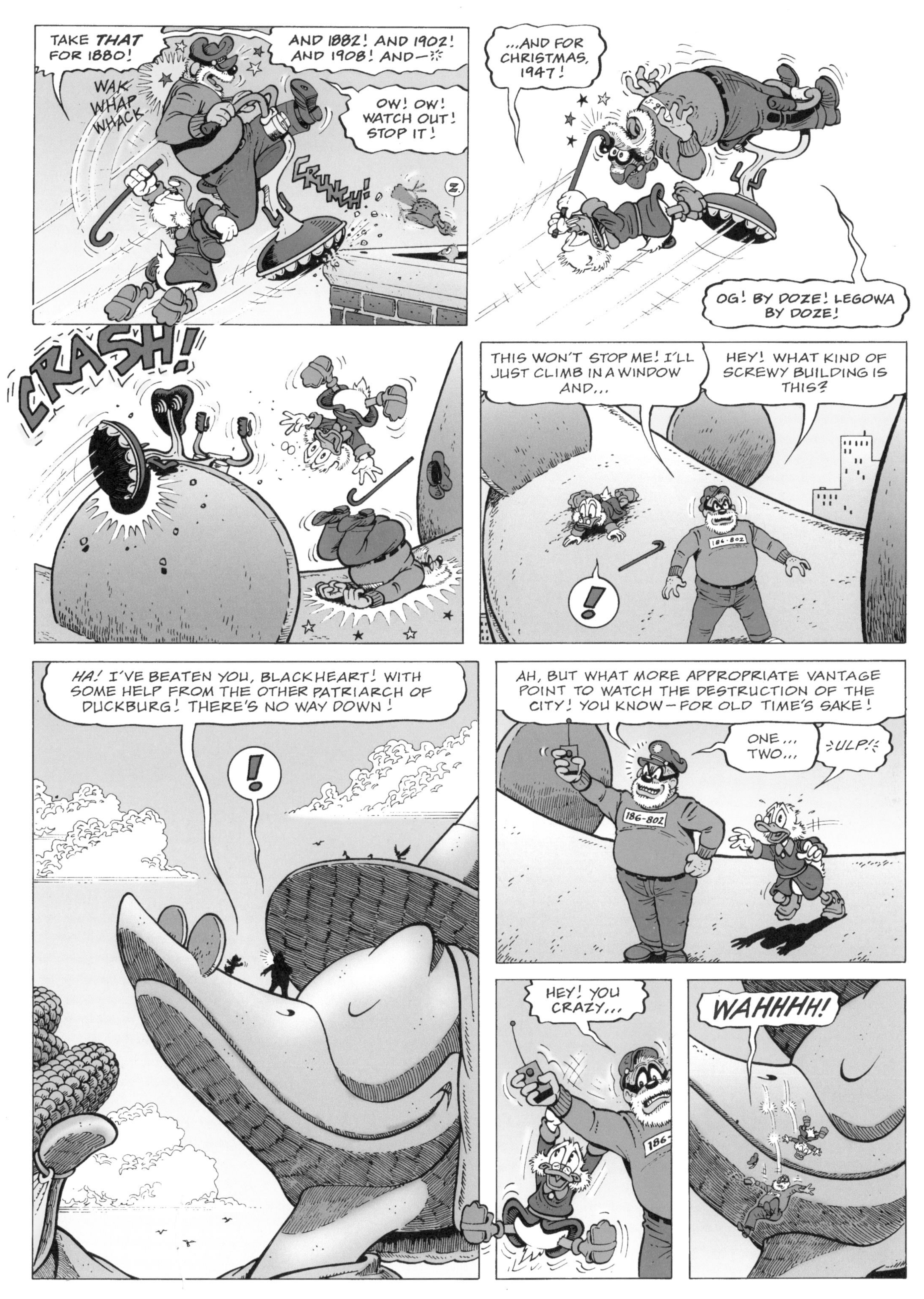
TAKE THAT FOR 1880!
AND 1882! AND 1902! AND 1908! AND—
WAK WHAP WHACK
OW! OW! WATCH OUT! STOP IT!
CRUNCH!
...AND FOR CHRISTMAS, 1947!
OG! BY DOZE! LEGOWA BY DOZE!
CRASH!
THIS WON'T STOP ME! I'LL JUST CLIMB IN A WINDOW AND...
HEY! WHAT KIND OF SCREWY BUILDING IS THIS?
!
186-802
HA! I'VE BEATEN YOU, BLACKHEART! WITH SOME HELP FROM THE OTHER PATRIARCH OF DUCKBURG! THERE'S NO WAY DOWN!
!
AH, BUT WHAT MORE APPROPRIATE VANTAGE POINT TO WATCH THE DESTRUCTION OF THE CITY! YOU KNOW—FOR OLD TIME'S SAKE!
ONE... TWO...
ULP!
HEY! YOU CRAZY...
WAHHHH!

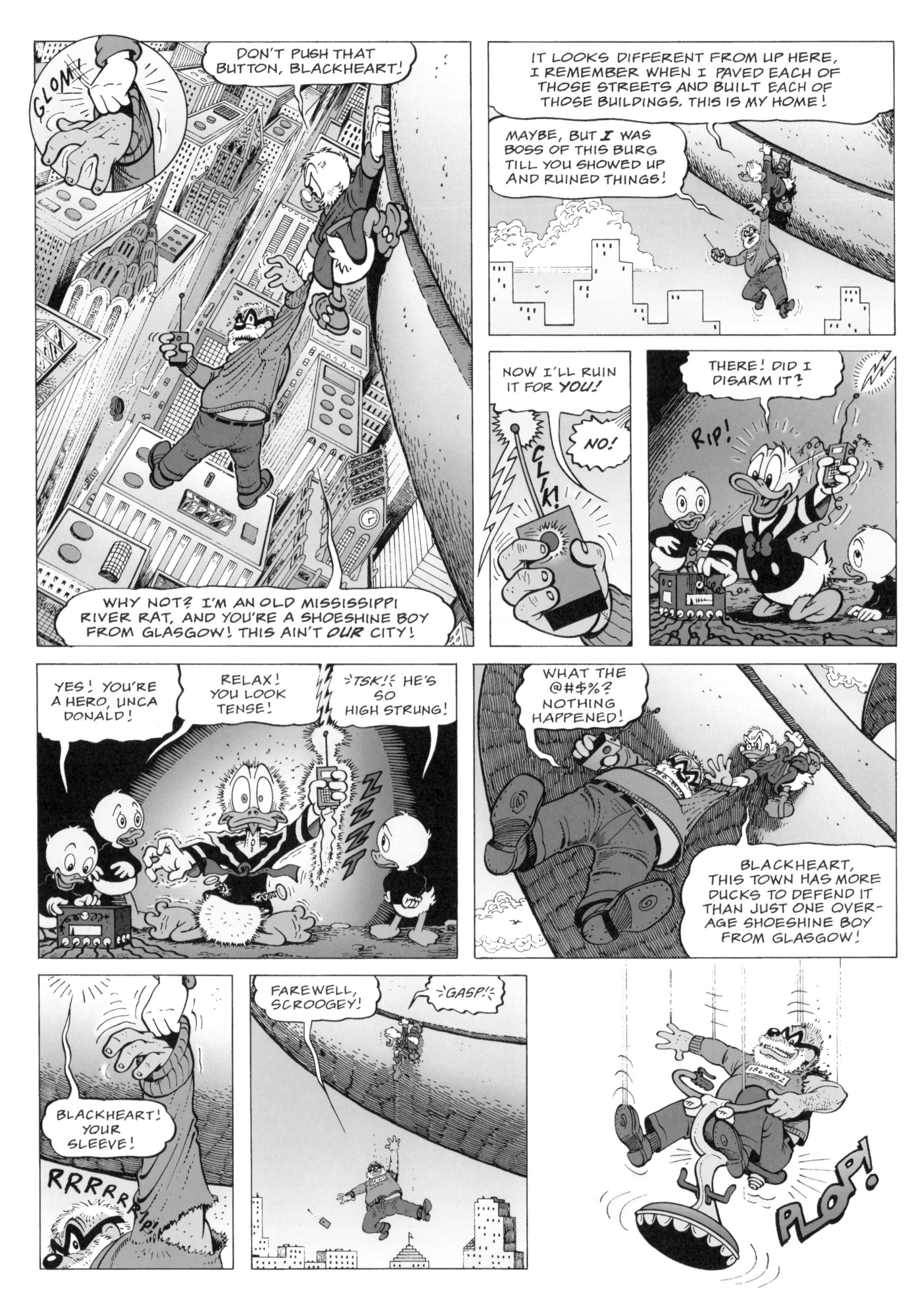
DON'T PUSH THAT BUTTON, BLACKHEART!
GLOM!
WHY NOT? I'M AN OLD MISSISSIPPI RIVER RAT, AND YOU'RE A SHOESHINE BOY FROM GLASGOW! THIS AIN'T OUR CITY!
IT LOOKS DIFFERENT FROM UP HERE, I REMEMBER WHEN I PAVED EACH OF THOSE STREETS AND BUILT EACH OF THOSE BUILDINGS. THIS IS MY HOME!
MAYBE, BUT I WAS BOSS OF THIS BURG TILL YOU SHOWED UP AND RUINED THINGS!
NOW I'LL RUIN IT FOR YOU!
NO!
CLIK!
THERE! DID I DISARM IT?
RIP!
YES! YOU'RE A HERO, UNCA DONALD!
RELAX! YOU LOOK TENSE!
TSK! HE'S SO HIGH STRUNG!
ZZZT
WHAT THE @#$%? NOTHING HAPPENED!
BLACKHEART, THIS TOWN HAS MORE DUCKS TO DEFEND IT THAN JUST ONE OVER-AGE SHOESHINE BOY FROM GLASGOW!
BLACKHEART! YOUR SLEEVE!
RRRRRRIP!
FAREWELL, SCROOGEY!
GASP!
176-802
PLOP!

YOU DIDN'T THINK I'D LET IT ALL END SO EASILY, DID YOU? I SPOTTED THIS CONTRAPTION HOVERING BELOW ME!
I'LL BE BACK!
WAIT UNTIL MY CENTENNIAL, OKAY?
DID YOU SAY THAT'S THE FOUNDER OF THE BEAGLE BOYS?
YES! AND HE'S GETTING AWAY!
MAYBE I CAN HELP!
CHIEF! PUT A REWARD ON HIS HEAD! FAST!
ER... OKAY... I SET A... UH... THOUSAND-DOLLAR REWARD ON... ER... WHOEVER THAT IS!
NOW WHAT?
JUST WAIT!
LAND-O-GOSHEN! WHAT A WIND IS KICKING UP!
50
HEY!
MMF!
OOF!
UF!
MF!
GPH!
@#%☆@
BOINK!
PLOP!
GOOD WORK, MR. GANDER! HERE'S A DOLLAR THIRTY-SEVEN. I'LL HAFTA OWE YOU THE REST!
NO HURRY!
MERCY! WHAT ABOUT THE REST OF THE GANG?

THAT QUERY TAKES US TO THE OUTLET OF THE MAIN DUCKBURG SEWER LINE...
EEW!
MADAM, I BELIEVE YOUR EAU-DE-COLOGNE HAS BEEN OVERCOME!
EEK! WHAT ARE THEY DOING HERE?
OH, MY TRANSMUTATION WAND CAME ON AGAIN! THESE EXPENSIVE MAGIC DEVICES ARE TOO SENSITIVE FOR MY TASTE!
ZZT
POP
SPUT
176-671
I'LL FIX THAT OL' WAND! UG, GRUNT!
HERE! LET ME!
176-176
STEP STEP
POP
ZT
STOMP
CRACK!
THAT'S BETTER!
I HOPE THIS TRANSPORT DUST ISN'T TOO WET FOR AN ESCAPE FROM THIS STUPID TOWN!
176-167
176-617
176-176
ESCAPE?! HEY! COUNT US IN ON THAT!
WHY NOT? SCROOGE GAVE ME AN IDEA THAT YOU BOYS COULD HELP WITH! GATHER 'ROUND!
176-167
THE VALLEY OF THE LIMPOPO!
FOOM!
BAH! GOOD RIDDANCE! I KNEW THAT PACK OF IDIOTS WOULD RUIN THE PLAN AND...
WAIT! THE VALLEY OF...?... THAT'S WHERE I... UH-OH!
GLOMGOLD TO HOVER-JET! PICK ME UP IMMEDIATELY! I MUST GET BACK TO SOUTH AFRICA ...NOW!

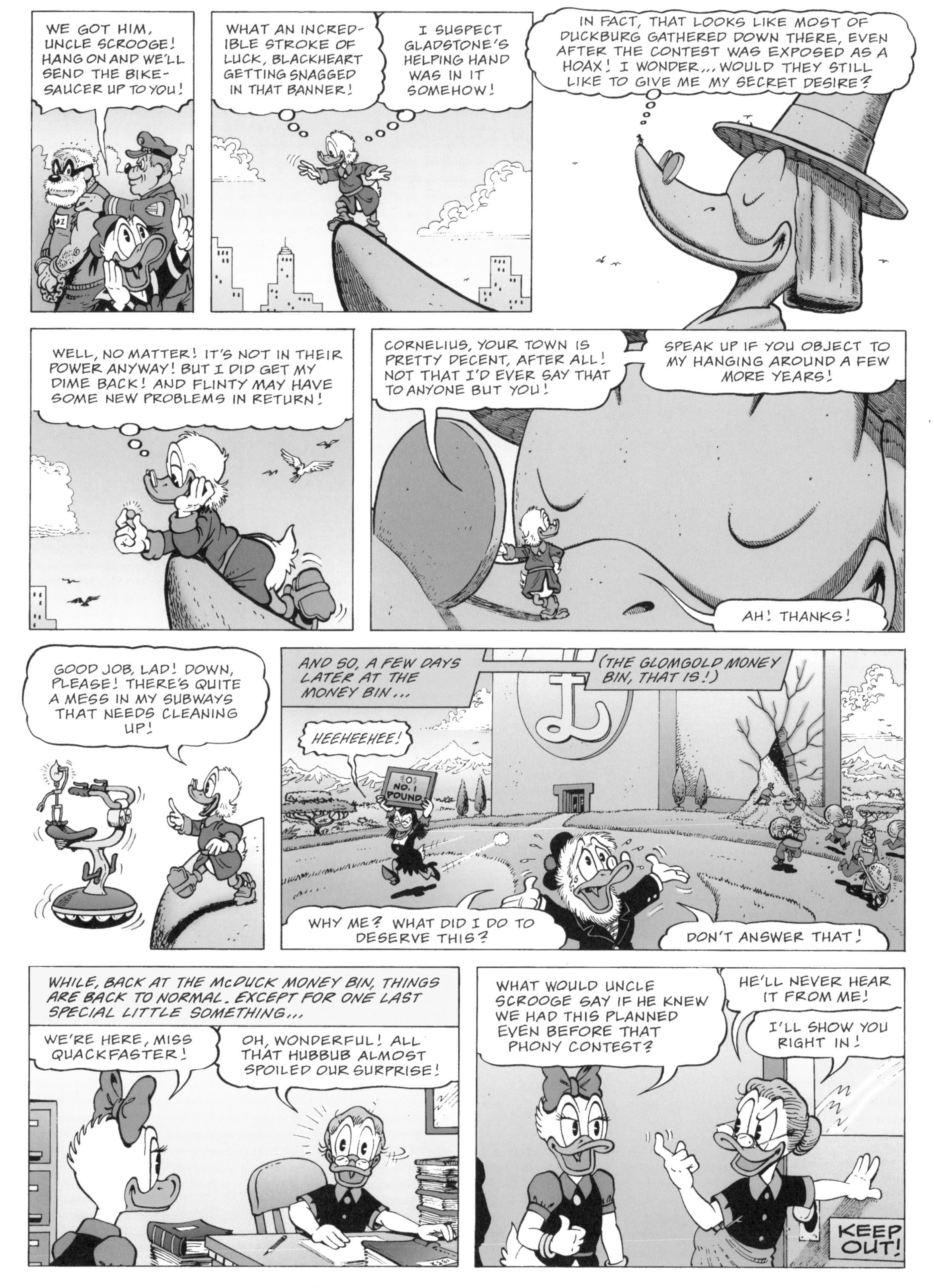
WE GOT HIM, UNCLE SCROOGE! HANG ON AND WE'LL SEND THE BIKE-SAUCER UP TO YOU!
WHAT AN INCREDIBLE STROKE OF LUCK, BLACKHEART GETTING SNAGGED IN THAT BANNER!
I SUSPECT GLADSTONE'S HELPING HAND WAS IN IT SOMEHOW!
IN FACT, THAT LOOKS LIKE MOST OF DUCKBURG GATHERED DOWN THERE, EVEN AFTER THE CONTEST WAS EXPOSED AS A HOAX! I WONDER... WOULD THEY STILL LIKE TO GIVE ME MY SECRET DESIRE?
WELL, NO MATTER! IT'S NOT IN THEIR POWER ANYWAY! BUT I DID GET MY DIME BACK! AND FLINTY MAY HAVE SOME NEW PROBLEMS IN RETURN!
CORNELIUS, YOUR TOWN IS PRETTY DECENT, AFTER ALL! NOT THAT I'D EVER SAY THAT TO ANYONE BUT YOU!
SPEAK UP IF YOU OBJECT TO MY HANGING AROUND A FEW MORE YEARS!
AH! THANKS!
GOOD JOB, LAD! DOWN, PLEASE! THERE'S QUITE A MESS IN MY SUBWAYS THAT NEEDS CLEANING UP!
AND SO, A FEW DAYS LATER AT THE MONEY BIN...
(THE GLOMGOLD MONEY BIN, THAT IS!)
HEEHEEHEE!
NO. 1 POUND
WHY ME? WHAT DID I DO TO DESERVE THIS?
DON'T ANSWER THAT!
WHILE, BACK AT THE McDUCK MONEY BIN, THINGS ARE BACK TO NORMAL. EXCEPT FOR ONE LAST SPECIAL LITTLE SOMETHING...
WE'RE HERE, MISS QUACKFASTER!
OH, WONDERFUL! ALL THAT HUBBUB ALMOST SPOILED OUR SURPRISE!
WHAT WOULD UNCLE SCROOGE SAY IF HE KNEW WE HAD THIS PLANNED EVEN BEFORE THAT PHONY CONTEST?
HE'LL NEVER HEAR IT FROM ME!
I'LL SHOW YOU RIGHT IN!
KEEP OUT!

MR. McDUCK, THERE'S A SOMEONE HERE WITH SOMETHING SPECIAL FOR YOU!
WELL, THROW HIM OUT! I'M BUSY TRYING TO MAKE SURE EVERY PENNY OF MY MONEY IS BACK IN THE BIN!
SAY, ISN'T THAT...
SHHH!
NOW RUN ALONG! THIS WON'T BE SOMETHING FOR THE EYES OF A JUNIOR WOODCHUCK!
NO KIDDING!!!
AND, MISS QUACKFASTER—TELL WHOEVER IT IS THAT THE CONTEST WAS A HOAX! THEY WERE NEVER GOING TO GIVE ME MY SECRET DESIRE!
YOU KNOW, SCROOGE—THIS IS ALSO THE FIFTIETH ANNIVERSARY OF SOMETHING ELSE!
SNAP!
IT'S BEEN FIFTY YEARS SINCE YOU LEFT THE KLONDIKE!
GOLDIE!
WH-WH-WHAT DO YOU W-W-WANT?
YOUR FAMILY AND FRIENDS CHIPPED IN TO FLY ME HERE FOR YOUR GOLDEN JUBILEE! THEY ALL WANTED TO GIVE SOMETHING TO THE DUCK WHO HAS EVERYTHING THAT MONEY CAN BUY!
L-L-L-LIKE WH-WH-WHAT?
SOMETHING ONLY I CAN GIVE HIM! JUST A LITTLE SOMETHING... SPECIAL!

DAGNABBIT! I'M TOO BUSY FOR THIS KIND OF FOOLISHNESS!
I KNOW, I KNOW!
I'LL BET THAT IDIOT NEPHEW OF MINE PUT YOU UP TO THIS! WAIT'LL I GET MY HANDS ON HIM!
HIM AND A BUNCH OF OTHER "IDIOTS"!
I HAVE A WORLDWIDE EMPIRE TO RUN! I CAN'T JUST DROP EVERYTHING AND FRITTER AWAY TIME ON NONSENSE!
I KNOW! I KNOW!
I'LL WAIT!
BYE, SCROOGE!
CLIK!
GRUMBLE, GRUMBLE!
SIGH!
SCRAM
HANDS OFF!!
FIRST 50 YEARS in DUCKBURG
$CROOGE McDUCK
Finis!

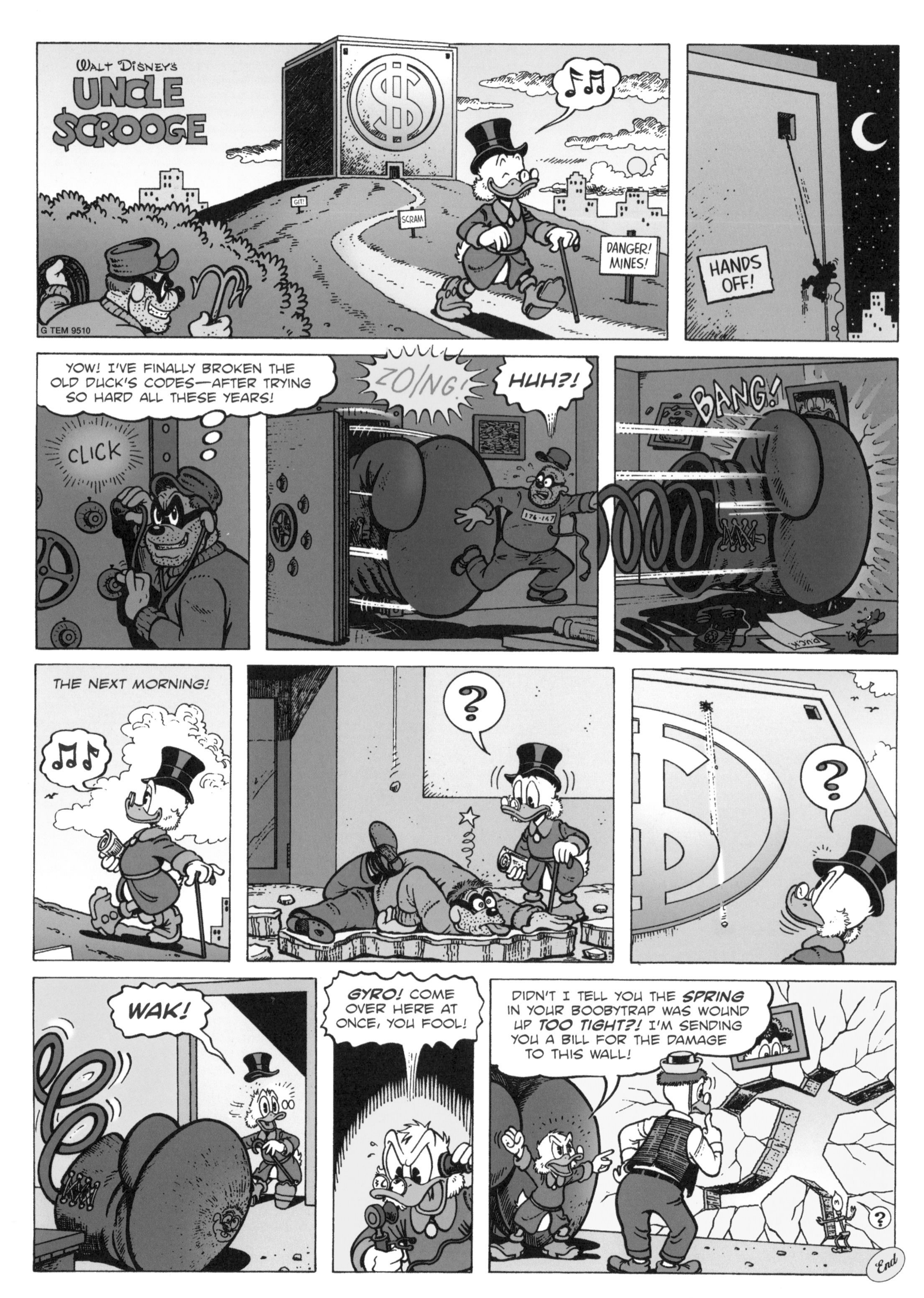
WALT DISNEY'S
UNCLE SCROOGE
GIT!
SCRAM
DANGER! MINES!
G TEM 9510
HANDS OFF!
YOW! I'VE FINALLY BROKEN THE OLD DUCK'S CODES—AFTER TRYING SO HARD ALL THESE YEARS!
CLICK
ZOING!
HUH?!
176-167
BANG!
THE NEXT MORNING!
?
?
WAK!
GYRO! COME OVER HERE AT ONCE, YOU FOOL!
DIDN'T I TELL YOU THE SPRING IN YOUR BOOBYTRAP WAS WOUND UP TOO TIGHT?! I'M SENDING YOU A BILL FOR THE DAMAGE TO THIS WALL!
?
End

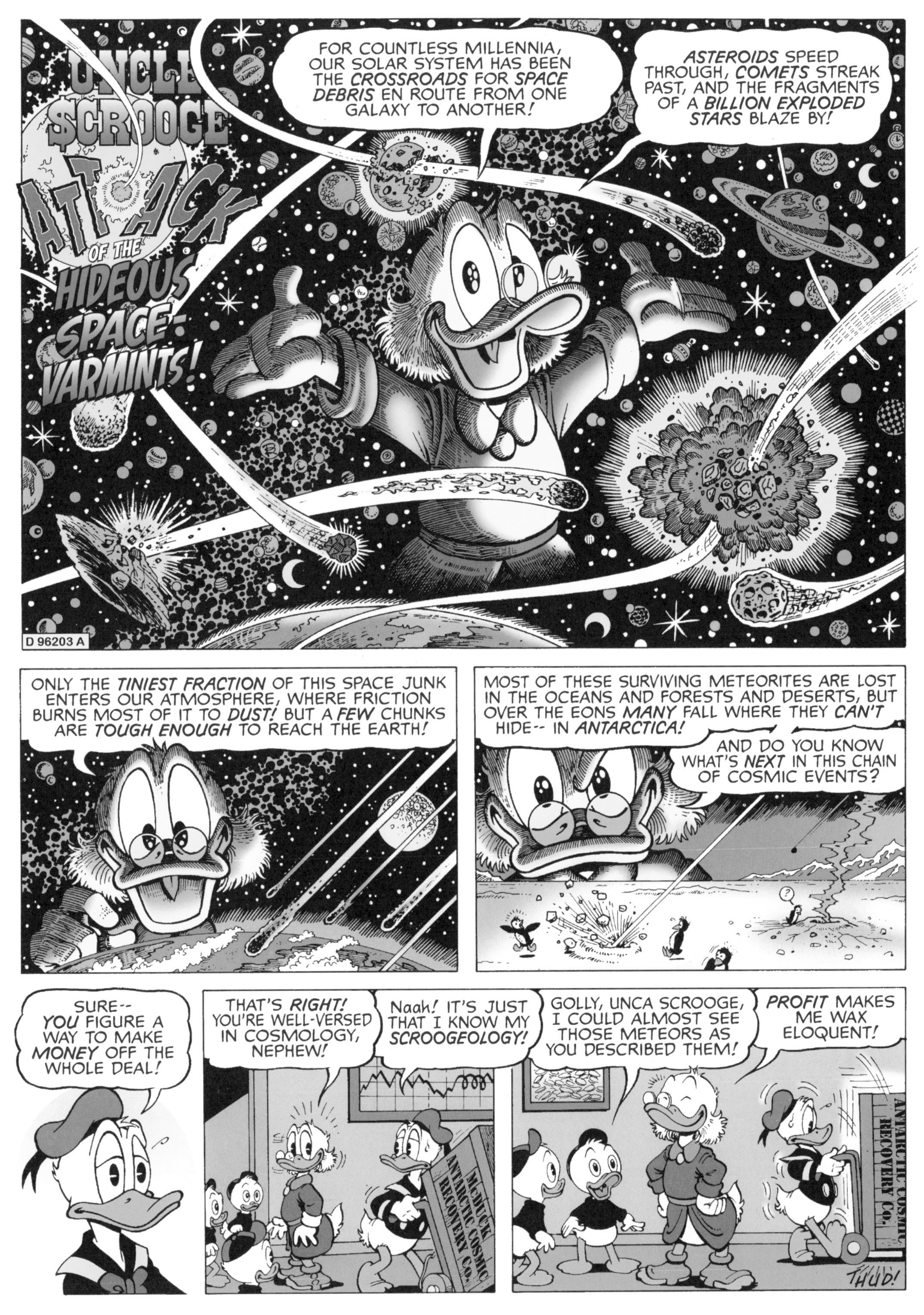
UNCLE $CROOGE
ATTACK OF THE HIDEOUS SPACE-VARMINTS!
FOR COUNTLESS MILLENNIA, OUR SOLAR SYSTEM HAS BEEN THE CROSSROADS FOR SPACE DEBRIS EN ROUTE FROM ONE GALAXY TO ANOTHER!
ASTEROIDS SPEED THROUGH, COMETS STREAK PAST, AND THE FRAGMENTS OF A BILLION EXPLODED STARS BLAZE BY!
D 96203 A
ONLY THE TINIEST FRACTION OF THIS SPACE JUNK ENTERS OUR ATMOSPHERE, WHERE FRICTION BURNS MOST OF IT TO DUST! BUT A FEW CHUNKS ARE TOUGH ENOUGH TO REACH THE EARTH!
MOST OF THESE SURVIVING METEORITES ARE LOST IN THE OCEANS AND FORESTS AND DESERTS, BUT OVER THE EONS MANY FALL WHERE THEY CAN'T HIDE-- IN ANTARCTICA!
AND DO YOU KNOW WHAT'S NEXT IN THIS CHAIN OF COSMIC EVENTS?
?
SURE-- YOU FIGURE A WAY TO MAKE MONEY OFF THE WHOLE DEAL!
THAT'S RIGHT! YOU'RE WELL-VERSED IN COSMOLOGY, NEPHEW!
Naah! IT'S JUST THAT I KNOW MY SCROOGEOLOGY!
McDUCK ANTARCTIC COSMIC RECOVERY CO.
GOLLY, UNCA SCROOGE, I COULD ALMOST SEE THOSE METEORS AS YOU DESCRIBED THEM!
PROFIT MAKES ME WAX ELOQUENT!
ANTARCTIC COSMIC RECOVERY CO.
THUD!

AND I EXPECT BIG PROFITS FROM MY NEW ANTARCTIC COSMIC RECOVERY Co.! IT WAS SET UP TO FIND PRECIOUS METALS OR JEWELS IN THE METEORS THAT LITTER THE ICEPACK!
HANDS OFF
SCRAM
SO THIS IS A CRATE OF SPACE TRASH FROM PENGUIN LAND?
YES, BUT MY SALVAGERS SAID THIS WAS A PARTICULARLY INTERESTING METEOR!
McDUCK ANTARCTIC COSMIC RECOVERY Co.
DON'T YOU HAVE ENOUGH WAYS TO MAKE MONEY?
IT... IT'S JUST THAT I'VE CONQUERED EVERY CORNER OF THIS WORLD! I MISS THE NEW FRONTIERS I HAD IN THE OLD DAYS!
CREAK!
SEARCHING FOR VALUABLE METEORS IS A FRESH CHALLENGE! IT'S AS CLOSE AS I CAN GET TO THE FRONTIERS OF THE STARS!
WOW! LOOK!
THIS IS AN ODD METEOR! IT'S MADE OF METAL!
AND IT'S HOLLOW! HOW COULD THAT BE?
BONG! BONG!
HERE'S A CRACK-- LET'S PRY IT APART!
WOW! THIS ISN'T A METEOR! IT'S FULL OF MACHINERY!
CRONK!
BAH! IT MUST BE AN OLD SPUTNIK MELTED DOWN DURING RE-ENTRY! WORTHLESS!
NO! THIS MECHANISM IS NOT OF THIS EARTH!
AND LOOK AT THIS HOLE! AS IF IT WAS SHOT DOWN BY SOME ALIEN POWER!
!
⇒GULP!⇐ YOU MEAN BY BIG GREEN MONSTERS HAVING A SPACE WAR?
UNCLE SCROOGE, LET'S RECRATE THAT THING AND SHIP IT BACK TO THE SOUTH POLE!
NOT SO FAST!

LET'S HAVE A CLOSER LOOK! MAYBE I CAN FIND A NEW TECHNOLOGY THAT I CAN SELL FOR BILLIONS OF "EARTHLING" DOLLARS!
THIS SEEMS TO BE THE MAIN MECHANISM IN THE THING!
LOOKS LIKE WHATEVER BLASTED THE HOLE KNOCKED THAT DOOHICKEY LOOSE!
I WONDER WHAT WOULD HAPPEN IF I RECONNECTED THE DOO TO THE HICKEY?
THE FIRST THING THAT WILL HAPPEN IS THAT YOUR NEPHEWS WILL HASTILY DEPART BEFORE YOU DISINTEGRATE THIS SIDE OF DUCKBURG!
ZZT!
TOO LATE! I CAN FEEL MY ATOMS COMING LOOSE!
RUMBLE
FLOP!
WAIT! THE ALIEN "BOX" ISN'T DOING ANYTHING! IT'S THE MONEY BIN THAT'S VIBRATING! IT'S AN EARTHQUAKE!!!
RUMBLE
EVERYBODY OUT-SIDE BEFORE A WALL FALLS ON US!
RUMBLE
KEEP OUT!
!
THERPLUNK!
HEY! WHEN DID YOU DIG THIS MOAT?!
I DIDN'T! SOME-THING STRANGE IS HAPPENING!
IT'S YOUR BIN! IT'S MOVING OFF ITS FOUNDATION!
RUMBLE

Er.... AREN'T THERE VARIOUS AND SUNDRY LAWS OF PHYSICS BEING VIOLATED HERE?
HANDS OFF
SCRAM
I'LL SAY! THIS IS NO EARTHQUAKE! IT HAS TO BE THE RESULT OF UNCA SCROOGE TURNING ON THAT ALIEN CONTRAPTION!
YOU'RE RIGHT! PERHAPS I SHOULD DISCONNECT THE HICKEY FROM THE DOO!
TOO LATE! IT'S OUT OF REACH!
YOUR BIN IS ENVELOPED IN SOME SORT OF ENERGY FIELD THAT'S TAKING IT SOMEWHERE!
BUT... WHERE?
HOP IN MY CAR AND WE'LL CHASE IT!
YIPES! IT'S HEADING FOR MY BRAND-NEW OFFICE BUILDINGS!
CRUNCH!
CLUNK!
LOOKS LIKE YOU JUST LOST TWO RENTAL PROPERTIES!
Hm... BUT MAYBE I GAINED A NICE TOURIST ATTRACTION?
LOOK OUT!
HEY, McDUCK! YOUR BIN JUST KNOCKED THE TOP OFF OF CITY HALL!
MY BIN? I SUPPOSE I HAVE THE ONLY THREE-CUBIC-ACRE MONEY BIN IN TOWN OR SOMETHING?
FASTER, NEPHEW, FASTER!!!
IT'S NO USE, UNCA SCROOGE! YOUR BIN IS GETTING HIGHER EVERY MINUTE!

THAT STRANGE ALIEN BOX IS TAKING YOUR BIN STRAIGHT TO OUTER SPACE! IT'S LOST!
I'M NOT LICKED YET! TAKE A RIGHT ON CORNTASSEL ROAD JUST AHEAD AND STOP AT THE FIRST FARM!
MR. McDUCK! THE RENT CHECK IS THE MAIL! HONEST!
RELAX, CLEM! I JUST WANT TO GET SOMETHING OUT OF MY OLD HAY BARN!
SCREECH!
THIS HAD BETTER BE A SPACEPORT I DIDN'T HAPPEN TO KNOW ABOUT!
YOU DON'T KNOW HOW RIGHT YOU ARE, WISEGUY! I'VE KEPT SOMETHING STORED HERE FOR YEARS, IN CASE OF EMERGENCY!
Oh, YES-- THIS IS JUST WHAT WE NEED! BUT WHERE DO YOU KEEP THE FLUBBER?
HMPH! MY 1902 ROLLS-REGAL IS NOT WHAT WE CAME FOR!
IT'S HERE-- IN THE SILO!
OMIGOSH! A ROCKET SHIP!!!
IT'S A MOON ROCKET THAT GYRO GEARLOOSE BUILT FOR ME! I ONLY MADE ONE TRIP, SO IT'S BARELY GOT A HALF-MILLION MILES ON THE ODOMETER!
WHAT ABOUT FUEL? AND AIR?
HERE'S ENOUGH IN THE TANKS FOR A FEW DAYS-- THAT'S ALL WE'LL NEED!
MOO!
ALL ASHORE, BOSSY! WE DON'T HAVE SPACESUITS IN YOUR SIZE!
GET THAT OLD GOAT OUT OF THE PILOT SEAT!
HECK, NO! LET HIM FLY HIS OWN ROCKET! YOU KIDS AND I ARE STAYING ON MOTHER EARTH!

WAITAMINNIT! OPEN THE AIRLOCK AND LET US OUT!
CRASH!
ROAR!
NO TIME, NEPHEW! MY BIN IS GETTING FURTHER AWAY EVERY SECOND!
CLEAR THAT STUFF OUT OF THE WAY AND CHECK THOSE GAUGES FOR ME!
SEEMS YOUR RESIDENT FARMER WAS USING THIS HULK AS HIS CORN CRIB!
AND HIS ROOT CELLAR! LOOK-- HE WON A BLUE RIBBON AT THE COUNTY FAIR FOR THESE PRESERVES!
THE RADAR SHOWS YOUR BIN IS JUST AHEAD, UNCA SCROOGE!
BUT SO WHAT IF WE CATCH IT?! HOW DO WE TURN IT AROUND?
DO SOMETHING TO THAT ALIEN BOX, MAYBE! I... I'LL THINK OF SOMETHING!
I HOPE!
THEN THINK FAST, BECAUSE WE'RE ALMOST THERE!
IT SURE IS MOVING SLOWLY! WHERE COULD THE BOX EVER HOPE TO GO AT THAT SPEED?
JUST COUNT OUR BLESSINGS AND PREPARE TO LAND! BUCKLE UP, AND PUT YOUR TRAY TABLES IN THEIR FULL UPRIGHT AND LOCKED POSITIONS!
HOLY COW! THIS IS ONE WEIRD MOON ROCKET!
YOU KNOW THAT GYRO!
PIGEONS KEEP OFF!

SUIT UP AND FOLLOW ME! WE'LL--
WAIT, UNCA SCROOGE! SUDDENLY THE INSTRUMENTS ARE REGISTERING A POWER SURGE!
WHAT HAPPENED TO THE STARS? THEY BECAME STREAKS OF LIGHT!
YIPES! THE BIN IS GOING INTO SOME SORT OF HYPERDRIVE, AND TAKING US WITH IT!
HURRY! TAKE OFF!
BUT... I CAN'T LEAVE MY BIN!
WE HAVE TO, UNCA SCROOGE! THAT ALIEN BOX COULD DRAG US TOO FAR FROM HOME TO EVER RETURN!
WHEW! THE STARS ARE BACK!
BUT... BUT THAT LARGE LIGHT STREAK IS MY BIN-- DASHING OFF TO PARTS UNKNOWN!
FORGET YOUR DARN MONEY, UNCLE SCROOGE! WE'RE JUST LUCKY WE'RE NOT TOO FAR FROM EARTH TO GET BACK!
Uh... YOU'D BETTER LOOK AGAIN, UNCA DONALD! THAT'S NOT EARTH!
IT'S JUPITER! WE MUST BE ABOUT 200 MILLION MILES FROM EARTH!
GULP! SO HOW LONG WILL IT TAKE US TO GET HOME?
AT OUR TOP SPEED OF 5,000 MPH IT WOULD TAKE OVER FOUR YEARS! WE HAVE ENOUGH AIR AND FOOD FOR FOUR DAYS!
Oog!
WAIT! MAYBE UNCLE SCROOGE HAS SOME AIR TANKS HIDDEN AWAY THAT THE OLD MISER FORGOT ABOUT!
EVEN I DON'T HOARD AIR, NEPHEW!
SPLAT! SPLAT!

WELL, NO SPARE AIR TANKS, BUT WE'RE IN GOOD SHAPE IN THE INTERPLANETARY-HEN-FRUIT DEPARTMENT!
HEY! LOOK AT THIS GAUGE!
THIS SENSOR SHOWS ANOTHER POWER-SURGE NEARBY! THAT MEANS YOUR BIN MUST HAVE STOPPED RIGHT AFTER WE HOPPED OFF!
WHERE? WHERE?
25¢
WOW!
A FEW DAYS' FLIGHT-- THATAWAY! WE COULD JUST ABOUT REACH IT WITH OUR FUEL AND AIR!
THERE MUST BE A REASON THAT BLASTED BOX TOOK MY BIN THERE!
MAYBE THERE'S AN ALIEN SPACE STATION OR MOTHERSHIP!
PACKED FULL OF SLIMY GREEN MONSTERS? NO, THANK YOU! I'LL STAY RIGHT HERE AND EAT EGGS!
DON'T BE A DOPE, NEPHEW! WHENEVER I WAS LOST AND STARVING IN THE WILDER NESS, EVEN AN ENEMY CAMP WAS A WEL- COME SIGHT! FULL SPEED... THATAWAY!
3½ DAYS, 400,000 MILES, AND SEVERAL OMELETS LATER, THE DUCKS APPROACH THEIR UNKNOWN DESTINATION!
THIS IS WHERE MY BIN ENDED ITS LITTLE JOYRIDE?
WHAT IS IT? SOME KIND OF AN OUTER SPACE MOUNTAIN RANGE?
IT'S A DENSE SECTION OF THE ASTEROID BELT-- A BAND OF LARGE AND SMALL PLANETARY DEBRIS THAT ORBITS THE SUN BETWEEN MARS AND JUPITER!
LOOK! TWELVE O'CLOCK HIGH!
THERE IT IS! THE MONEY BIN!
BUT LOOK AT IT! SOMETHING WEIRD HAS HAPPENED!!!

SOMEBODY-- OR SOMETHING-- HAS ANCHORED MY BIN TO THAT ASTEROID!
AND THERE'S A RING OF MONEY DRIFTING AROUND IT!
IT'S BEING EJECTED THROUGH A HOLE BUSTED IN THE FRONT OF YOUR BIN!
OUR AIR IS DANGEROUSLY LOW! EVEN IF THAT'S THE WORK OF MARTIAN BEAGLE BOYS, WE NEED TO BEG THEM TO SAVE OUR LIVES!
I'M LANDING! SUIT UP, DONALD!
ME?!
WHAT HAS TAKEN POSSESSION OF UNCLE SCROOGE'S MONEY BIN? WHAT STRANGE ALIEN BEASTS ARE DESPOILING HIS BILLIONS? AND WHY? TO FIND OUT, WE SHIFT OUR POINT OF VIEW TO SEE...
HOOO--EEEE! AH'M GITTIN' PLUMB TUCKERED OUT! THIS IS POW'RFUL HARD WORK!
JUNIOR! SKEE-DADDLE DOWN TA YER MAW AN' ASK HER TA FETCH ME UP A COLD-DRANK!
SHORE THANG, PAW!

AIN'T YOU DONE GITTIN' SHET A' ALL THET DANG JUNK YET?
IT MIGHT GO A LICK FASTER IF'N YOU WUZ TA HE'P ME A MITE, GRAMPS!
AH AIN'T-A GONTA' BE COTCHED A-MESSIN' WITH THET STUFF! WHEN THE MININ' COMP'NY FINDS YOU IN THAR STOREHOUSE, THEY'LL SIC THE LAW ON YA'!
GRAMPS, YOU KNOW THAT THE BIG MININ' OU'FITS STOPPED WORKIN' THIS AS-TEE-ROID BELT A FLERN'S AGE AGO! ANYTHIN' THEY LEFT BEHIND 'EM IS FAIR PICKIN'S!
?
AH CAIN'T FIGGER WHY THEY LEFT THIS OLD SHED FULLA' USELESS METAL CHIPS, BUT IT'LL MAKE A RIGHT NICE HOMESTEAD WHEN AH CLEANS IT OUT!
MEBBE...
DADBURN IT! WHAR'S MAH COLD-DRANK?
HEY, MAAAW!
AH, PLEEZ, MAW! WHY CAIN'T AH HAVE ONE A' MAH VIDDY-BOOKS?
ON ACCOUNT A' YOU HAIN'T DONE YORE CHORES! YOU HIGHTAIL IT OUT AND PUT UP THOSE "KEEP OUT" SIGNS LIKE YORE PAW SAID!
B'SIDES, THEM SILLY STORIES WILL LAIK TA GIVE A BODY NIGHTMARES!
THEM'S "FIKSHUNAL SCIENCE" STORIES, MAW! THEY AIN'T SILLY! THEY... AW, SKIP IT!
NOBODY LISSENS TA A WORD AH SEZ! THEY STILL TREAT ME LAIK AH WUZ ONLY FIFTY YEARS OLD OR SUMP'N! THEY'LL SEE! SOMEDAY I'LL--
KEEP OUT!
DONALD, THE KIDS WILL STAY ABOARD WHILE YOU AND I SCOUT AROUND!
!!!!

GOSH-ALL-FISHHOOKS! JES' LAIK IN THE VIDDY-BOOKS! MONSTERS FUM OUTTA' SPACE! AH... AH GOTTA TELL PAW!
PAW! GRAMPS! THEY'S HERE! THEY'S A-SWARMIN' OUTTA THAR SHIPS TA GIT US! RUN!
GUCK!
AH TOLJA! THEM GUMMINT MEN WILL TOSS US IN THE HOOSEGOW AN' THROW THE KEY IN A SPACEWARP!
NO, IT AIN'T THE PO-LEECE! IT'S MONSTERS FUM OUTTA' SPACE!!!
THAT DANG KID AND HIS IMAGINASHUN! HE ALMOST MADE ME SPLIT MAH QUARTZ!
JUNIOR, IF'N YOU DO THET AGIN, AH'LL TAN YORE LI'L FIZBOT!
BUT, PAW-- IT'S TRUE! WHITE MONSTERS WITH TWO EYES!
SAME AS LAST TIME? HOW CUM YORE IMAGINARY SPACE CRITTERS AIN'T NEVER A NORMAL COLOR-- LAIK PURPLE?
AN' THEY ALLUS' HAS MORE EYEBALLS THAN YOU KIN SHAKE A STICK AT! CACKLE!
OOGA BOOGA!
ON TH' OTHER HAND, GRAMPS, WE DON'T REALLY KNOW WHY THE GUMMINT WON'T LET US GET NO CLOSER TA THE SUN THAN THIS HERE ASTEROID BELT! WHO KNOWS WHUT'S OUT THAR?!
WAL, IF'N YORE WORRIED 'BOUT MONSTERS, GO TAKE A SQUINT!
SAY, JUNIOR-- JUST WHO IS THIS A STATUE OF?
CAREFUL, NOW! WE DON'T KNOW WHAT'S INSIDE!
!!!!
MONSTERS! AND THEY'S EVEN MORE HIDEOUS THAN JUNIOR SAID! THEY'S GOT DISGUSTIN' ORANGE GROWTHS ON THEIR UGLY FACES!
AN' THEY'S MAKIN' ICKY GURGLIN' SOUNDS!

SOUNDS LAIK MINDLESS CRITTERS BENT ON INVADIN' OUR NEW HOMESTEAD! SHOOT 'EM DAID AFORE THEY EATS US RAW!
YORE RIGHT!
HUH? WHAT WAS THAT?
ZAP!
GULP! IT... IT'S THE ALIENS! BUT... THEY DON'T LOOK TOO FEROCIOUS!
WE-COME-IN-PEACE! TAKE-US-TO-YOUR-LEADER!
!
JEE-HOSAPHAT! THEY TOOK A FULL ZETA BLAST AN' IT DIDN'T FAZE 'EM!
OUR GUNS ONLY WORK ON HOOMIN ATOMIC STRUCTURE, PAW! BUT THEY'S NOT HOOMIN BEANS!
THE STORYBOOKS SAY YA NEEDS TO SHOOT BULLETS TO KILL ALIEN MONSTERS!
A BULLET GUN? SWELL! WHERE WE GONTA' GIT SUCHA' NONSENSICAL THANG?
RUN FO' YO' LIFE!
AM I CRAZY, OR DO I HEAR THEM SPEAKING ENGLISH?
AND IT'S HILLBILLY ENGLISH... LIKE THEY SPEAK IN THE KENTUCKY BACKWOODS! I DON'T GET IT!
THEY'RE RUNNING LIKE THEY'RE SCARED OF US!
HURRY! IF THEY HIDE FROM US, WE'LL RUN OUT OF AIR BEFORE WE CAN FIND THEM!
DIG OUT, MAW! IT'S GIANT WHITE MONSTERS CUM TA EAT OUR BRAINS!
LAND SAKES! AH AIN'T A-GONTA GIVE UP THIS NEW HOMESTEAD! AH JES' MOPPED IT!

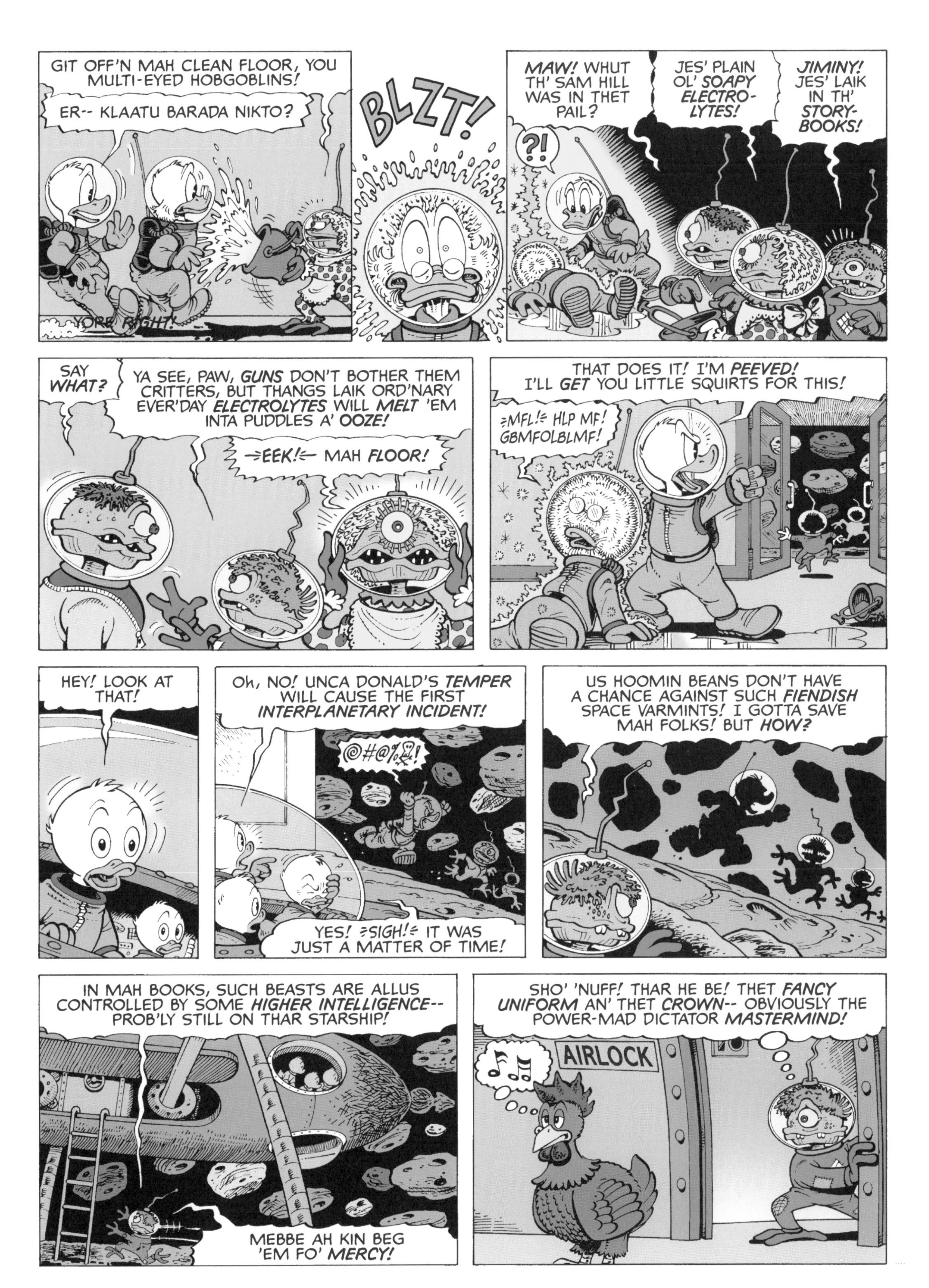

GIT OFF'N MAH CLEAN FLOOR, YOU MULTI-EYED HOBGOBLINS!
ER-- KLAATU BARADA NIKTO?
YORE RIGHT!
BLZT!
MAW! WHUT TH' SAM HILL WAS IN THET PAIL?
JES' PLAIN OL' SOAPY ELECTRO-LYTES!
JIMINY! JES' LAIK IN TH' STORY-BOOKS!
?!
SAY WHAT?
YA SEE, PAW, GUNS DON'T BOTHER THEM CRITTERS, BUT THANGS LAIK ORD'NARY EVER'DAY ELECTROLYTES WILL MELT 'EM INTA PUDDLES A' OOZE!
EEK! MAH FLOOR!
THAT DOES IT! I'M PEEVED! I'LL GET YOU LITTLE SQUIRTS FOR THIS!
MFL! HLP MF! GBMFOLBLMF!
HEY! LOOK AT THAT!
Oh, NO! UNCA DONALD'S TEMPER WILL CAUSE THE FIRST INTERPLANETARY INCIDENT!
YES! SIGH! IT WAS JUST A MATTER OF TIME!
US HOOMIN BEANS DON'T HAVE A CHANCE AGAINST SUCH FIENDISH SPACE VARMINTS! I GOTTA SAVE MAH FOLKS! BUT HOW?
IN MAH BOOKS, SUCH BEASTS ARE ALLUS CONTROLLED BY SOME HIGHER INTELLIGENCE-- PROB'LY STILL ON THAR STARSHIP!
MEBBE AH KIN BEG 'EM FO' MERCY!
SHO' 'NUFF! THAR HE BE! THET FANCY UNIFORM AN' THET CROWN-- OBVIOUSLY THE POWER-MAD DICTATOR MASTERMIND!
AIRLOCK

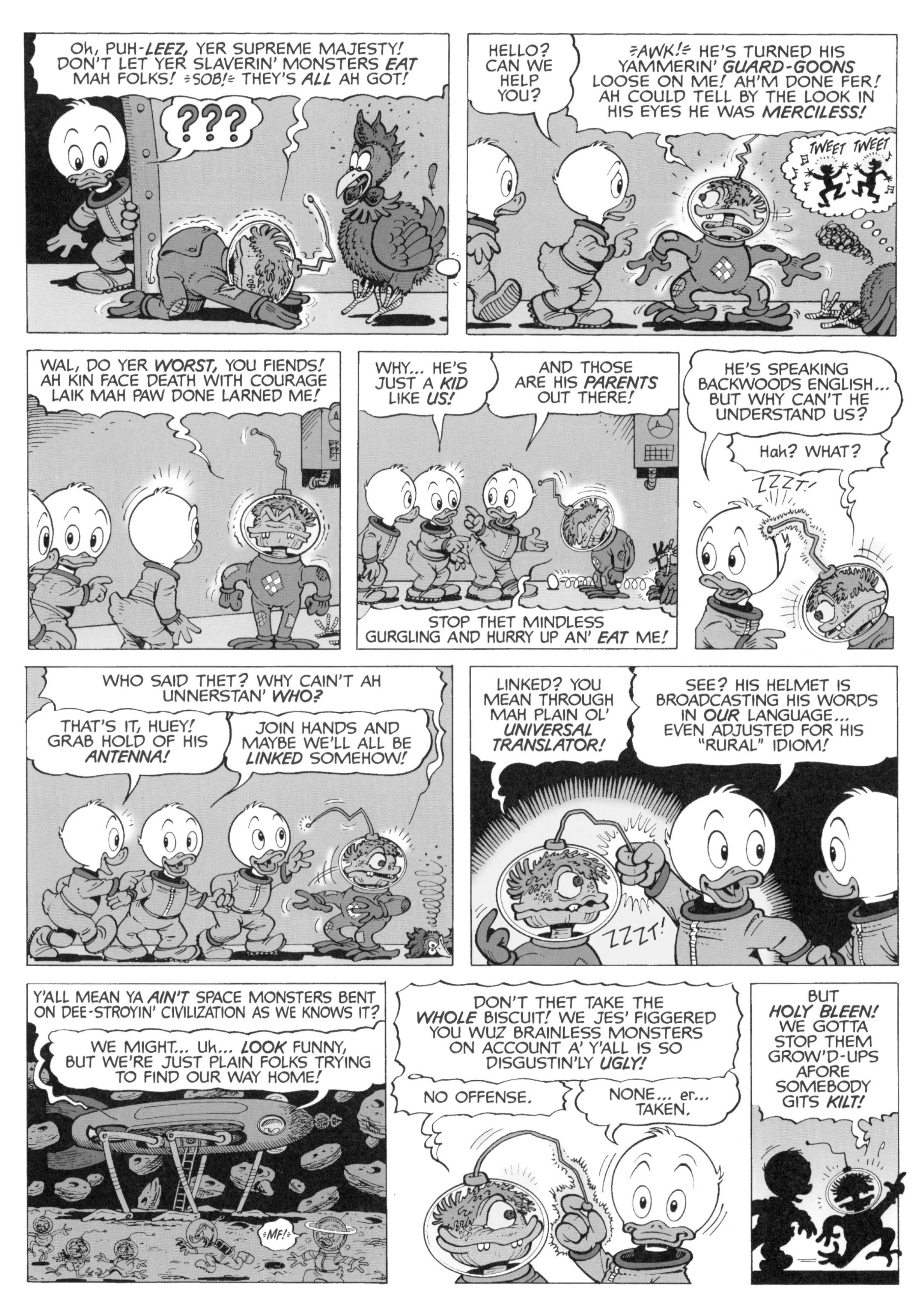
Oh, PUH-LEEZ, YER SUPREME MAJESTY! DON'T LET YER SLAVERIN' MONSTERS EAT MAH FOLKS! SOB! THEY'S ALL AH GOT!
???
HELLO? CAN WE HELP YOU?
AWK! HE'S TURNED HIS YAMMERIN' GUARD-GOONS LOOSE ON ME! AH'M DONE FER! AH COULD TELL BY THE LOOK IN HIS EYES HE WAS MERCILESS!
TWEET TWEET
WAL, DO YER WORST, YOU FIENDS! AH KIN FACE DEATH WITH COURAGE LAIK MAH PAW DONE LARNED ME!
WHY... HE'S JUST A KID LIKE US!
AND THOSE ARE HIS PARENTS OUT THERE!
STOP THET MINDLESS GURGLING AND HURRY UP AN' EAT ME!
HE'S SPEAKING BACKWOODS ENGLISH... BUT WHY CAN'T HE UNDERSTAND US?
Hah? WHAT?
ZZZT!
WHO SAID THET? WHY CAIN'T AH UNNERSTAN' WHO?
THAT'S IT, HUEY! GRAB HOLD OF HIS ANTENNA!
JOIN HANDS AND MAYBE WE'LL ALL BE LINKED SOMEHOW!
LINKED? YOU MEAN THROUGH MAH PLAIN OL' UNIVERSAL TRANSLATOR!
SEE? HIS HELMET IS BROADCASTING HIS WORDS IN OUR LANGUAGE... EVEN ADJUSTED FOR HIS "RURAL" IDIOM!
ZZZT!
Y'ALL MEAN YA AIN'T SPACE MONSTERS BENT ON DEE-STROYIN' CIVILIZATION AS WE KNOWS IT?
WE MIGHT... Uh... LOOK FUNNY, BUT WE'RE JUST PLAIN FOLKS TRYING TO FIND OUR WAY HOME!
MF!
DON'T THET TAKE THE WHOLE BISCUIT! WE JES' FIGGERED YOU WUZ BRAINLESS MONSTERS ON ACCOUNT A' Y'ALL IS SO DISGUSTIN'LY UGLY!
NO OFFENSE.
NONE... er... TAKEN.
BUT HOLY BLEEN! WE GOTTA STOP THEM GROW'D-UPS AFORE SOMEBODY GITS KILT!

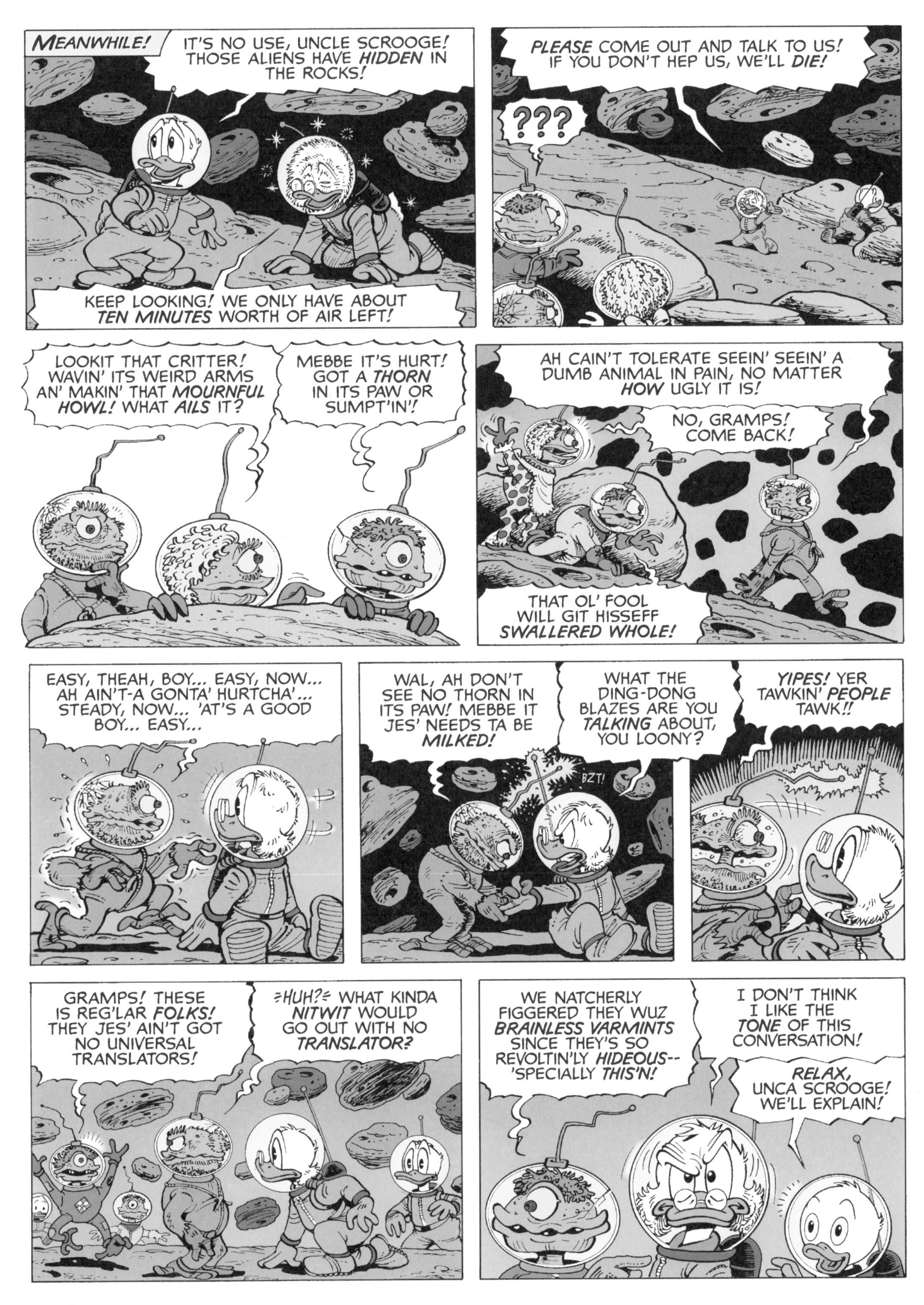
MEANWHILE!
IT'S NO USE, UNCLE SCROOGE! THOSE ALIENS HAVE HIDDEN IN THE ROCKS!
KEEP LOOKING! WE ONLY HAVE ABOUT TEN MINUTES WORTH OF AIR LEFT!
PLEASE COME OUT AND TALK TO US! IF YOU DON'T HEP US, WE'LL DIE!
???
LOOKIT THAT CRITTER! WAVIN' ITS WEIRD ARMS AN' MAKIN' THAT MOURNFUL HOWL! WHAT AILS IT?
MEBBE IT'S HURT! GOT A THORN IN ITS PAW OR SUMPT'IN'!
AH CAIN'T TOLERATE SEEIN' SEEIN' A DUMB ANIMAL IN PAIN, NO MATTER HOW UGLY IT IS!
NO, GRAMPS! COME BACK!
THAT OL' FOOL WILL GIT HISSEFF SWALLERED WHOLE!
EASY, THEAH, BOY... EASY, NOW... AH AIN'T-A GONTA' HURTCHA'... STEADY, NOW... 'AT'S A GOOD BOY... EASY...
WAL, AH DON'T SEE NO THORN IN ITS PAW! MEBBE IT JES' NEEDS TA BE MILKED!
WHAT THE DING-DONG BLAZES ARE YOU TALKING ABOUT, YOU LOONY?
BZT!
YIPES! YER TAWKIN' PEOPLE TAWK!!
GRAMPS! THESE IS REG'LAR FOLKS! THEY JES' AIN'T GOT NO UNIVERSAL TRANSLATORS!
HUH? WHAT KINDA NITWIT WOULD GO OUT WITH NO TRANSLATOR?
WE NATCHERLY FIGGERED THEY WUZ BRAINLESS VARMINTS SINCE THEY'S SO REVOLTIN'LY HIDEOUS-- 'SPECIALLY THIS'N!
I DON'T THINK I LIKE THE TONE OF THIS CONVERSATION!
RELAX, UNCA SCROOGE! WE'LL EXPLAIN!

SOON THE DUCKS ARE GIVEN UNIVERSAL TRANSLATORS AND ALL RETURN TO THE BIN FOR EXPLANATIONS!
...AND YA SAY SOME THINGAMAJIG HIJACKED YORE WAREHOUSE AN' BRANG IT HERE?
YES, THAT'S THE DOOHICKEY! AND IT SEEMS TO BE HOLDING THE AIR INSIDE THE BIN, TOO!
WHY, THIS IS A HYPERDRIVE HOMING DEVICE, LIKE I USETA' PUT IN MAH LI'L ORE-PROBES A FEW THOUSAND YEARS BACK!
THE SHIP IT WAS IN LOOKED LIKE IT WAS SHOT DOWN!
UP-- SOME GUMMINT AYJINTS PROB'LY GOT 'ER! AH USETA' SEND PROBES INTO THE FORBIDDEN ZONE IN THE OL' DAYS! CACKLE!
THEY SAY GRAMPS WAS QUITE A TERROR IN HIS YOUTH!
YES... I CAN FEEL A KIND OF... KINSHIP!
SLAP
ARE YOU SAYING YOU WERE A... A SPACE PROSPECTOR?
STILL AM! IT'S THE ONLIEST LIFE FER ME! LIVIN' ON MAH OWN TERMS IN TH' OUTER REGIONS!
THERE'S NUTHIN' LAIK IT! THIS IS AN INFINITE WILDERNESS OF LIMITLESS OPPORTUNITIES! YA CAIN'T IMAGINE THE WONDROUS SIGHTS AND ADVENTURES AWAITIN' OUT THAR!
YES... IT'S... IT'S THE FINAL FRONTIER! IT'S JUST WHAT I'VE FELT A... YEARNING FOR! IT'S... WONDERFUL!
CAN THIS HYPERDRIVER TAKE THE BIN BACK TO OUR PLANET?
IT'S A MITE OLD, BUT IT SHOULD HAVE JEST ENUFF JUICE TO GIT YA THAR!
GREAT! LET'S GO!
NOT SO FAST, DONALD! NOW THAT OUR NEW FRIENDS ARE OFFERING US AIR TO BREATHE, I THINK I'LL STAY AWHILE!
ER... BUT JUST A LITTLE WHILE, RIGHT?
WE'LL SEE, NEPHEW! WE'LL SEE...

YEEE-HAW!
WE'VE BEEN CRUISING THESE ASTEROIDS FOR DAYS NOW, AND UNCLE SCROOGE SHOWS NO SIGNS OF GETTING BORED!
YOU'RE NOT KIDDING! HE'S HAVING A FLASHBACK TO HIS YUKON DAYS!
THIS IS GETTING SERIOUS! WHAT IF HE DECIDES NOT TO... TO... GULP!
DON'T EVEN THINK THAT!
HEY, PARDNER! TEN BUCKS SAYS I FIND THE NEXT IMPERVIUM CRYSTAL!
Hah! AH'LL FIND IT, AND YOU KIN KEEP YER "TENBUX"!
THIS LI'L ASTEROID LOOKS LAIK JES' THE SPOT, TOO!
YESSIREEBOB-- THIS IS CRYSTAL-BEARING ROCK IF'N AH EVER SEED IT!
WHAT TH--
EUREKA!
SORRY, GRAMPS! I COULD TELL THE CRYSTAL ORE WAS CLOSER TO THE OTHER SIDE!
JEE-HOSAPHAT! YORE SLICKER'N FLOONBEEN ON A DOORKNOB!

I BEEN SPACE-PROSPECTIN' FER 837 YEARS, BUT YER ALREADY LARNIN' ME THANGS!
TUT! THIS IS JUST LIKE BACK HOME-- ONLY NO GRAVITY TO SLOW YOU DOWN!
WHAT A TEAM WE'LL BE! WE'LL DRILL FOR KRELIAN OIL ON ALTAIR-4! WE'LL DIG FER NEBULITE IN TH' CRYSTAL MOUNTAINS OF KENODON! AH'LL SHOW YOU SIGHTS YOU NEVER DREAMT OF!
SIGH! I'VE MISSED THIS SO MUCH!
ME, TOO! AH AIN'T FELT SO ALIVE SINCE... SINCE BACK IN THE OLD DAYS... LIKE WHEN AH FUHST MET ASTRA AT THE FRONTIER DANCEPORT!
WAS ASTRA YOUR... GIRL?
YEP! TWINKLIN' ASTRA, THE STAR OF THE NORTH STAR! HER HEART WAS AS COLD AS A BLACK HOLE... TILL I MADE HER MINE!
THAT'S ONE CHANCE I... I FLUBBED! TELL ME ABOUT HER?
UNCLE SCROOGE!
POP!
ALL YOUR YESTERDAYS ARE GONE! YOU CAN'T RECAPTURE THEM IN THE VOID OF SPACE!
"CRUELTY, THY NAME IS DONALD!"
LEAVE ME ALONE!
NO! DECIDE NOW! ARE YOU STAYING OR GOING HOME WITH US?
STAY, FRIEND! THE UNIVERSE IS OURS!
NO, UNCA SCROOGE! NO!
NEPHEWS... I'VE DECIDED THAT I'M GOING TO--
HEY! LOOKY THAR! THAT'S A HYPERDRIVE WARP FORMIN'!
IT'S A GUMMINT PATROL SHIP A-COMIN'! THEY MUSTA DETECTED YORE OUTLAW HYPERDRIVER FRUM ONE A' THEIR FRONTIER OUTPOSTS!

IF'N THEY COTCH YA, THEY'LL LOCK Y'ALL UP IN A LAB AN' STUDY YA SIX WAYS TA' GLUNGDAY!
JUNIOR'S RIGHT! YA GOTTA LEAVE NOW-- ALL OF YA!
BUT THE HYPERDRIVE BOX IS STILL BACK IN UNCLE SCROOGE'S BIN!
YA KNOW HOW TO WORK IT! HIGHTAIL IT BACK THAR! WE CAN'T HE'P YA NOW!
I DON'T KNOW WHAT TO DO! I...
SORRY, PARDNUH, BUT YER KIN IS RI HT--YOU CAIN'T RECAPTURE YORE PAST! YA BEST SKEEDADDLE WHILST YA STILL GOT A FUTURE!
SHO' 'NUFF! IT IS A GUMMINT PATROL SHIP!
GIT READY TA DO SUM FANCY ACTIN'!
ALL RIGHT! WHO HAS THE ILLEGAL HYPERDRIVER HERE? HAND IT OVER!
!!!
IT MUSTA BEEN SOME ALIEN CRITTERS, SIR!
YEAH! THEY WENT THATAWAY!
HEY! THE ALIENS ARE GETTING AWAY!
THERE'S NO SUCH THING AS ALIENS! YOU ONLY SAW SWAMP GAS OR A WEATHER BALLOON!
WEATHER BALLOON? WHUT'S THAT?
THERE'S NO SUCH THING AS A WEATHER BALLOON, EITHER! FORGET I SAID IT!
Uh-oh! THAT SAUCER IS ON OUR TAILFIN! STEP ON IT!
GULP!
TROUBLE IS, I DON'T KNOW HOW TO FLY THIS THING!
LOOKS LIKE THOSE BACKCOUNTRY YOKELS HAD CONTACT WITH THE ALIENS!
DON'T WORRY... NO ONE WILL BELIEVE THEM! THAT'S WHY WE ONLY CONTACT RURAL HAYSEEDS WHEN OUR PATROLS VISIT THEIR PLANET!

YIKES! THERE WENT MY WINDSHIELD!
NOW I'LL GET ALL THE BUGS RIGHT IN MY TEETH!
EMERGENCY! WE'VE LOST OUR AIR PRESSURE!
IT'S OKAY... I GOT OUR POOR CHICKEN INTO A SPARE SUIT JUST IN TIME!
GIVE ME THOSE CONTROLS BEFORE THE RESALE VALUE OF THIS CRAFT BECOMES NIL!
TOO LATE! THE HELM IS NOT RESPONDING!
WHAT LUCK! WE FELL RIGHT ON OUR ASTEROID!
LEAVE IT TO YOU TO SAY THAT!
THE SHIP IS DONE FOR! WE'LL HAVE TO FLY THE BIN HOME!
GO ON WITHOUT ME! I HAVE TO... eh... WAIT HERE FOR MY INSURANCE ADJUSTER TO FILE A CLAIM!
YOU CAN'T CHANGE YOUR MIND NOW! THAT "GUMMINT" SHIP IS COMING!
BESIDES, YOUR HELMET IS CRACKED! YOU MUST GET IN THE BIN WHERE THERE'S AIR!
GULP! I... I GUESS YOU'RE RIGHT!
WHOA! THOSE ALIENS ANCHORED THE BIN PRETTY GOOD! I HOPE THE DRIVE-BOX CAN MOVE THIS ASTEROID, TOO!
IT HAD BETTER! BUT THE EXTRA MASS WILL USE EXTRA POWER!
AT LEAST WE WON'T HAVE ALL THAT MONEY ADDING TO OUR WEIGHT!
YOU THOUGHT I'D LEAVE FOR HOME WITH-OUT IT? Hah! GO OPEN THE ROOF HATCH!
SCOOT

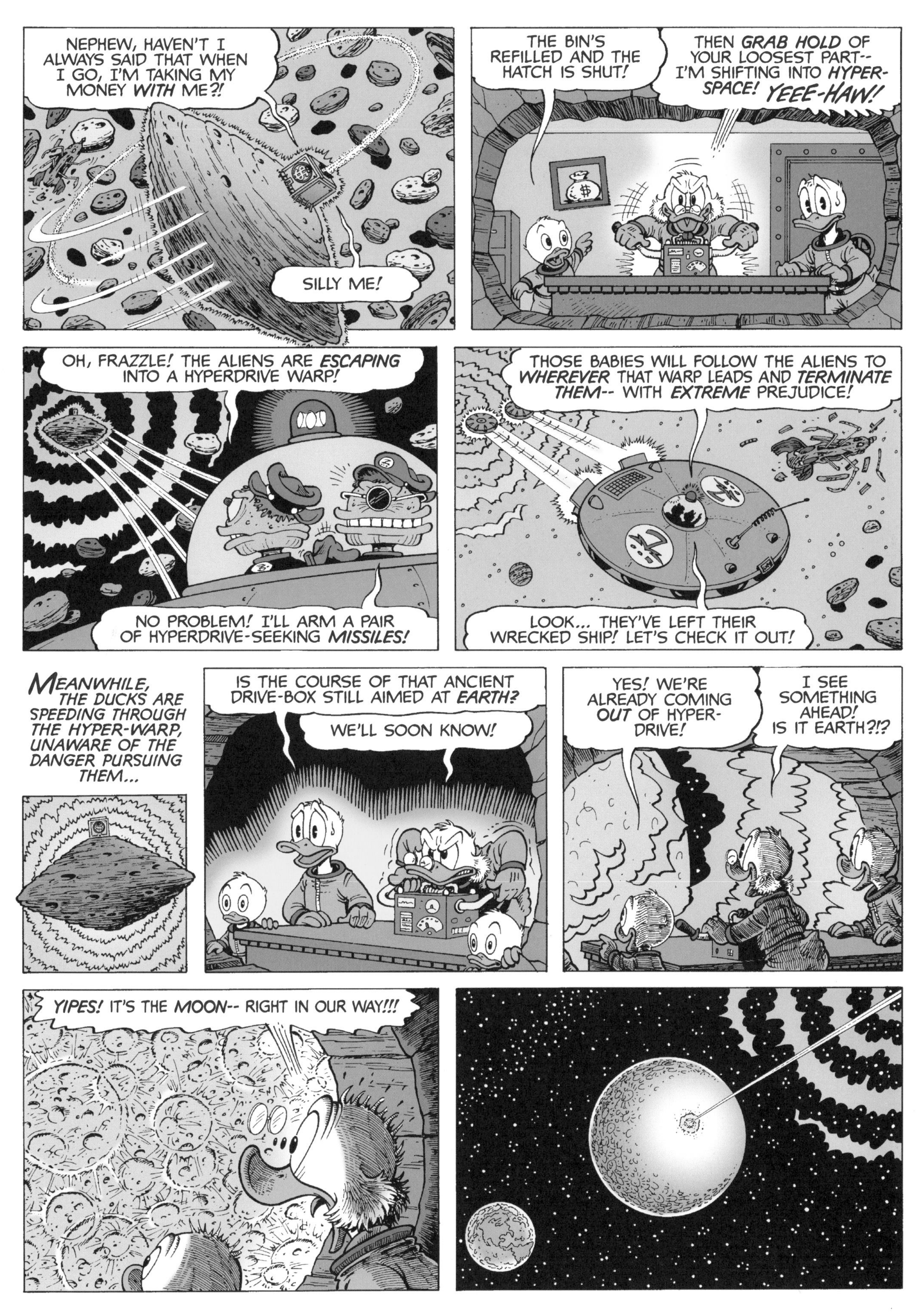
NEPHEW, HAVEN'T I ALWAYS SAID THAT WHEN I GO, I'M TAKING MY MONEY WITH ME?!
SILLY ME!
THE BIN'S REFILLED AND THE HATCH IS SHUT!
THEN GRAB HOLD OF YOUR LOOSEST PART-- I'M SHIFTING INTO HYPER-SPACE! YEEE-HAW!
OH, FRAZZLE! THE ALIENS ARE ESCAPING INTO A HYPERDRIVE WARP!
NO PROBLEM! I'LL ARM A PAIR OF HYPERDRIVE-SEEKING MISSILES!
THOSE BABIES WILL FOLLOW THE ALIENS TO WHEREVER THAT WARP LEADS AND TERMINATE THEM-- WITH EXTREME PREJUDICE!
LOOK... THEY'VE LEFT THEIR WRECKED SHIP! LET'S CHECK IT OUT!
MEANWHILE, THE DUCKS ARE SPEEDING THROUGH THE HYPER-WARP, UNAWARE OF THE DANGER PURSUING THEM...
IS THE COURSE OF THAT ANCIENT DRIVE-BOX STILL AIMED AT EARTH?
WE'LL SOON KNOW!
YES! WE'RE ALREADY COMING OUT OF HYPER-DRIVE!
I SEE SOMETHING AHEAD! IS IT EARTH?!?
YIPES! IT'S THE MOON-- RIGHT IN OUR WAY!!!

WOW! HOW DID WE SURVIVE SUCH A SUDDEN STOP?
THE HYPERDRIVE BOX MUST ELIMINATE INERTIA! THAT'S WHY WE DIDN'T FEEL ANY ACCELERATION WHEN IT SHIFTED INTO WARP-DRIVE!
WELL, HURRY AND BACK OUT OF HERE! WE NEED TO GET HOME BEFORE OUR POWER FAILS!
OKAY... EASY... BRING HER BACK... BACK... A LITTLE MORE... NOW CUT IT HARD... C'MON BACK... OKAY... YOU'RE CLEAR!
UNCA SCROOGE! LOOK! SOME SORT OF MISSILES COMING THROUGH OUR WARP!
GULP! HANG ON! WE GOTTA MOVE FAST!
WHEW! THAT WAS CLOSE!
LOOK AT THE CRATERS WE MADE ON THE POOR MOON! ER... CAN ANYONE SEE THAT FROM EARTH?
NO... THAT'S THE BACKSIDE OF THE MOON!
THAT'S A RELIEF! I WAS AFRAID WE MIGHT HAVE SOME LEGAL PROBLEMS!
NEXT STOP-- DUCKBURG!
CAN YOU FIND DUCKBURG FROM THIS ALTITUDE?
LUCKILY I HAD SOME MAPS IN MY DESK DRAWER! JUST GIVE ME A MOMENT TO UNFOLD ONE, WILL YOU?

THAT LOOKS LIKE THE CALISOTA COASTLINE!
IS THAT MOUNT DEMONTOOTH?
AND THAT MIGHT BE THE BLACK FOREST!
SURE! AND THERE'S THE TULEBUG RIVER!
I SEE DUCKBURG!!!
Er... A FUNNY RED LIGHT JUST LIT UP ON THE BOX!
Uh-oh! THIS HYPER-DRIVER MUST HAVE ONLY A FEW SECONDS OF POWER LEFT!
THERE'S KILLMOTOR HILL! I THINK WE'RE GONNA MAKE IT!
THIS RED LIGHT IS STARTING TO FLASH!
I DON'T THINK WE'RE GONNA MAKE IT!
YOW! OUT OF POWER! WE'RE IN FREEFALL!
CRASH!
???
WE'RE DOWN! IS EVERYONE OKAY?
YES! THERE MUST HAVE BEEN A SAFETY MARGIN OF ANTI-INERTIA TO PROTECT US IN A CRASH!
AND MY BIN, TOO! GOOD OL' HYPERDRIVER!
BUT WHERE DID WE LAND? NOT IN THE HIGH-RENT DISTRICT, I HOPE! WE MIGHT'VE WIPED OUT A FEW CITY BLOCKS OF DUCKBURG!

HOLY COW! WE LANDED RIGHT ON YOUR HILL! GOOD JOB, UNCA SCROOGE!
NOTHING TO IT! IT WASN'T NEAR AS TRICKY AS PILOTING RIVERBOATS ON THE MISSISSIPPI!
HEY-- WHO TURNED OUT THE LIGHTS?
IS IT AN ECLIPSE?
NAH! IT'S JUST THAT McDUCK NUT, SHOWING OFF WITH ANOTHER OF HIS SCREWBALL STUNTS! IGNORE HIM!
HOW WILL YOU EVER GET RID OF THIS ASTEROID SO YOUR BIN CAN BE PUT BACK IN PLACE, UNCLE SCROOGE?
I'VE ALREADY FIGURED THAT OUT!
I'LL SLOWLY BUST UP THIS ROCK AND SELL THE PIECES IN A "BAG-O-ASTEROID" AT A BUCK EACH! AND THE PROFIT WILL PAY TO LOWER THE BIN BACK TO ITS FOUNDATION!
AH! THEN YOU HAVEN'T LOST ANYTHING FROM THIS MISADVENTURE!
ONLY THE HORIZONS OF A NEW FRONTIER! BUT MAYBE THAT CHANCE WILL COME AGAIN... SOMEDAY...
GOSH-- I JUST REMEMBERED! WE LEFT OUR POOR STOWAWAY CHICKEN IN OUTER SPACE!
HOW AWFUL!!!
JEEPERS! I HOPE SHE'S OKAY!
NOT TO WORRY, POULTRY-LOVERS! SHE'S JUST FINE!
WE'VE BEEN INTERROGATING THIS ALIEN FOR DAYS, BUT IT WON'T SAY A TRANSLATABLE WORD!
KEEP TRYING! THE PRESIDENT SAID TO KEEP IT COMFORTABLE AND WELL-FED UNTIL IT REVEALS THE SECRETS OF ITS CIVILIZATION-- NO MATTER HOW LONG IT TAKES!
BUT JUST LOOK AT THAT GLEAM IN ITS EYE... AS IF ITS SCOFFING AT OUR INFERIOR INTELLECTS!
End

Walt Disney's UNCLE SCROOGE
THE LAST LORD OF ELDORADO
A SCHOONER DROPS ANCHOR IN THE CARIBBEAN SEA, ITS CREW LITTLE REALIZING THEY WILL SOON BE LAUNCHED ON AN OCEAN-SPANNING QUEST FOR THE GREATEST TREASURE OF THE AMERICAS... THE LOST "CITY OF GOLD" THAT WAS THE PRIMARY REASON FOR THE ORIGINAL EXPLORATION OF THE NEW WORLD--ELDORADO!
STAND BY TO COME TO!
DOWN HELM!
CAST OFF THE SHEETS!
CLOSE HAUL!
LET GO THE ANCHOR!
HIT THE BRAKES!
D 96066
-HMPH!- STOP BEING SUCH A SMART ALECK!
AYE, AYE! WHY ARE WE STOPPING, CAPTAIN UNCLE, SIR?
BECAUSE YOUR NEPHEWS HAVE JUST FINISHED CLEANING THE SILVER "PIECES OF EIGHT" WE SALVAGED OFF THAT SPANISH TREASURE GALLEON THIS MORNING...
...AND I CAN'T WAIT TO TAKE A QUICK DIP IN THE COINS! ONE SIDE, BOYS!
WAIT, UNCA SCROOGE! YOU CAN'T—
NONSENSE, LAD! YOU'VE SEEN ME DIVE INTO COINS BEFORE! I HAVE A KNACK FOR IT!
AH!
KONK!

THOSE COINS WERE IN THE SEA FOR OVER 400 YEARS! THEY'RE FUSED INTO A SOLID MASS!
OH, YEAH. MY EXCITEMENT MADE ME FORGET THAT LITTLE FACT!

WE NEED SOME GOLD COINS! GOLD NEVER DECOMPOSES!
THEN MAYBE I HAVE SOME GOOD NEWS FOR YOU, UNCLE SCROOGE!

ACCORDING TO YOUR PHOTOSTAT OF THAT 17TH CENTURY SALVAGE CHART, WE HAPPEN TO BE NEAR THE SITE OF ANOTHER SUNKEN SPANISH SHIP!

GREAT! SO FAR CAPTAIN MELIAN'S CHART HAS BEEN ACCURATE! NO WONDER HE WAS IN CHARGE OF KING PHILLIP IV'S TREASURE-SALVAGE FLEET!

YEAH!

TOO BAD FOR KING PHIL THAT MELIAN DIDN'T HAVE OUR MODERN DIVING EQUIPMENT! ALL HE COULD DO WAS CHART THE LOCATIONS OF THE WRECKS, NOT ACTUALLY SALVAGE THE TREASURE!
THE CHART SANK WITH MELIAN'S FLAGSHIP IN 1655 AND WAS FORGOTTEN UNTIL WE FOUND IT! NOW SALVAGING THE TREASURES OF THE SPANISH MAIN IS A CINCH!
I KNOW ALL THAT! WHAT ARE YOU, A RECAP CAPTION IN SOME SILLY COMIC BOOK?
LOOK, UNCA SCROOGE! YOUR CHART IS RIGHT ON THE MONEY AGAIN!
AN EXPRESSION I LIKE TO HEAR! LET'S SEE!
YES... THAT LUMP IN THE SEABED MUST BE ANOTHER ANCIENT WRECK! LET'S HOPE IT'S A TREASURE GALLEON!

IS THE DIVE TEAM READY?
NOT ONLY IS HE READY, HE'S HALFWAY DOWN THE LADDER AND ALREADY GRIPING!
-GRUMBLE!- A REAL DIVE TEAM WOULD QUIT IF HE TRIED TO PAY THEM ONLY 30¢ AN HOUR!
TRY TO FIND SOME CLUE TO THE SHIP'S IDENTITY! THEN I CAN CHECK MY LOGS OF THE OLD TREASURE FLEETS TO SEE WHAT ITS CARGO IS!
RADIO.
I KNOW THE ROUTINE!
YOU'RE IN LUCK! I ALREADY FOUND A BRASS NAMEPLATE READING "DUKATENESEL"! SPANISH?
NO... GERMAN! I'LL NEED TO LOOK IN A DIFFERENT SET OF OLD LOGS!
Dukatenesel
HERE IT IS... THE "DUKATENESEL"... LOST IN 1581 EN ROUTE FROM CORO, VENEZEULA, TO HAMBURG... A PASSENGER SHIP! DRAT!
WAIT! THE METAL DETECTOR IS PICKING UP SOMETHING ELSE!
JUST ONE PIECE... BUT IT'S GOLD!
WHATIZZIT? WHATIZZIT?
IT'S SOME SORT OF PLAQUE WITH SOME GUY'S PICTURE AND LOTS OF GERMAN!
WHAT ELSE? WHAT ELSE?
ist auffgericht worden und beschworn / das Consortium der Herrn Welser von Augspurg in Nova Granada / an sein obristen der heylgen seen / den 21. Feb. A.D. MDXXXIX.
WELL, THERE'S AN ENGRAVING ON THE BACK SIDE, TOO!
OF WHAT? OF WHAT?
HM... IT LOOKS LIKE SOME KINDA BIG FISH!
OH... SORRY... IT'S NOT AN ENGRAVING! IT'S ONLY A REFLECTION OF...
...WUHHHH-OHHHHHH!

WHAT'S HAPPENING? IS UNCA DONALD OKAY?
I THINK I SEE HIM COMING TO THE SURFACE!
YES, HE'S SWIMMING STRAIGHT UP! AND HE LOOKS EXCITED! I'LL BET HE FOUND SOMETHING EXTRA SPECIAL!

NO, HE— HEY! EVERYTHING WENT BLACK!
OMIGOSH! UNCA SCROOGE!

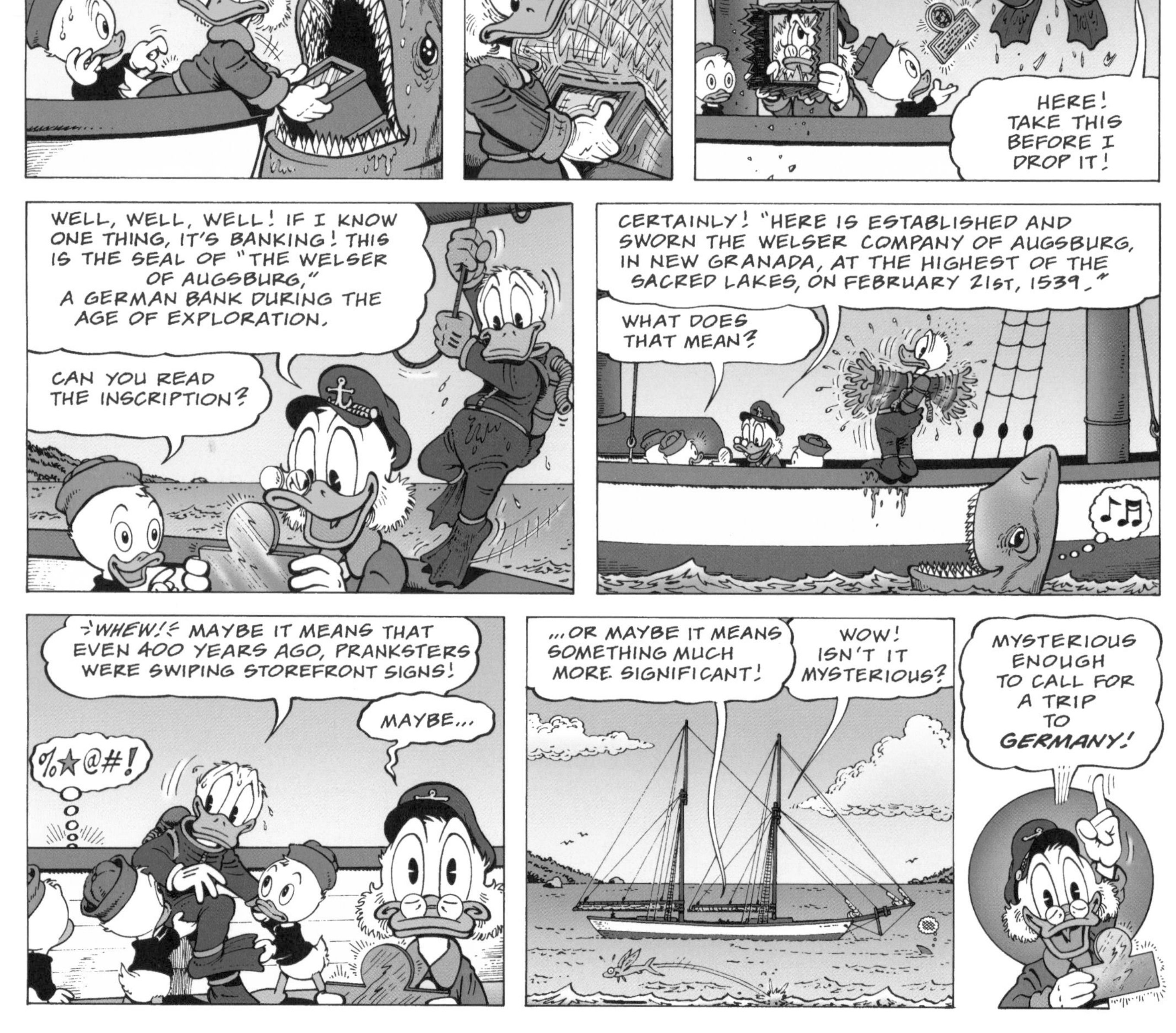
YES? WHAT DO YOU—
SNAP!
DAGGONNIT! THAT VIEWER COST ME TWO DOLLARS IN KEY WEST IN 1909!
HERE! TAKE THIS BEFORE I DROP IT!
WELL, WELL, WELL! IF I KNOW ONE THING, IT'S BANKING! THIS IS THE SEAL OF "THE WELSER OF AUGSBURG," A GERMAN BANK DURING THE AGE OF EXPLORATION.
CAN YOU READ THE INSCRIPTION?
CERTAINLY! "HERE IS ESTABLISHED AND SWORN THE WELSER COMPANY OF AUGSBURG, IN NEW GRANADA, AT THE HIGHEST OF THE SACRED LAKES, ON FEBRUARY 21ST, 1539."
WHAT DOES THAT MEAN?
WHEW! MAYBE IT MEANS THAT EVEN 400 YEARS AGO, PRANKSTERS WERE SWIPING STOREFRONT SIGNS!
MAYBE...
%★@#!
...OR MAYBE IT MEANS SOMETHING MUCH MORE SIGNIFICANT!
WOW! ISN'T IT MYSTERIOUS?
MYSTERIOUS ENOUGH TO CALL FOR A TRIP TO GERMANY!

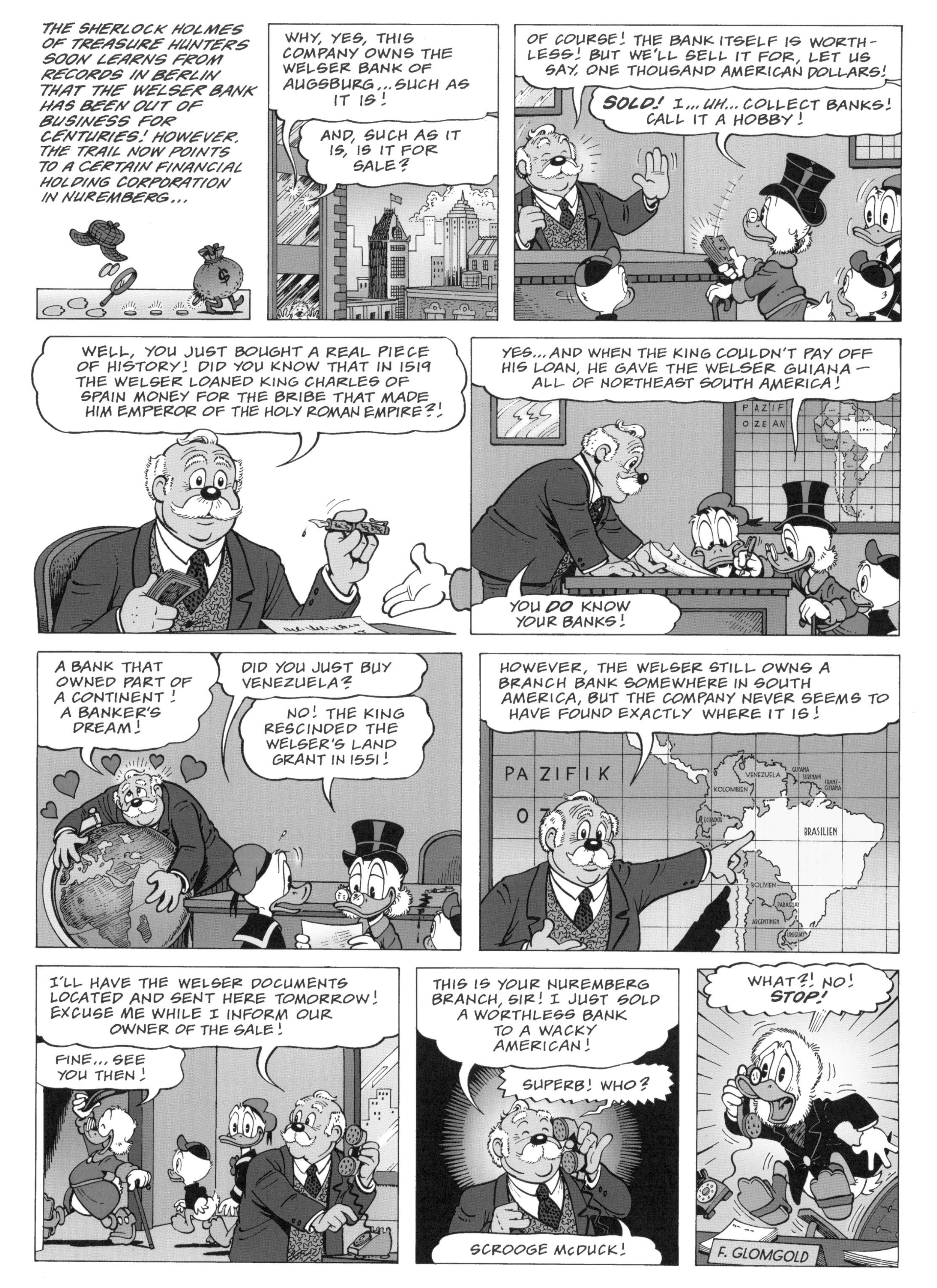
THE SHERLOCK HOLMES OF TREASURE HUNTERS SOON LEARNS FROM RECORDS IN BERLIN THAT THE WELSER BANK HAS BEEN OUT OF BUSINESS FOR CENTURIES! HOWEVER, THE TRAIL NOW POINTS TO A CERTAIN FINANCIAL HOLDING CORPORATION IN NUREMBERG...
WHY, YES, THIS COMPANY OWNS THE WELSER BANK OF AUGSBURG... SUCH AS IT IS!
AND, SUCH AS IT IS, IS IT FOR SALE?
OF COURSE! THE BANK ITSELF IS WORTHLESS! BUT WE'LL SELL IT FOR, LET US SAY, ONE THOUSAND AMERICAN DOLLARS!
SOLD! I... UH... COLLECT BANKS! CALL IT A HOBBY!
WELL, YOU JUST BOUGHT A REAL PIECE OF HISTORY! DID YOU KNOW THAT IN 1519 THE WELSER LOANED KING CHARLES OF SPAIN MONEY FOR THE BRIBE THAT MADE HIM EMPEROR OF THE HOLY ROMAN EMPIRE?!
YES... AND WHEN THE KING COULDN'T PAY OFF HIS LOAN, HE GAVE THE WELSER GUIANA — ALL OF NORTHEAST SOUTH AMERICA!
PAZIF OZEAN
YOU DO KNOW YOUR BANKS!
A BANK THAT OWNED PART OF A CONTINENT! A BANKER'S DREAM!
DID YOU JUST BUY VENEZUELA?
NO! THE KING RESCINDED THE WELSER'S LAND GRANT IN 1551!
HOWEVER, THE WELSER STILL OWNS A BRANCH BANK SOMEWHERE IN SOUTH AMERICA, BUT THE COMPANY NEVER SEEMS TO HAVE FOUND EXACTLY WHERE IT IS!
PAZIFIK
O
KOLOMBIEN
VENEZUELA
GUYANA
SURINAM
FRANZ-GUYANA
ECUADOR
BRASILIEN
BOLIVIEN
PARAGUAY
ARGENTINIEN
URUGUAY
I'LL HAVE THE WELSER DOCUMENTS LOCATED AND SENT HERE TOMORROW! EXCUSE ME WHILE I INFORM OUR OWNER OF THE SALE!
FINE... SEE YOU THEN!
THIS IS YOUR NUREMBERG BRANCH, SIR! I JUST SOLD A WORTHLESS BANK TO A WACKY AMERICAN!
SUPERB! WHO?
SCROOGE McDUCK!
WHAT?! NO! STOP!
F. GLOMGOLD

BUT IT'S... ER... TOO LATE HERR GLOMGOLD! THE PAPERS ARE ALREADY SIGNED!
GRR! THEN DELAY DELIVERING THE DOCUMENTATION TO HIM UNTIL I CAN FLY THERE TO NUREMBERG!
McDUCK KNOWS SOMETHING OR HE'D NEVER BUY A WORTHLESS COMPANY! I'D BETTER SEE HOW I CAN GET MY BANK BACK FROM THE OLD WRETCH!
THE NEXT AFTERNOON...
SO, ALL THAT'S LEFT OF THE MIGHTY HOUSE OF WELSER IS THAT FANCY OLD DOCUMENT CASE?
YES, THAT'S ALL!
BUT MY OLD SOURDOUGH SNOOT TELLS ME I'M ON THE TRAIL OF SOMETHING BIG!
I CAN'T WAIT! LET'S STEP IN HERE AND OPEN THIS CASE!
Biergarten
THIS SAYS... "CHARTER OF THE WELSER BANK OF NEW GRANADA."
THAT'S A ROYAL CHARTER SIGNED BY THE KING'S GOVERNOR, SO IT'S STILL VALID!
"ASSETS — THE DEED TO THE CITY OF OMAGUA! DEPOITORS — THE THREE LORDS OF OMAGUA"!
THE PLOT THICKENS!
LIKE DÜSSELDORF MUSTARD.
"SIGNED BY JIMÉNEZ de QUESADA, NICOLAUS FEDERMANN AND SEBASTIÁN de BELALCÁZAR"... AND THAT'S ALL THE BOX CONTAINS!
CHECK THOSE NAMES IN THE JUNIOR WOODCHUCKS GUIDEBOOK!
THIS GETS BETTER ALL THE TIME! THOSE WERE THE THREE MEN INVOLVED IN THE MOST DRAMATIC MOMENT IN THE EXPLORATION OF THE NEW WORLD!
WELL, DO READ ON!
?

"JIMÉNEZ de QUESADA – A FORMER LAWYER, WAS APPOINTED GOVERNOR-GENERAL OF NEW GRANADA! BUT HE DESERTED HIS OFFICE IN 1536 TO LEAD AN EXPEDITION INTO THE JUNGLES OF WHAT IS NOW COLOMBIA!

"NICOLAUS FEDERMANN – FROM THE WELSER BANK, WAS PLACED IN CHARGE OF GUIANA! BUT HE ALSO DESERTED, IN 1537, TO LEAD AN EXPEDITION INTO THE SWAMPS OF WHAT IS NOW VENEZUELA!

"SEBASTIÁN de BELALCÁZAR – PIZARRO'S TOP CAPTAIN IN THE CONQUEST OF THE INCAS! PIZARRO SENT HIM TO CONQUER EQUADOR, BUT HE TOO DESERTED HIS POST IN 1537 TO LEAD HIS ARMY INTO THE MOUNTAINS!

EACH RENEGADE EXPEDITION TRAVELED NEARLY A THOUSAND MILES THROUGH THE HARSHEST UNEXPLORED TERRAIN! EACH WAS UNAWARE OF THE EXISTENCE OF THE OTHER TWO GROUPS!

"YET IN FEBRUARY, 1539, THE THREE EXPEDITIONS MET SIMULTANEOUSLY AT WHAT THEY'D EACH THOUGHT WAS THEIR PRIVATE, SECRET, OBJECTIVE ON THE HIGH CUNDINAMARCA PLATEAU – OMAGUA!

"HISTORY DOES NOT KNOW WHAT BARGAIN WAS STRUCK THAT DAY, BUT THE THREE LEADERS LATER SAILED TOGETHER TO REPORT THEIR DISCOVERY TO THEIR EUROPEAN MASTERS!"

AND MY PLAQUE TELLS THE LOCATION OF THIS "OMAGUA"!
DEWEY, LOOK UP WHAT "OMAGUA" MEANS!
UH-OH! HUEY, LOUIE... GET A GOOD GRIP ON UNCA SCROOGE!
WOOO BOY! THIS IS GONNA BE GOOD, EH?
I'LL SAY! "OMAGUA" WAS THE ORIGINAL INDIAN NAME FOR THE LOST CITY OF GOLD – ELDORADO!
TWANG!

GET SOME SMELLING SALTS! UNCA SCROOGE FAINTED!
WAITRESS!
SORRY, MEIN HERR, THE WAITRESS HAS ALSO FAINTED!
VAS IST LOS MIT DER PRETZELS?
I'M OKAY! KEEP READING!
WOW! UPON RETURNING FROM EUROPE, BELALCÁZAR WAS ARRESTED IN SPAIN FOR DESERTION, AND FEDERMANN WAS ARRESTED BY THE WELSER FOR FRAUD! THEY DIED IN PRISON!
WHAT ABOUT THE THIRD GUY?
THE KING REMOVED QUESADA FROM HIS GOVERNORSHIP OF NEW GRANADA, AND IT WAS 30 YEARS BEFORE HE COULD AFFORD TO RETURN TO AMERICA WITH MEMBERS OF HIS OLD EXPEDITION!
AHA! TO GET THEIR TREASURE TROVE!
?
QUESADA WAS FOLLOWED BY AGENTS OF THE WELSER, BUT HE NEVER LED THEM TO A CITY OF GOLD! HOWEVER, HE LIVED THE REST OF HIS LIFE AS A MYSTERIOUSLY WEALTHY MAN IN BOGOTÁ, WHICH HE FOUNDED IN 1538!
HE RETIRED NEAR HIS HIDDEN "BANK," NO DOUBT! HE AND HIS MEN COULD SNEAK INTO THE MOUNTAINS AND MAKE "WITHDRAWALS" WHENEVER THEY WANTED! PRETTY SLY, HUH?
!!!
KISS!
BUT I STILL NEED THE MISSING CONTRACT BETWEEN THE CONSPIRATORS TO PROVE I OWN ELDORADO, OR THE GOLD BELONGS TO COLOMBIA!
THEN GET THIS! WHEN QUESADA DIED IN 1579, HE WILLED ALL HIS PAPERS TO THE CONVENT OF SANTO TOMAS OF BOGOTÁ!
AHA!!
TO BOGOTÁ!!
DAS IST GUT, FRAULEIN, BUT COULD YOU GET SOME FRESH PRETZELS BEFORE YOU GO?

SEVERAL DAYS LATER, IN AN ANCIENT CONVENT ON THE CRAGS OF THE CUNDINAMARCA PLATEAU ABOVE BOGOTÁ...
I AM SORRY, SEÑOR, WE NEVER ALLOW OUTSIDERS TO VIEW OUR ARCHIVES!
WHY IS THAT, MOTHER SUPERIOR?

BECAUSE, IT IS WRITTEN THAT IN 1580, A THIEF IN DISGUISE STOLE A GOLDEN RELIC ENTRUSTED TO US BY THE GREAT FOUNDER OF THE CITY OF BOGOTÁ!
I'LL BET THAT THIEF WAS AN AGENT OF THE WELSER! HE LOST HIS BOOTY WHEN THE "DUKATEN-ESAL" SANK!
YES...
I HAVE AN IDEA, MOTHER SUPERIOR! WHAT IF I RETURN THAT VERY RELIC?
MADRE DE DIOS! THE QUESADA PLAQUE! BLESS YOU, SEÑOR! OF COURSE THE ARCHIVES ARE OPEN TO YOU!
GRACIAS!
THAT WAS UNUSUALLY GENEROUS OF YOU, UNCA SCROOGE! AFTER ALL, THAT GOLDEN GEEGAW WAS YOURS BY RIGHT OF SALVAGE!
AND THAT'S WHY I FEEL FAINT! BUT I HOPE IT'LL PAY OFF!
SO BEGINS A SEARCH THROUGH BOOKS AND PAPERS COVERED WITH THE DUST OF NEARLY FOUR CENTURIES!
POOR BOX DONATIONS FROM 1563... CANDLE RECEIPTS FROM 1599... AHA!
WHAT?! WHAT IS IT?
A SPIDER FROM 1587! CUTE, HUH?
PRECIOUS!
HOW ARE YOU KIDS DOING?
WE MIGHT HAVE SOMETHING! WE FOUND SOME THICK BOOKS MARKED "QUESADA"!
HEY! WHAT'S THIS PARCHMENT?
Quesada

"CAPITULACION DE ELDORADO"! IT'S THE CONTRACT!
UNCA SCROOGE!
Capitulacion de Eldorado
OH, I AM SO SORRY! THE LIBRARY IS CLOSING FOR TODAY! COME AGAIN!
ZOW!
SLAM!
THIS CONTRACT WILL GIVE ME A CLAIM ON ELDORADO!
ER... YES... SISTER?
WHAT'S GOING...
YOUR STUDY HALL TIME HAS ALL RUN OUT, DUCKY BOY! TA TA!
BWAH-HA HA-HA-HA-HAAAA!
!!!
WHAT THE SAM HILL WAS THAT ALL ABOUT?
MY GUESS IS THAT SISTER HAS BEEN DRINKING TOO MUCH 100% COLOMBIAN COFFEE... MAYBE WITH COLA MIXED WITH IT!
UNCA SCROOGE! WE FOUND THE CONTRACT!
WHERE?
THAT... ER... NUN TOOK IT!
HM...
SOMETHING IS FISHY ABOUT THIS!
!
HEY— YOU WITH THE BEARD! I DON'T KNOW WHAT YOU'RE UP TO IN THAT DISGUISE, BUT HAND OVER THAT BOOK!
GASP!
BIFF! SOK!

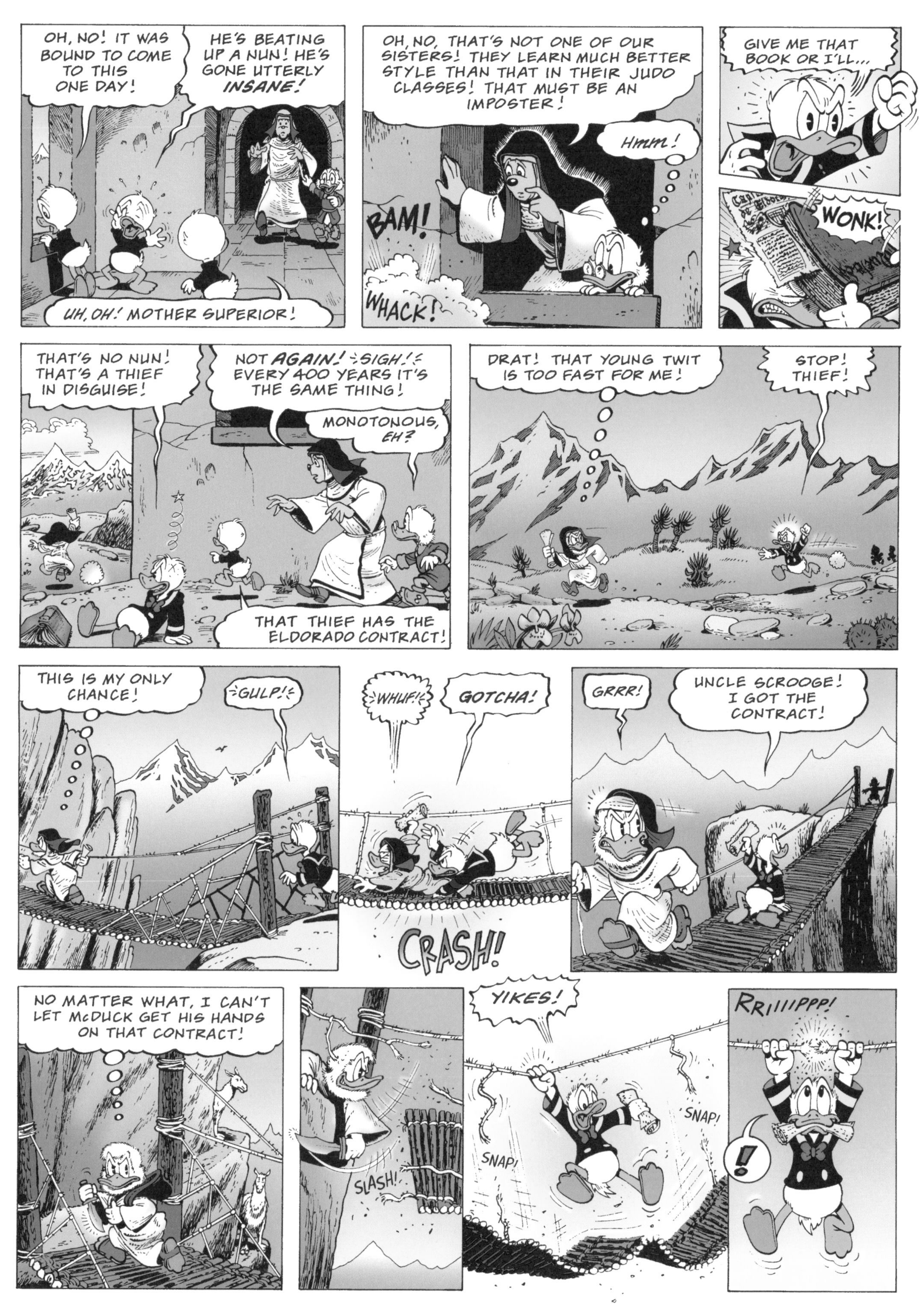
OH, NO! IT WAS BOUND TO COME TO THIS ONE DAY!
HE'S BEATING UP A NUN! HE'S GONE UTTERLY INSANE!
UH, OH! MOTHER SUPERIOR!
OH, NO, THAT'S NOT ONE OF OUR SISTERS! THEY LEARN MUCH BETTER STYLE THAN THAT IN THEIR JUDO CLASSES! THAT MUST BE AN IMPOSTER!
Hmm!
BAM!
WHACK!
GIVE ME THAT BOOK OR I'LL...
WONK!
THAT'S NO NUN! THAT'S A THIEF IN DISGUISE!
NOT AGAIN! -SIGH!- EVERY 400 YEARS IT'S THE SAME THING!
MONOTONOUS, EH?
THAT THIEF HAS THE ELDORADO CONTRACT!
DRAT! THAT YOUNG TWIT IS TOO FAST FOR ME!
STOP! THIEF!
THIS IS MY ONLY CHANCE!
-GULP!-
-WHUF!-
GOTCHA!
CRASH!
GRRR!
UNCLE SCROOGE! I GOT THE CONTRACT!
NO MATTER WHAT, I CAN'T LET McDUCK GET HIS HANDS ON THAT CONTRACT!
SLASH!
YIKES!
SNAP!
SNAP!
RRIIIIPPP!
!

SNAP!
OOG!
HLLP! WHT DU AH DU NW? HLP!
HORRORS! HOLD ON NEPHEW! I'M COMING!
UNCA SCROOGE! WAIT! YOU CAN'T...
OW OW OG UH ARG!
STEADY, NEPHEW, STEADY!
GAH! UNCL SCRJ! YR KILIN MIH! HRY!
JUST ANOTHER FEW FEET, DONALD, AND EVERYTHING WILL BE ALL RIGHT!
THERE! WHEW! THAT WAS CLOSE!
YOU KIDS BETTER THINK OF SOMETHING! I'LL BET DONALD'S ARMS ARE HURTING LIKE ALL GET OUT!
WE'RE ALREADY WORKING ON IT!
WAIT! WE DIDN'T CALCULATE THE COEFFICIENT OF ROPE STRETCH DUE TO MASS!
RIGHT! QUICK, REINTERPOLATE THAT SINE CURVE!
h=r-r(sin x) r=17m x=20°
h=17-17(.3420) ⇒ h=11.186 m
UH, OH!
SNAP!
GULP! I HOPE I HIT A SOFT SECTION OF ROCK!
SWISH!
GOT IT! IF UNCA DONALD LETS GO OF THE OTHER ROPE, HE'LL IMPACT HERE, ON THE CLIFF!
WE NEED SOME PADDING, A TAPE MEASURE... WHO'S GOT THE BAROMETER?
?
WHUMP
OH, NO! WHAT WAS THAT AWFUL SOUND?
WE'RE TOO LATE! UNCA DONALD FELL INTO THE CHASM!

I... I DON'T SEE ANYTHING! WHERE DID HE HIT?
PRY YOUR UNCLE OUT OF THAT LLAMA WHILE WE HEAD BACK TO THE CONVENT AND EXAMINE THIS CONTRACT!
MHF

SHORTLY...
THE FIRST THING THE EXPLORERS AGREED TO DO WHEN THE MET UNEXPECTEDLY AT ELDORADO WAS DRIVE OFF THE CHIBCHA INDIANS AND THEIR KING, THE GILDED MAN...
...TO BRITISH GUIANA!
HOW DO YOU KNOW THAT?
NEVER MIND! KEEP READING!
ALL THREE MEN WERE GUILTY OF DESERTING THEIR POSTS, SO THEY KNEW THEIR CLAIM ON THE GOLD MIGHT NOT BE HONORED, UNLESS THEY HAD AN ANGLE!
"FEDERMANN, THE BANKER, ESTABLISHED A WELSER BANK; QUESADA, THE LAWYER, WROTE UP A LEGAL CHARTER; AND BELALCÁZAR, THE CONQUISTADOR, ORDERED THE SOLDIERS TO COOPERATE!"
A BANKER, A LAWYER, AND A SOLDIER! WOTTA TEAM! SHUDDER!
THEY NAMED THEMSELVES THE LORDS OF THE CITY AND THE OWNERS OF THE GOLD DEPOSITED IN THEIR BANK! BRILLIANT!
BUT NOW I OWN THE BANK AND I ALSO OWN THE GOLD!
YOU'VE OVERLOOKED ONE SMALL DETAIL — YOU HAVE TO FIND YOUR BANK!
THE GOLD PLAQUE TOLD US THAT! "AT THE HIGHEST OF THE SACRED LAKES"!
WE'LL RENT SOME DIGGING EQUIPMENT IN TOWN, AND OUR NEXT STOP WILL BE — ELDORADO!

THE NEXT MORNING, A DUCK-LADEN TRUCK AND BULLDOZER TRUNDLES OUT OF BOGOTÁ—BUT NOT QUITE YET ON THE HIGH ROAD TO THE CITY OF GOLD!
HERE'S THE LAKE SHOWN ON THE MAP AS THE HIGHEST IN ALTITUDE! BUT, IS THERE A ROAD TO THAT REMOTE REGION?
RMRMRMR
TOURIST GUIDE
STOP THERE FOR DIRECTIONS!
BUENOS DIAS, AMIGO! CAN YOU DIRECT US TO LAKE TEUSACÁ?
SO, LAKE TEUSACÁ, IS IT?
TEUSACÁ? YOU GRINGOS MUST BE CHASING AFTER THAT SILLY GOLDEN CITY! EVERYONE IN COLOMBIA KNOWS THAT'S ONLY A LEGEND!
HO HO HO! IT IS TO LAUGH!
MY ADVICE TO YOU, GRINGO, IS TO SELL WHATEVER BANK... ER... TREASURE MAP YOU MUST HAVE BOUGHT BACK TO THE CROOK WHO SOLD IT TO YOU!
HEY!
WHEN YOU OFFERED TO WATCH MY STAND WHILE I GRABBED A BURGER, YOU DIDN'T SAY YOU WERE GONNA HORN IN ON MY TERRITORY! SCRAMBO!
AHA! SOME GRINGO TREASURE HUNTERS! I HAVE JUST THE 100% AUTHENTIC TREASURE MAPS YOU NEED!
HMM...
Maps to lost TEMPLES
YOU'LL LOVE THIS! A VISITOR'S GUIDE TO THE SEVEN CITIES OF CIBOLA!
TRIED IT! COULDN'T FIND EVEN ONE SUBURB OF ANY CIBOLA!
YOU'RE IN LUCK! TODAY'S SPECIAL, THE HIDDEN GOLD MINES OF THE INCAS!
BEEN THERE! DONE THAT!
NO, WE'RE LOOKING FOR ELDORADO!
OHO! THE GILDED MAN HIMSELF! I HAVE HIS HOME ADDRESS IN... IN... BRITISH GUIANA!
FORGET IT! JUST TELL US WHICH WAY TO LAKE TEUSACÁ!
LIBRE de TELEPHONO

TEUSACÁ? YOU GRINGOS MUST BE CHASING AFTER THAT SILLY GOLDEN CITY! EVERYONE IN COLOMBIA KNOWS THAT'S A LEGEND!
HO HO HO! IT IS TO LAUGH!
NEVER MIND! I'LL FIND THE STUPID LAKE MYSELF! DONALD — WIPE THAT BOOK OFF YOUR FACE AND START DRIVING! SNORT!
SPECIAL! LOST MAPS TO FOUND TREASURES CHEAP!
THE HIGHEST SIERRA AND DEEPEST BARRANCA ARE NOT ENOUGH TO BAR SCROOGE'S ROAD TO ELDORADO! SEVERAL DAYS' TRAVEL FINDS THE DUCKS AGAIN IN THE ANDES, TRUNDLING OVER THE LOFTY SPINE OF THE CORDILLERA ORIENTAL...
RMRMRMR
MEANWHILE, HIGH ABOVE...
POOR SCROOGEY! THAT'S VERY DANGEROUS TERRAIN FOR SUCH A HUGE TRUCK! WHY, AT ANY MOMENT A BOULDER COULD FALL AND KNOCK THEM RIGHT OFF!
GLOMGOLD ENT.
CHOP-CHOP-CHOP!
OH, NO! OH, MY WORD! LOOK AT THAT! HORRORS!
I WAS UNGH RIGHT!
GLOMGOLD ENT.
CRUMBLE

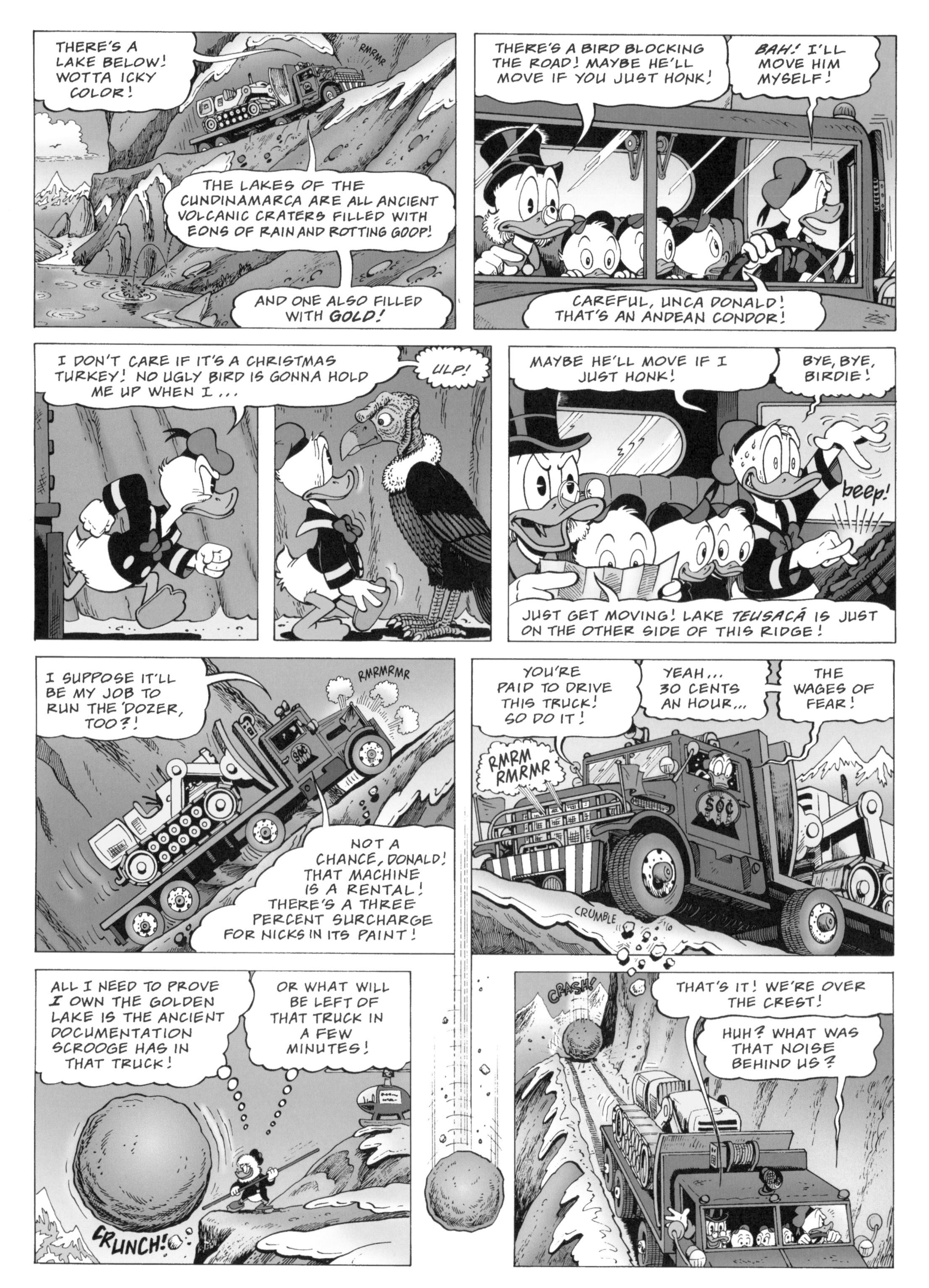
THERE'S A LAKE BELOW! WOTTA ICKY COLOR!
RMRMR
THE LAKES OF THE CUNDINAMARCA ARE ALL ANCIENT VOLCANIC CRATERS FILLED WITH EONS OF RAIN AND ROTTING GOOP!
AND ONE ALSO FILLED WITH GOLD!
THERE'S A BIRD BLOCKING THE ROAD! MAYBE HE'LL MOVE IF YOU JUST HONK!
BAH! I'LL MOVE HIM MYSELF!
CAREFUL, UNCA DONALD! THAT'S AN ANDEAN CONDOR!
I DON'T CARE IF IT'S A CHRISTMAS TURKEY! NO UGLY BIRD IS GONNA HOLD ME UP WHEN I...
ULP!
MAYBE HE'LL MOVE IF I JUST HONK!
BYE, BYE, BIRDIE!
beep!
JUST GET MOVING! LAKE TEUSACÁ IS JUST ON THE OTHER SIDE OF THIS RIDGE!
I SUPPOSE IT'LL BE MY JOB TO RUN THE 'DOZER, TOO?!
RMRMRMR
NOT A CHANCE, DONALD! THAT MACHINE IS A RENTAL! THERE'S A THREE PERCENT SURCHARGE FOR NICKS IN ITS PAINT!
YOU'RE PAID TO DRIVE THIS TRUCK! SO DO IT!
YEAH... 30 CENTS AN HOUR...
THE WAGES OF FEAR!
RMRM RMRMR
CRUMBLE
ALL I NEED TO PROVE I OWN THE GOLDEN LAKE IS THE ANCIENT DOCUMENTATION SCROOGE HAS IN THAT TRUCK!
OR WHAT WILL BE LEFT OF THAT TRUCK IN A FEW MINUTES!
CRUNCH!
CRASH!
THAT'S IT! WE'RE OVER THE CREST!
HUH? WHAT WAS THAT NOISE BEHIND US?

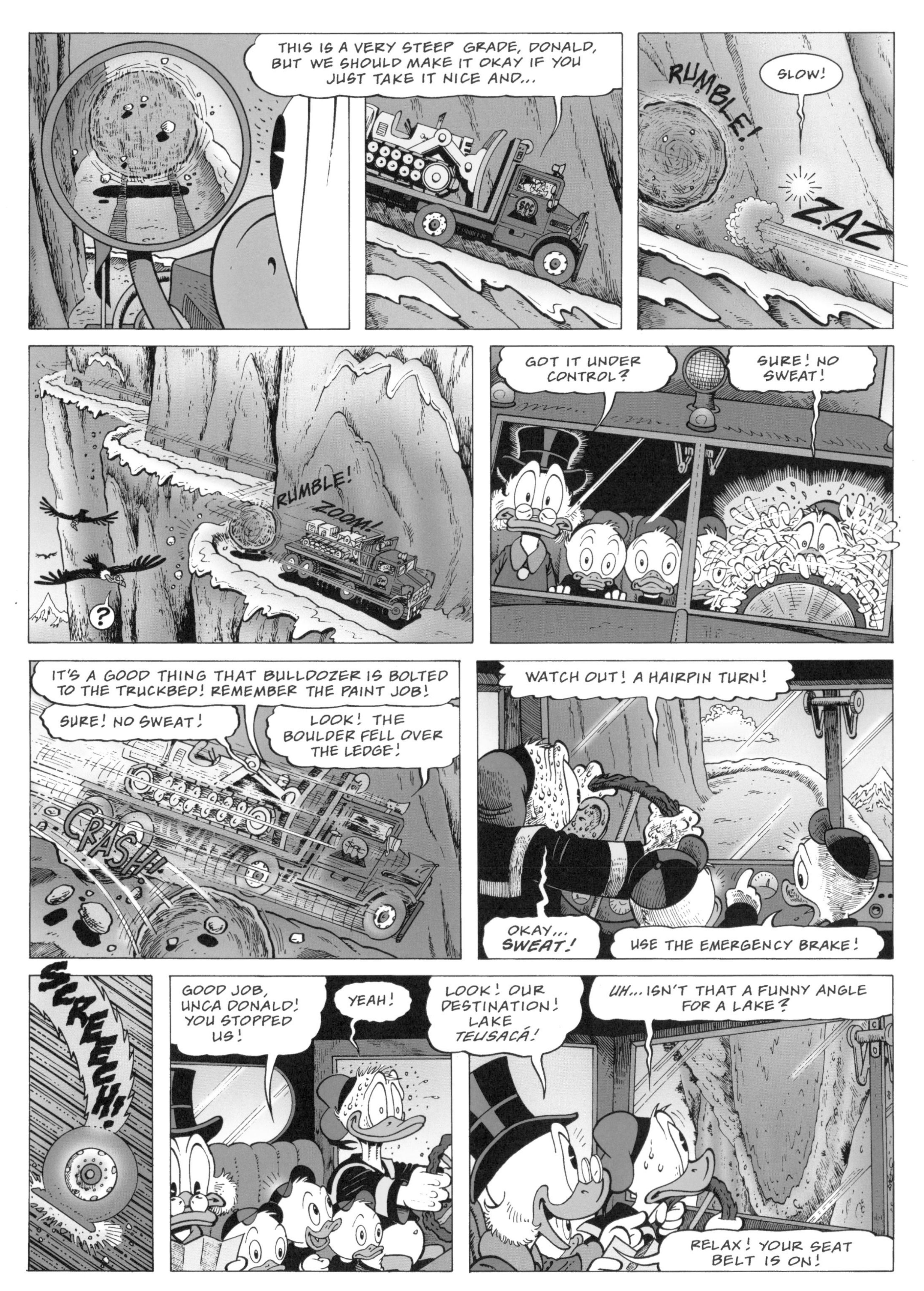

THIS IS A VERY STEEP GRADE, DONALD, BUT WE SHOULD MAKE IT OKAY IF YOU JUST TAKE IT NICE AND...
RUMBLE!
SLOW!
ZAZ
RUMBLE!
ZOOM!
?
GOT IT UNDER CONTROL?
SURE! NO SWEAT!
IT'S A GOOD THING THAT BULLDOZER IS BOLTED TO THE TRUCKBED! REMEMBER THE PAINT JOB!
SURE! NO SWEAT!
LOOK! THE BOULDER FELL OVER THE LEDGE!
CRASH!
WATCH OUT! A HAIRPIN TURN!
OKAY... SWEAT!
USE THE EMERGENCY BRAKE!
SCREEECH!
GOOD JOB, UNCA DONALD! YOU STOPPED US!
YEAH!
LOOK! OUR DESTINATION! LAKE TEUSACÁ!
UH... ISN'T THAT A FUNNY ANGLE FOR A LAKE?
RELAX! YOUR SEAT BELT IS ON!

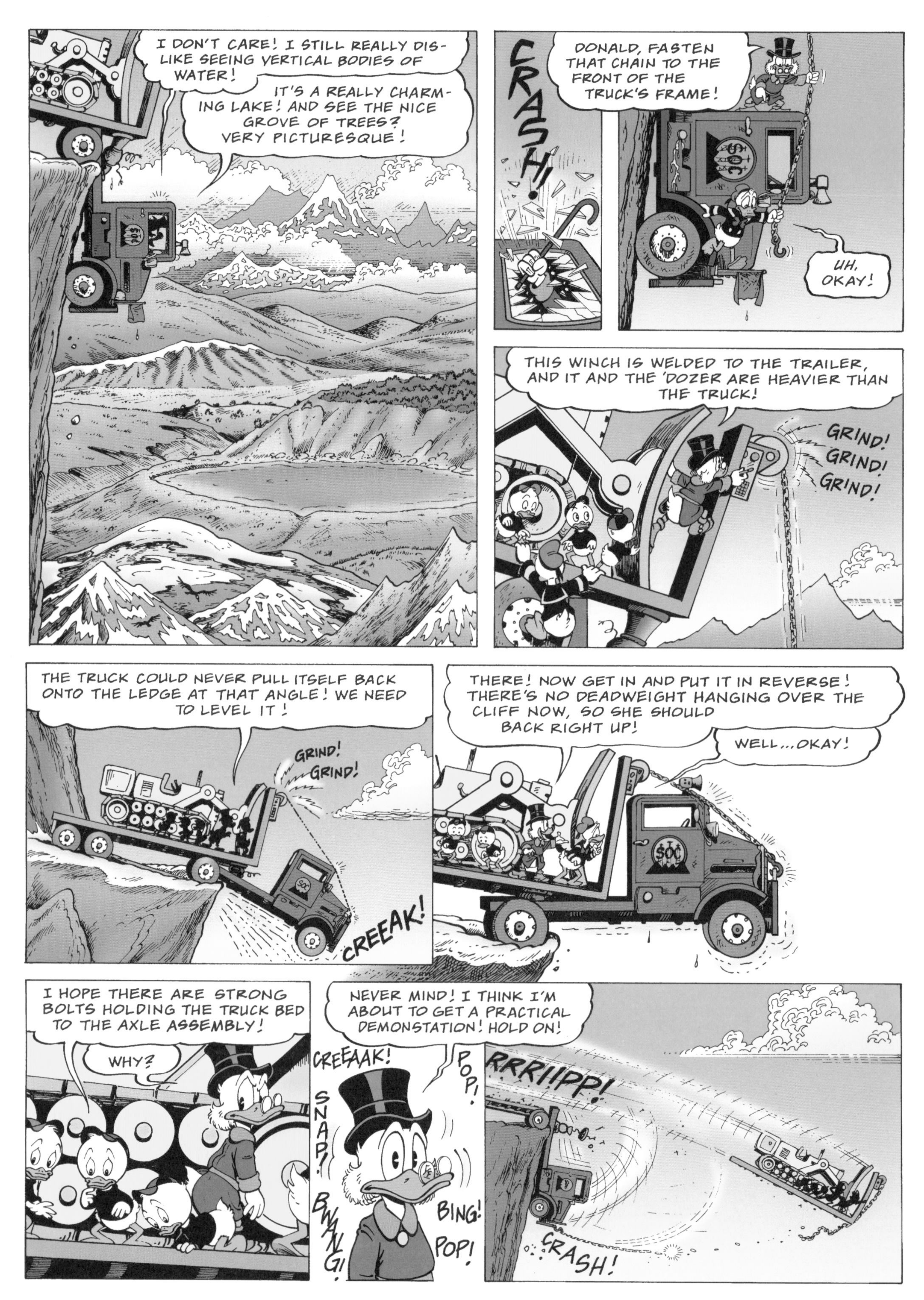
I DON'T CARE! I STILL REALLY DIS-LIKE SEEING VERTICAL BODIES OF WATER!
IT'S A REALLY CHARMING LAKE! AND SEE THE NICE GROVE OF TREES? VERY PICTURESQUE!
CRASH!
DONALD, FASTEN THAT CHAIN TO THE FRONT OF THE TRUCK'S FRAME!
UH, OKAY!
THIS WINCH IS WELDED TO THE TRAILER, AND IT AND THE 'DOZER ARE HEAVIER THAN THE TRUCK!
GRIND! GRIND! GRIND!
THE TRUCK COULD NEVER PULL ITSELF BACK ONTO THE LEDGE AT THAT ANGLE! WE NEED TO LEVEL IT!
GRIND! GRIND!
CREEAK!
THERE! NOW GET IN AND PUT IT IN REVERSE! THERE'S NO DEADWEIGHT HANGING OVER THE CLIFF NOW, SO SHE SHOULD BACK RIGHT UP!
WELL...OKAY!
I HOPE THERE ARE STRONG BOLTS HOLDING THE TRUCK BED TO THE AXLE ASSEMBLY!
WHY?
NEVER MIND! I THINK I'M ABOUT TO GET A PRACTICAL DEMONSTATION! HOLD ON!
CREEAAK!
POP!
SNAP!
BWANG!
BING!
POP!
RRRIIPP!
CRASH!

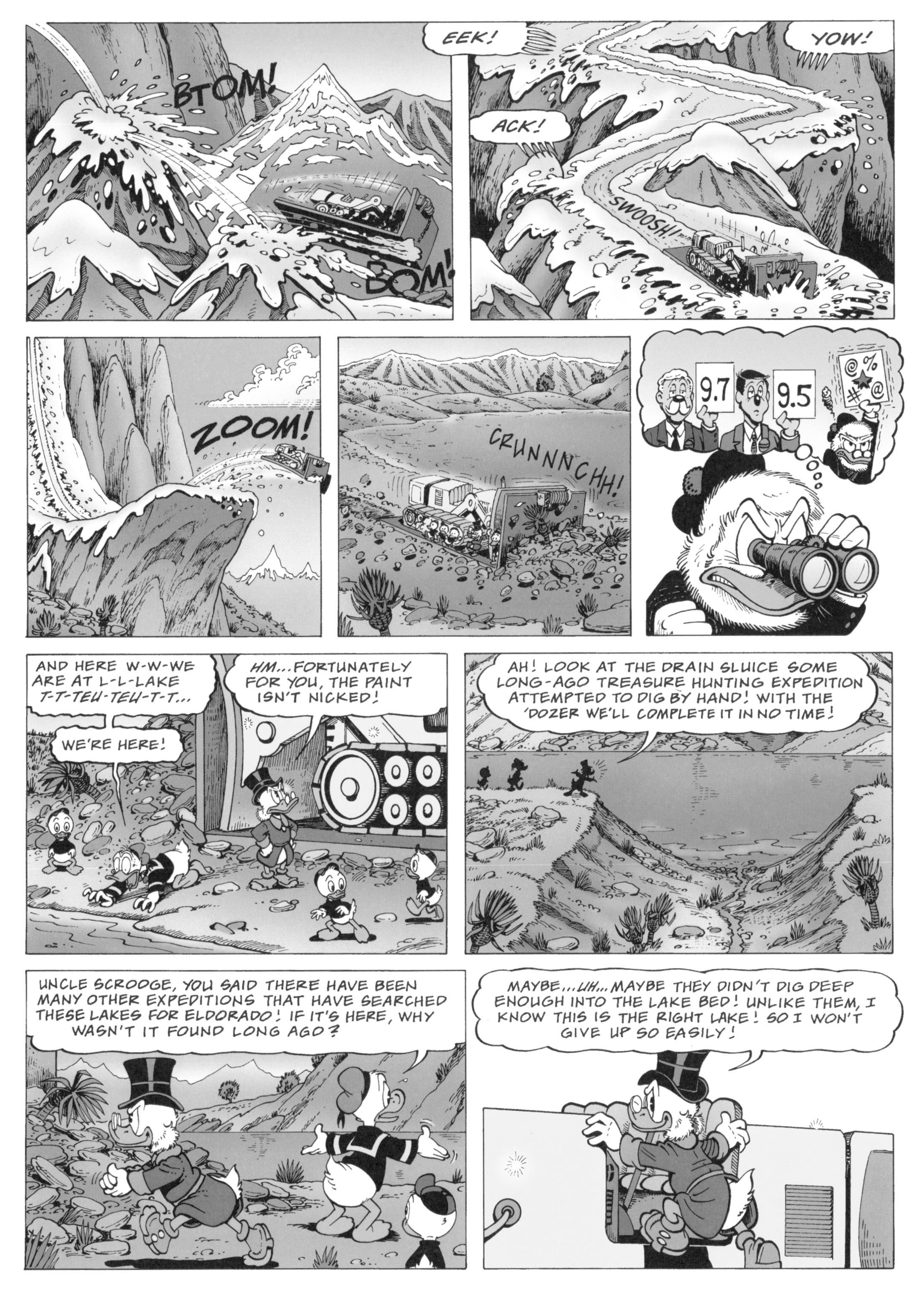
EEK!
YOW!
BTOM!
ACK!
SWOOSH!
BOM!
ZOOM!
CRUNNNCHH!
9.7
9.5
AND HERE W-W-WE ARE AT L-L-LAKE T-T-TEH-TEH-T-T...
WE'RE HERE!
HM... FORTUNATELY FOR YOU, THE PAINT ISN'T NICKED!
AH! LOOK AT THE DRAIN SLUICE SOME LONG-AGO TREASURE HUNTING EXPEDITION ATTEMPTED TO DIG BY HAND! WITH THE 'DOZER WE'LL COMPLETE IT IN NO TIME!
UNCLE SCROOGE, YOU SAID THERE HAVE BEEN MANY OTHER EXPEDITIONS THAT HAVE SEARCHED THESE LAKES FOR ELDORADO! IF IT'S HERE, WHY WASN'T IT FOUND LONG AGO?
MAYBE... UH... MAYBE THEY DIDN'T DIG DEEP ENOUGH INTO THE LAKE BED! UNLIKE THEM, I KNOW THIS IS THE RIGHT LAKE! SO I WON'T GIVE UP SO EASILY!

ONCE I GET THIS OLD LAKE DRAINED, WE CAN START HAULING GOLD!
CHUG CHUG CHUG
WHY DOES UNCLE SCROOGE THINK THE GOLDEN CITY IS UNDERWATER?
WELL, THE "CITY" REALLY IS JUST A LEGEND! BUT IT'S BASED ON THE TRUE STORY OF THE CHIBCHA INDIANS' RELIGIOUS RITES!
HM, I SMELL A GUIDEBOOK LECTURE COMING UP!
CHUG CHUG CHUG
"THE CHIBCHA DIDN'T HAVE GREAT TEMPLES OR ADVANCED SCIENCES LIKE THE AZTECS AND INCAS! ALL THEY HAD WAS LOTS OF GOLD!
"FOR UNTOLD CENTURIES, THE CHIBCHA'S LEADER PERFORMED THE RITUAL OF DUMPING ALL OF THEIR ACCUMULATED WEALTH INTO THEIR SACRED LAKE AS AN OFFERING!"
WHERE'D THEY GET ALL THEIR GOLD? MINES?
THEY HAD MINES, BUT THEY WERE MINES OF SALT! SOMETHING THE OTHER INDIAN NATIONS VALUED MORE THAN GOLD!
CHUG CHUG CHUG
THEY GOT THEIR GOLD IN TRADE FOR SALT?
AND FOR POTATOES! ALL THE POTATOES IN THE WORLD ORIGINATED FROM THOSE THE SPANIARDS FOUND HERE, ON THE CHIBCHA PLATEAU!
THE POOR CHIBCHA! TO HAVE LOST A TREASURE SO PRECIOUS!
YES! IT'S SUPPOSED TO HAVE BEEN THE GREATEST TROVE OF GOLD IN HISTORY!.
GOLD? NO, I MEAN THE SALT AND POTATOES! IF THEY HAD HELD THE CORNER ON THE POTATO CHIP MARKET, THEY'D BE THE WORLD'S RICHEST INDIANS!
SIGH!
HM... PROBABLY SO!

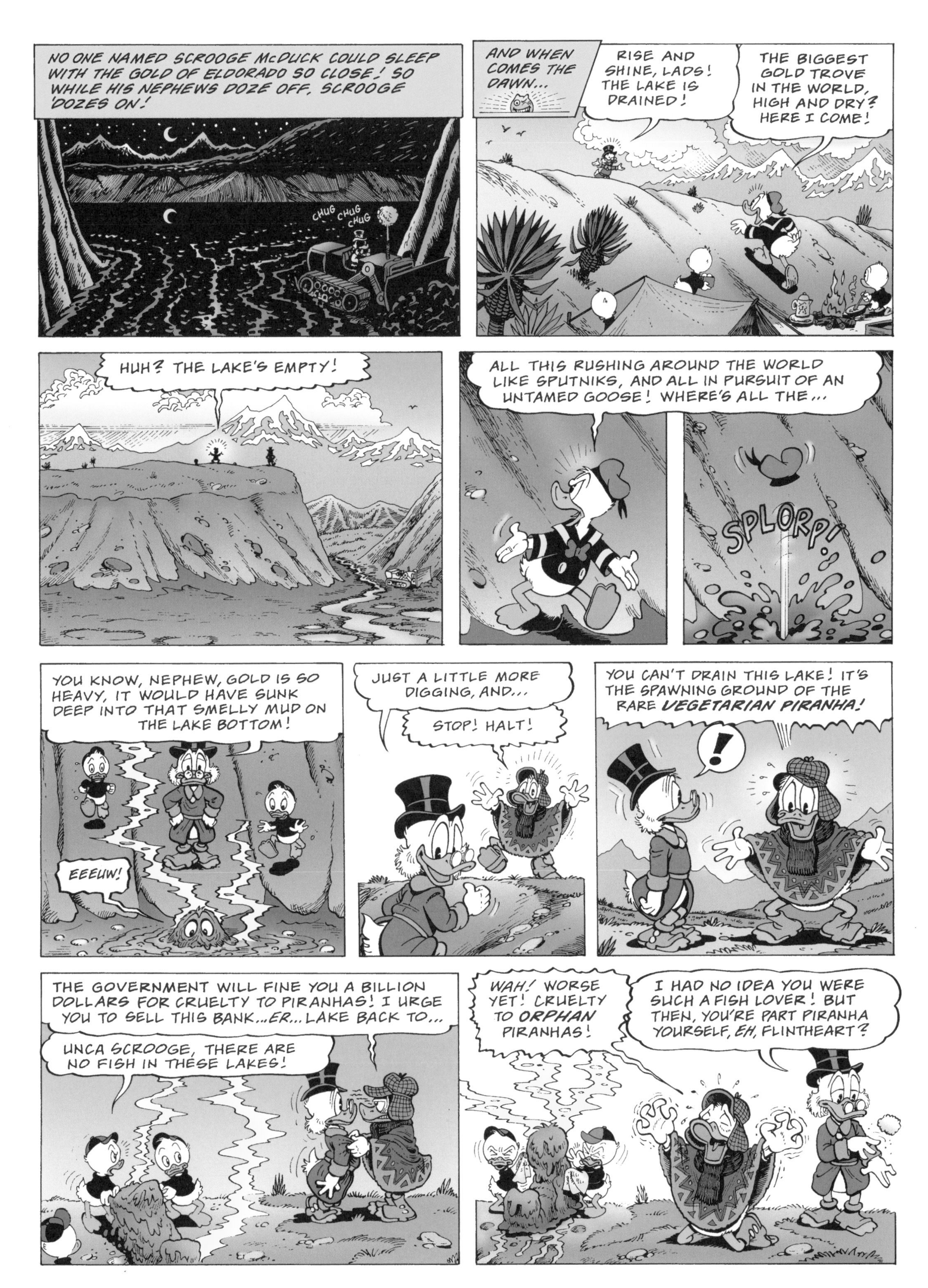
NO ONE NAMED SCROOGE McDUCK COULD SLEEP WITH THE GOLD OF ELDORADO SO CLOSE! SO WHILE HIS NEPHEWS DOZE OFF, SCROOGE 'DOZES ON'!
CHUG CHUG CHUG
AND WHEN COMES THE DAWN...
RISE AND SHINE, LADS! THE LAKE IS DRAINED!
THE BIGGEST GOLD TROVE IN THE WORLD, HIGH AND DRY? HERE I COME!
HUH? THE LAKE'S EMPTY!
ALL THIS RUSHING AROUND THE WORLD LIKE SPUTNIKS, AND ALL IN PURSUIT OF AN UNTAMED GOOSE! WHERE'S ALL THE...
SPLORP!
YOU KNOW, NEPHEW, GOLD IS SO HEAVY, IT WOULD HAVE SUNK DEEP INTO THAT SMELLY MUD ON THE LAKE BOTTOM!
EEEUW!
JUST A LITTLE MORE DIGGING, AND...
STOP! HALT!
YOU CAN'T DRAIN THIS LAKE! IT'S THE SPAWNING GROUND OF THE RARE VEGETARIAN PIRANHA!
!
THE GOVERNMENT WILL FINE YOU A BILLION DOLLARS FOR CRUELTY TO PIRANHAS! I URGE YOU TO SELL THIS BANK...ER...LAKE BACK TO...
UNCA SCROOGE, THERE ARE NO FISH IN THESE LAKES!
WAH! WORSE YET! CRUELTY TO ORPHAN PIRANHAS!
I HAD NO IDEA YOU WERE SUCH A FISH LOVER! BUT THEN, YOU'RE PART PIRANHA YOURSELF, EH, FLINTHEART?

I... YOU... HUH?
I WAS ALSO SURPRISED YOU'RE A TOURIST GUIDE AND PART-TIME WAITRESS, BUT I'D AGREE A STAY IN A CONVENT MIGHT DO YOU SOME GOOD!
YOU SHOULD RECALL THAT SOUTH AMERICA IS BAD LUCK FOR YOU! HAS IT BEEN SO LONG SINCE I WHIPPED YOU IN OUR RACE TO FIND THE GOLD OF THE INCAN EMPIRE?
YOU REMEMBER? THE TEMPLE OF MANCO CAPAC, THE SON OF THE SUN?
WHAT'S FLINTHEART DOING HERE?
I SUSPECT HE WAS THE PREVIOUS OWNER OF MY "BANK"! CHUCKLE! HE'LL SURE BE STEAMED WHEN I DIG UP THE GOLD OF ELDORADO!
OR GULP! I'LL LOOK MIGHTY BAD IF I DON'T!
FOR THE NEXT FEW DAYS, SCROOGE REAMS OUT THE LAKE BED, WITHOUT UNCOVERING SO MUCH MUCH AS A GILDED MAN'S CUFF LINK.
UNCA SCROOGE, YOU'VE UNDERCUT THAT RIDGE SO SEVERELY, IT'S READY TO COLLAPSE ON YOU!
YOU'D BETTER STOP DIGGING BEFORE YOU BECOME A DEPOSIT IN YOUR OWN BANK!
THE CLUES THAT LED ME HERE WERE AUTHENTIC! THIS MUST BE ELDORADO!
BUT I'M ALMOST DOWN TO BEDROCK! I'LL HAVE TO PROCEED BY HAND!
DONALD! GET DOWN HERE WITH A SHOVEL!
YOU RUN THE BULLDOZER! BUT BE CAREFUL! I'M STILL SUBJECT TO THAT THREE PERCENT SURCHARGE!
AND I'M SUBJECT TO 100% SQUISHING!

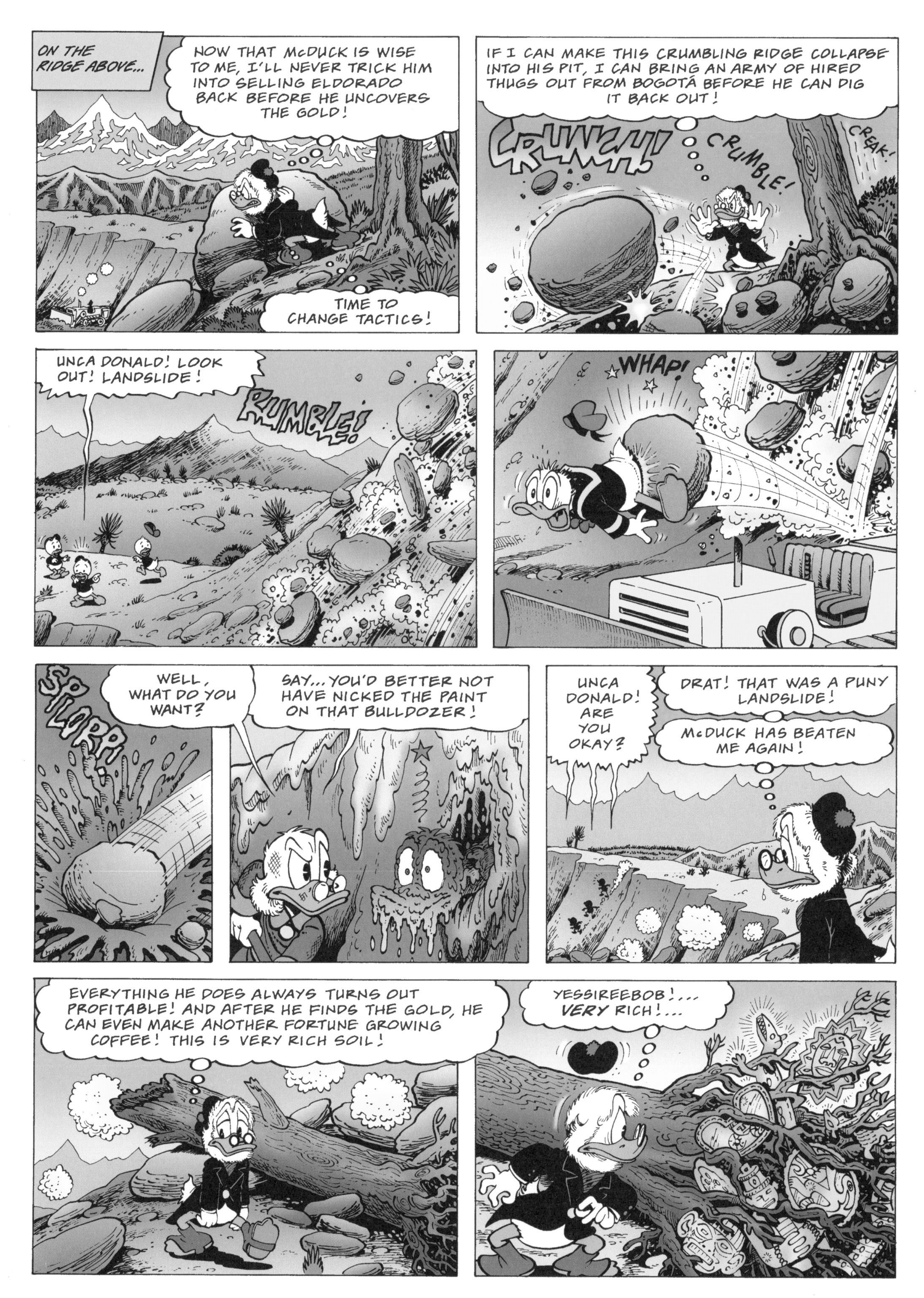

ON THE RIDGE ABOVE...
NOW THAT McDUCK IS WISE TO ME, I'LL NEVER TRICK HIM INTO SELLING ELDORADO BACK BEFORE HE UNCOVERS THE GOLD!
TIME TO CHANGE TACTICS!
IF I CAN MAKE THIS CRUMBLING RIDGE COLLAPSE INTO HIS PIT, I CAN BRING AN ARMY OF HIRED THUGS OUT FROM BOGOTÁ BEFORE HE CAN DIG IT BACK OUT!
CRUNCH!
CRUMBLE!
CREAK!
UNCA DONALD! LOOK OUT! LANDSLIDE!
RUMBLE!
WHAP!
SPLORP!
WELL, WHAT DO YOU WANT?
SAY... YOU'D BETTER NOT HAVE NICKED THE PAINT ON THAT BULLDOZER!
UNCA DONALD! ARE YOU OKAY?
DRAT! THAT WAS A PUNY LANDSLIDE!
McDUCK HAS BEATEN ME AGAIN!
EVERYTHING HE DOES ALWAYS TURNS OUT PROFITABLE! AND AFTER HE FINDS THE GOLD, HE CAN EVEN MAKE ANOTHER FORTUNE GROWING COFFEE! THIS IS VERY RICH SOIL!
YESSIREEBOB!... VERY RICH!...

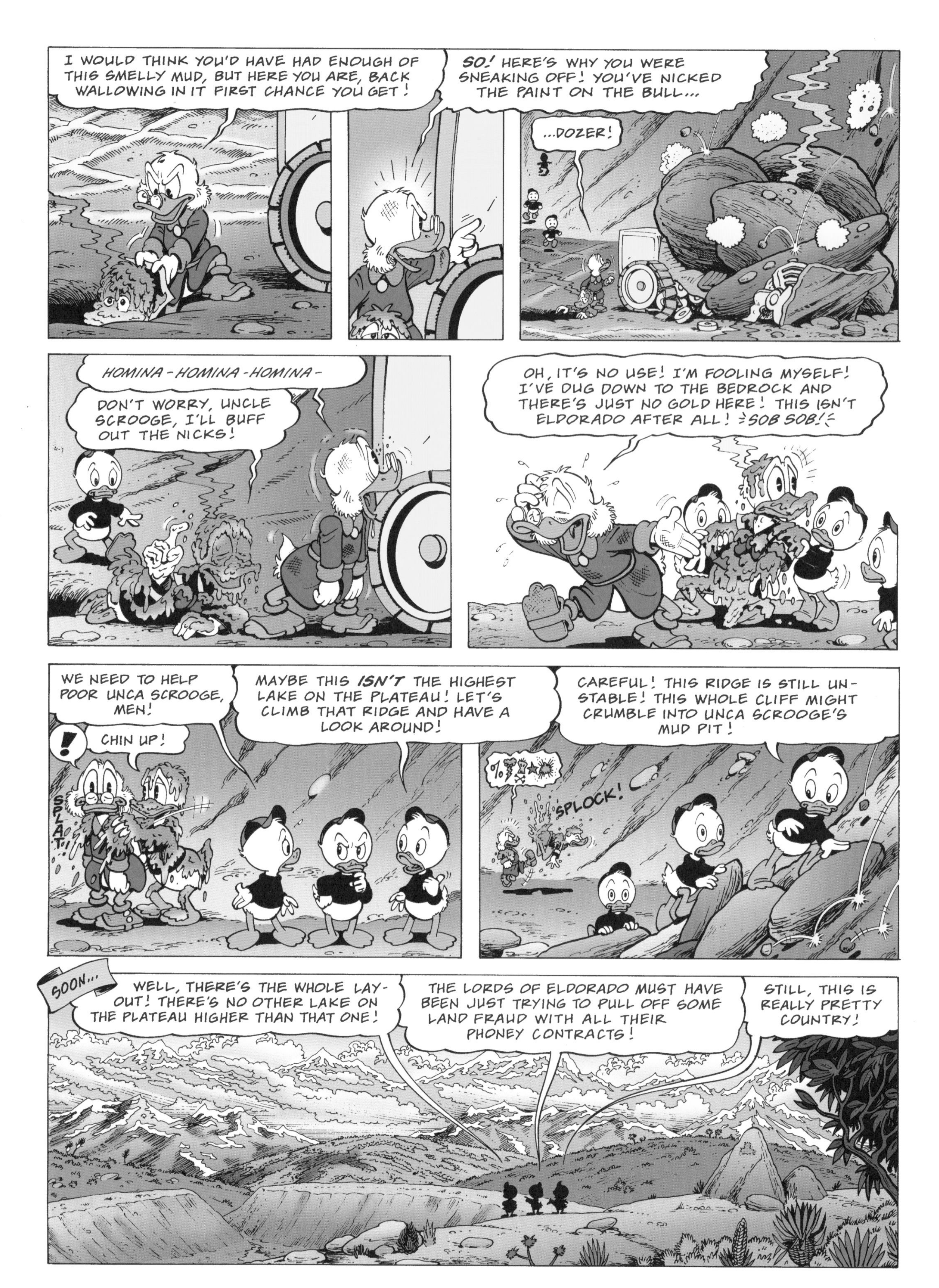
I WOULD THINK YOU'D HAVE HAD ENOUGH OF THIS SMELLY MUD, BUT HERE YOU ARE, BACK WALLOWING IN IT FIRST CHANCE YOU GET!
SO! HERE'S WHY YOU WERE SNEAKING OFF! YOU'VE NICKED THE PAINT ON THE BULL...
...DOZER!
HOMINA-HOMINA-HOMINA-
DON'T WORRY, UNCLE SCROOGE, I'LL BUFF OUT THE NICKS!
OH, IT'S NO USE! I'M FOOLING MYSELF! I'VE DUG DOWN TO THE BEDROCK AND THERE'S JUST NO GOLD HERE! THIS ISN'T ELDORADO AFTER ALL! SOB SOB!
WE NEED TO HELP POOR UNCA SCROOGE, MEN!
!
CHIN UP!
SPLAT!
MAYBE THIS ISN'T THE HIGHEST LAKE ON THE PLATEAU! LET'S CLIMB THAT RIDGE AND HAVE A LOOK AROUND!
SPLOCK!
CAREFUL! THIS RIDGE IS STILL UNSTABLE! THIS WHOLE CLIFF MIGHT CRUMBLE INTO UNCA SCROOGE'S MUD PIT!
SOON...
WELL, THERE'S THE WHOLE LAY-OUT! THERE'S NO OTHER LAKE ON THE PLATEAU HIGHER THAN THAT ONE!
THE LORDS OF ELDORADO MUST HAVE BEEN JUST TRYING TO PULL OFF SOME LAND FRAUD WITH ALL THEIR PHONEY CONTRACTS!
STILL, THIS IS REALLY PRETTY COUNTRY!

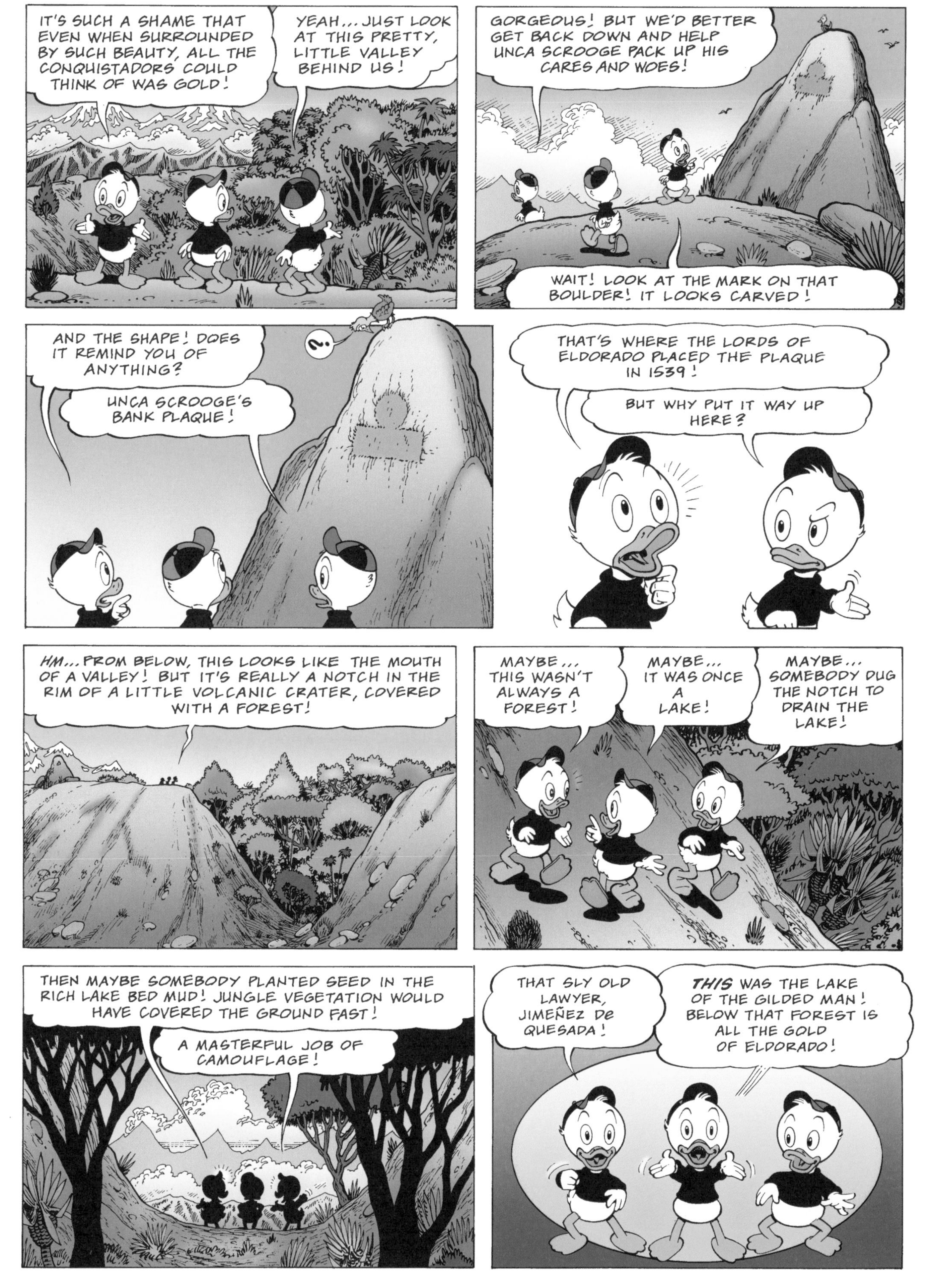
IT'S SUCH A SHAME THAT EVEN WHEN SURROUNDED BY SUCH BEAUTY, ALL THE CONQUISTADORS COULD THINK OF WAS GOLD!
YEAH... JUST LOOK AT THIS PRETTY, LITTLE VALLEY BEHIND US!
GORGEOUS! BUT WE'D BETTER GET BACK DOWN AND HELP UNCA SCROOGE PACK UP HIS CARES AND WOES!
WAIT! LOOK AT THE MARK ON THAT BOULDER! IT LOOKS CARVED!
AND THE SHAPE! DOES IT REMIND YOU OF ANYTHING?
UNCA SCROOGE'S BANK PLAQUE!
?
THAT'S WHERE THE LORDS OF ELDORADO PLACED THE PLAQUE IN 1539!
BUT WHY PUT IT WAY UP HERE?
HM... FROM BELOW, THIS LOOKS LIKE THE MOUTH OF A VALLEY! BUT IT'S REALLY A NOTCH IN THE RIM OF A LITTLE VOLCANIC CRATER, COVERED WITH A FOREST!
MAYBE... THIS WASN'T ALWAYS A FOREST!
MAYBE... IT WAS ONCE A LAKE!
MAYBE... SOMEBODY DUG THE NOTCH TO DRAIN THE LAKE!
THEN MAYBE SOMEBODY PLANTED SEED IN THE RICH LAKE BED MUD! JUNGLE VEGETATION WOULD HAVE COVERED THE GROUND FAST!
A MASTERFUL JOB OF CAMOUFLAGE!
THAT SLY OLD LAWYER, JIMEÑEZ De QUESADA!
THIS WAS THE LAKE OF THE GILDED MAN! BELOW THAT FOREST IS ALL THE GOLD OF ELDORADO!

WHEN QUESADA FINALLY RETURNED HERE IN 1569, HE REMOVED THE GOLD PLAQUE AND MANAGED, WITH HIS MEN, TO DRAIN THE LAKE, COMPLETELY HIDING ELDORADO!

THE KING OF SPAIN, THE WELSER BANK, AND 400 YEARS WORTH OF TREASURE HUNTERS LOOKED FOR A LAKE THAT NO LONGER EXISTED!
YEAH... BUT QUESADA COULD SNEAK UP HERE AND MAKE "WITHDRAWALS" FOR HIS OLD-AGE PENSION!

LET'S GO TELL UNCA SCROOGE THE GOOD NEWS!
I'LL BET FLINTHEART WOULD LIKE TO KNOW ABOUT THIS!

YOU LITTLE CHERUBS HAVE ALWAYS BEEN TOO SMART FOR YOUR OWN GOOD!
MMF!
NOW, NOW! JUNIOR GROUNDHOGS SHOULDN'T USE SUCH LANGUAGE!

SHORTLY...
GOOD NEWS, UNCLE SCROOGE! HERE'S A PART WITHOUT A SINGLE NICK!
SNORT!
UH, OH! I CAN GUESS WHO THAT IS!
CHOP-CHOP-CHOP!
I FIGURED THE NEXT TIME YOU POPPED IN, YOU'D BE DRESSED LIKE MICKEY MOUSE!
NO NEED FOR PERSONAL RANCOR, OLD FRIEND! I'M HERE TO HELP YOU!
DON'T TELL ME YOU STILL WANT TO BUY YOUR BANK BACK! I CAN'T HIDE THIS EMPTY HOLE!
BUT I'M IN A SPOT! I VIOLATED A GERMAN BANKING LAW WHEN I MADE THE SALE! I'M SUBJECT TO A STIFF FINE UNLESS I BUY THE BANK BACK!
WHILE YOU TWO NEGOTIATE, I'M GONNA SEE WHAT'S HAPPENING WITH THE KIDS! THIS RIDGE IS LOOKING MORE UNSTABLE!
UH, OH!

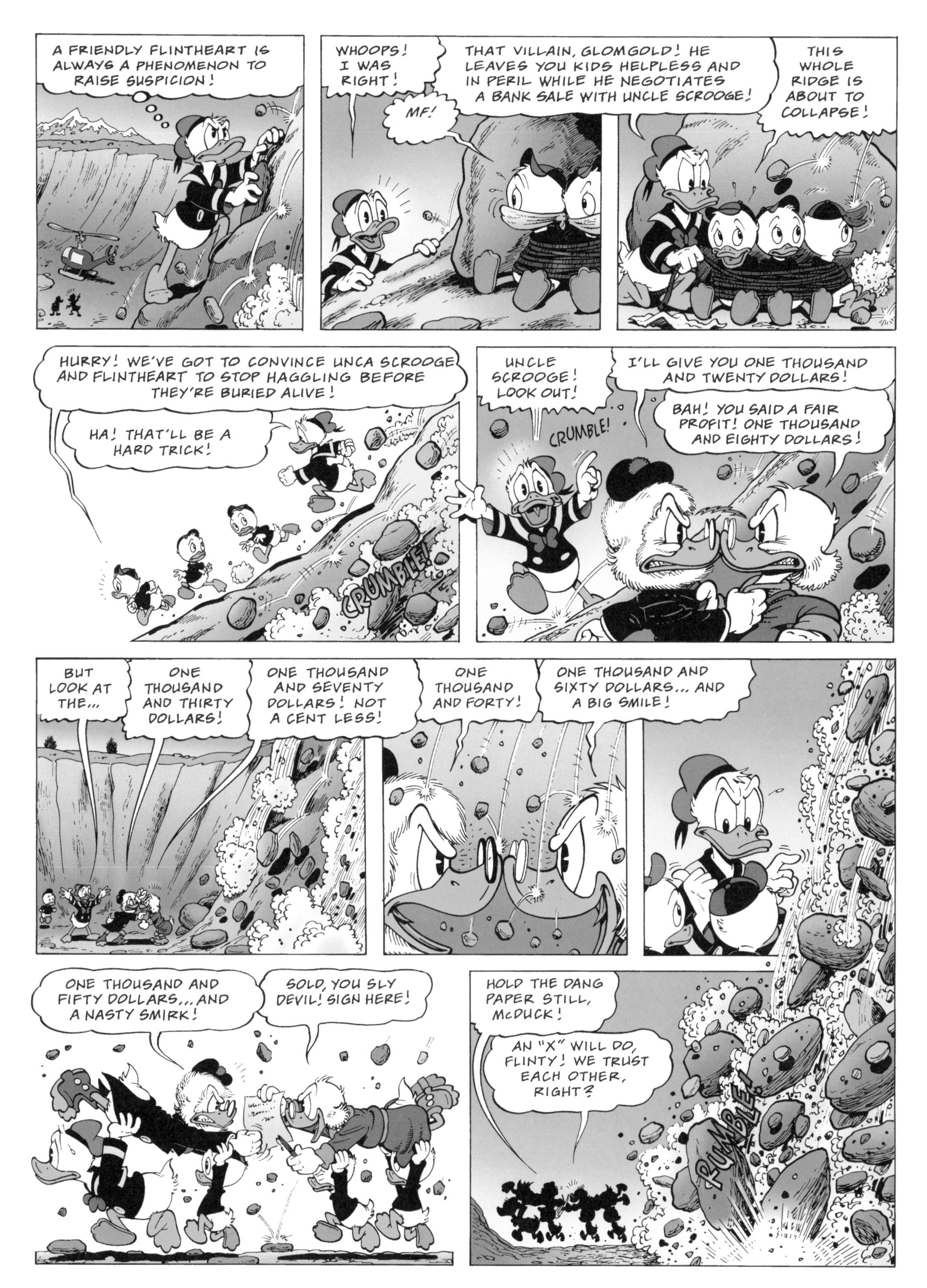
A FRIENDLY FLINTHEART IS ALWAYS A PHENOMENON TO RAISE SUSPICION!
WHOOPS! I WAS RIGHT!
MF!
THAT VILLAIN, GLOMGOLD! HE LEAVES YOU KIDS HELPLESS AND IN PERIL WHILE HE NEGOTIATES A BANK SALE WITH UNCLE SCROOGE!
THIS WHOLE RIDGE IS ABOUT TO COLLAPSE!
HURRY! WE'VE GOT TO CONVINCE UNCA SCROOGE AND FLINTHEART TO STOP HAGGLING BEFORE THEY'RE BURIED ALIVE!
HA! THAT'LL BE A HARD TRICK!
CRUMBLE!
UNCLE SCROOGE! LOOK OUT!
CRUMBLE!
I'LL GIVE YOU ONE THOUSAND AND TWENTY DOLLARS!
BAH! YOU SAID A FAIR PROFIT! ONE THOUSAND AND EIGHTY DOLLARS!
BUT LOOK AT THE...
ONE THOUSAND AND THIRTY DOLLARS!
ONE THOUSAND AND SEVENTY DOLLARS! NOT A CENT LESS!
ONE THOUSAND AND FORTY!
ONE THOUSAND AND SIXTY DOLLARS... AND A BIG SMILE!
ONE THOUSAND AND FIFTY DOLLARS... AND A NASTY SMIRK!
SOLD, YOU SLY DEVIL! SIGN HERE!
HOLD THE DANG PAPER STILL, McDUCK!
AN "X" WILL DO, FLINTY! WE TRUST EACH OTHER, RIGHT?
RUMBLE!

THE BANK OF ELDORADO IS MINE AGAIN! AND JUST IN TIME! LOOK!
WHAT? WHAT'S ALL THE GOLD DOING WAY UP THERE?
I'M AFRAID THAT'S WHERE ELDORADO ORIGINALLY WAS, UNCA SCROOGE!
WOW! AZTEC ARTIFACTS! INDIAN RELICS! MAYAN STATUARY! IT'S A SOLID GOLD HISTORY OF PRE-COLUMBIAN AMERICA!
WELL... I'LL BE SWOGGLED!
HAHAHAHA! YOU'RE TAKING THIS MIGHTY WELL FOR SOMEONE WHO JUST SOLD THE TREASURE OF ELDORADO FOR CHUMP CHANGE!
I ONLY SOLD YOU A BANK, FLINTY! I TRANSFERRED THE LAND GRANT OUT OF THE BANK'S ASSETS THE DAY I BOUGHT IT!
GIGGLE! SO WHAT? HEH, HEH, THE GOLD IS STILL, HEH, THE GOLD IS...
THE GOLD? THE GOLD IS DEPOSITED IN YOUR BANK, BUT IT'S THE PROPERTY OF THE OWNER OF THE TOWN OF OMAGUA, OF ELDORADO!
AND I, SCROOGE McDUCK, AM THE ONE AND ONLY LAST LORD OF ELDORADO!
DAWK!
BY THE WAY, AS YOUR ONLY DEPOSITOR, I'M TEMPTED TO COMPLAIN ABOUT YOUR SLOPPY STORAGE METHODS, TSK!

UNCLE SCROOGE GOT YOU AGAIN, FLINTY! BUT THIS TIME IT ONLY COST YOU FIFTY BUCKS!
I'M AFRAID HE WON'T GET OFF QUITE THAT LIGHT!
OH, NOW WHAT?
IT'S JUST THAT YOU OWN A BANK THAT HAS NEVER PAID INTEREST ON THIS MAGNIFI-CENT DEPOSIT!

HOLY COW! YOU MUST OWE UNCLE SCROOGE ALL THE MONEY IN YOUR BIN!
NO! YOUR UNCLE ISN'T SO MERCIFUL! HE KNOWS THAT COMPOUND INTEREST ON THAT MUCH GOLD FOR 418 YEARS IS...
SOB! I OWE HIM ALL THE MONEY IN THE WORLD!
BUT I'LL SETTLE FOR YOUR BIN! PLUS A FULL LIEN ON ALL YOUR FUTURE EARNINGS!
HEY! WHO'S THAT?
EXCUSE US, SEÑOR, WE HEARD THERE WAS SOMEONE SEARCHING FOR ELDORADO!
AND WHO ARE YOU, BESIDES TRESPASSERS?
GOVERNMENT TAX ASSESSORS! LOOKS LIKE WE FINALLY FOUND THE "BANK OF OMAGUA" THAT'S BEEN IN OUR FILES SINCE 1539!
HA! TOO BAD YOU CAN'T TOUCH THE GOLD IN IT!
SORRY, SIR, TAXES ON THIS CORPORATION HAVE NOT BEEN PAID SINCE JIMÉNEZ QUESADA DIED IN 1579!
THE BANK AND ITS ASSETS BECAME COLOMBIAN GOVERNMENT PROPERTY ON, UH... JUNE 29, 1637!
WHICHEVER ONE OF THESE TWO IS THE LAST LORD OF ELDORADO, HE WAS BANKRUPT CENTURIES BEFORE HE WAS BORN, AND NEVER KNEW IT!

AND SO...
HOW ARE YOU FEELING, UNCA SCROOGE?
OH, NOT SO BAD! THEY LET ME KEEP THE ANCIENT DEED TO ELDORADO FOR MY TROPHY COLLECTION!
BOGOTÁ 5 km
AND FOR ONE GLORIOUS MOMENT, FLINTY THOUGHT HE OWED ME ALL THE MONEY ON EARTH!
HA! EAT YOUR HEART OUT, McDUCK!
AHA! THE GRINGO TREASURE HUNTERS! I STILL HAVE SOME RED HOT TREASURE MAPS FOR SALE, SEÑOR!
Tourist Maps
WELL, I'M NOT BUYING! BUT I SEE ONE MAP HERE THE CHAP IN THE REAR WOULD LOVE TO HEAR ABOUT!
?
THANKS FOR THE TIP, SPORT!
SEÑOR! I CAN TELL YOU ARE JUST THE MAN WHO WOULD APPRECIATE THIS CHOICE MAP! THE SECRET OF THE LOST GOLD OF THE INCAS...
GRUNT!
...THE LEGENDARY TEMPLE OF MANCO CAPAC...
...YOU KNOW... THE SON OF THE SUN!
WHAT'S WITH FLINTHEART?
I HAVEN'T A CLUE!
BUT, I FEEL MUCH BETTER! CAN THE LAST LORD OF ELDORADO BUY SODAS ALL AROUND?
YOU BETCHA, YOUR ROYAL GOLDLESSNESS!
End

Behind the Scenes

BY

Don Rosa

"The Once and Future Duck" was first published in Europe as a three-part serialization, created by replacing the top halves of story pages 9 and 17 with these specially drawn recap panels. Color by Digikore Studios.

THE ONCE AND FUTURE DUCK *p. 9*

This story, as with several others I've done in the past, is a Duck version of an adventure I had written and drawn many years earlier, using my own character Lance Pertwillaby, and which was published in the preeminent comics fan-magazine of the 1970s, *The Rocket's Blast Comicollector*. And as with other of my Pertwillaby plots, it makes a pretty good story, but not necessarily a good *Duck* story. There is a certain "feeling" to a proper Barksian Duck adventure; I have my own ideas (as do we all) as to what that feeling is, and I know when I veer off that course. This story was too "science-fictiony," read too much like an exposé of the King Arthur myth, and had a bit too much bloodthirsty warfare to feel like a proper lighthearted Duck adventure.

For another thing, I personally don't like the idea that Barks' Gyro Gearloose could invent a time travel machine. Time travel is the subject of some of my favorite books and movies, but it's not a notion that Barks would have approved. His Gyro was a more "nuts and bolts" inventor, and never was involved in such abstract or absurd concepts as time travel. However, I know that many subsequent European stories have shown Gyro frequently allowing Scrooge or Donald to borrow time-travel machines from him, so many readers are used to the idea.

But worse yet, my original Pertwillaby story dealt with a very experimental time machine which did not operate properly, so how could I use that idea in a story to be read by people who were familiar with Gyro being proficient in time travel? As you'll see, my solution was to have Gyro experimenting with a mini-time-machine in the shape of a helmet, so that there was still the possibility of some operational problems to solve.

All the facts, places and names in the story that deal with what the original "King Arthur" might have been like, if he ever existed at all, are carefully researched. My purpose was to depict Arthur as the barbarian warlord he would actually have been in real life rather than the "knight in shining armor" as he has always been depicted in all the highly anachronistic (though enjoyable!) books and movies and comics of the past. But my resultant cast of characters comes off as a bit too "gritty" and unsavory for a Donald Duck story, don'tcha think?

I still had my usual amount of fun inserting lots of inside jokes. Donald's "magic words" are all modern references from the 1950s (when my present-day stories are set). The "bard" in my story suffers from a lack of artistic respect, an homage to the poor bard Cacaphonix in the *Asterix* stories. The dialogue mimics the general atmosphere of *Monty Python and the Holy Grail*. There are also numerous English puns in my dialogue that are integral to the story that I had to trust foreign translators to figure out how to deal with in many countries (with my apologies for making their jobs difficult!). But one aspect that might be enjoyed in any language is that I managed to make Gyro's Little Helper the hero of the day.

In a scene anticipating Rosa's "The Once and Future Duck," dynamic Donald prepares to scuttle his nephews' snow fort in Carl Barks' "The Duck in the Iron Pants" (*Walt Disney's Comics and Stories* 41, 1944)

D.U.C.K. SPOTTER'S GUIDE: "D.U.C.K." ("Dedicated to Unca Carl from Keno," Keno being my actual first name) is the special dedication to Carl Barks that I hide somewhere on the first page of most of my stories—in the opening splash panel, unless noted otherwise. In "The Once and Future Duck" splash, the dedication is written in the grass in the lower left of the first panel.

MOUSE SPOTTER'S GUIDE: I frequently hide li'l Mickey Mouse appearances or shapes in my stories, just for fun, to give readers one more detail to hunt for. In "The Once and Future Duck," Mickey appears on a clock face on page 10—and his *name* is used on page 25 in a bogus magic spell recited by Donald, leading others to believe that Gyro's Helper is a "magic mouse" of some kind.

INSANE DETAILS TO LOOK FOR: When I reread these old stories to write these texts, I often spot details in my own backgrounds that I'd forgotten. Notice that my seedy "King Arthur" always has two flies buzzing around him... until page 26, where they are both killed by a power blast. I'd forgotten that! (Chuckle!)

Some famous dialogue from a classic old Barks short story—"The Duck in the Iron Pants" in *Walt Disney's Comics and Stories* 41, 1944—is reused for the pleasure of fans. When Donald shouts "I am invincible! I am doom itself!" it mirrors his threat when attacking his nephews' snow fort in that long-ago tale. Another long-ago reference: in the story's opening panel, Barks scholars will recognize the concrete-from-foam wall that Gyro invented in Barks' second solo Gyro story (*Uncle Scrooge* 14, 1956): you can see the shatter marks where a car ran into it.

"Donald Duck & Co.," Donald's proposed corporate name in the story, is actually the name of *(Continued on Page 191)*

Above and opposite: two pages from Rosa's *Pertwillaby Papers* story "Knighttime" show many similarities with Rosa's later Donald adventure "The Once and Future Duck." *The Pertwillaby Papers* © and courtesy Don Rosa.

ZOW
PUNXSUTAWNEY, PENNSYLVANIA!
ZING
ZOW!
ZOOM!
JESUS CHRIST! MERL-- I DO NOT THINK I LIKE THIS OVERMUCH. THAT MYSTIC INCANTATION HE UTTERED...SUCH POWER RIVALS YOUR OWN!
UH...I...ER ... JUST A MOMENT, SIRE... I MUST CONCENTRATE
SWISH!
TIPPECANOE AND TYLER, TOO!
URANIUM TWO-THIRTY-EIGHT!
FLUB
FOOMP
SNORT.
ALCOA ALUMINUM!
SPLAT!
FOTOMAT!
... SIRE?
ZOUNDS! I AM BEWITCHED!
WOP
RUMBLE!

THE TREASURE OF THE TEN AVATARS
Norwegian *Donald Duck & Co.* 1996-26, June 1996; first American printing on *Uncle Scrooge Adventures* 51, October 1997.
Color by Raimo Hyvonen.

D.U.C.K. SPOTTER'S GUIDE:
Don Rosa's famous dedication to Carl Barks ("Dedicated to Unca Carl from Keno") is hidden in the petals on the red flower to the right.

the flagship Disney comic book in Norway, published by Egmont—the major European comics publisher for whom I did so much of my comics work over the years. The flagship comic books in Denmark and Sweden are also called something equating to "Donald Duck & Co."

How carefully researched were my King Arthur facts? Well, Riothamus—Arthur's surname in my story—comes from the king of Britain between 454 and 470 A.D., pinpointed as the "real" Arthur by Geoffrey Ashe and other modern-day scholars. I don't miss a trick!!!

Or do I? In all previous editions of this story, Palug's Monster Cat—a giant cat Arthur battled in legend—was misnamed as "Taurog's" Monster Cat. *Don Rosa Library* editor David Gerstein has corrected my mistake for this edition. I might have gotten "Taurog" from Norman Taurog, director of *Boys Town* (1938) and other classic films.

THE TREASURE OF THE TEN AVATARS *p. 33*

I began this story by deciding it was time to send Scrooge off on another quest for a fabled treasure of antiquity... so I simply looked at a world globe and considered an interesting locale... and for no particular reason I chose India. As usual, my next step was to amass a pile of books on Indian history and culture, and to dig into my sixty years of *National Geographics*. I seldom had a plot in mind until I started my research, since the best plots are hidden in the history books.

One of the entrance gates of Angkor Thom in Cambodia is the model for the gate into Rosa's fictional city Shambala. Image © and courtesy Egmont Serieforlaget AS.

The first fact I came across regarding India was that Alexander the Great's march of world conquest was turned back at the edge of India in 326 BC when his soldiers were struck with fear of some unknown terror. Here was my story-hook—was Big Al's conquest of India thwarted by some terrible guardian of a great treasure city that would catch Scrooge's fascination? Why not?

The next step was to figure out what that challenge or danger might be. Ancient India had more myths and gods than virtually any other culture in history, and the most fascinating ones I came across were the group of the Ten Avatars. Each of this group of ten were helpers to mankind in some particular aspect, so I decided that these gods would be the key to Scrooge's attaining his goal—they would each help him when called upon at the right time. However, this idea lead me to my most frequent problem—too much plot and too few pages. I was assigned a specific page limit for these stories, and that was not enough to deal with all ten Avatars. I was about to rewrite the story and title it "The Treasure of Only Some of the Ten Avatars", but my editor granted me several extra pages to cover the left-over Avatars, and I was all set.

If anyone is curious about other authentic details—the design for my lost city was borrowed from the Temples of Ajanta, an actual lost city stumbled upon by tiger hunters in 1819. It was carved into a single rock cliff deep in the Indian jungle, having apparently taken over 700 years to complete! The interior entrance hall is that of another cave-shrine of the Deccan Plateau, the Karli Temple.

The Gate to the Grand Staircase is copied from the "Gate of the Dead" entrance to Angkor Thom, yet another lost city of temples, this one built by Indian Hindus in Cambodia, and discovered by Henri Mouhot in 1800 after being hidden by jungle growth for 600 years. This city is the basis for most all the lost cities you've ever seen in movies and comic books! But it makes one wonder how people would lose cities so often in the old days! I mean, is an entire city so easy to misplace? Perhaps this problem was alleviated with the later invention of eyeglasses and auto-club roadmaps.

The second gate at the top of my staircase on the valley rim is copied from the gate to the Great Stupa at Sanchi in central India. The public bath of my city is copied from the Great Bath of the city of Mohenjo Daro, a mighty Indian city of 20,000 people which actually had running water in the homes, and was built 4,500 years ago when Europeans were living in huts and Stonehenge was new.

The only other detail I recall about this story was that the evil Maharajah in my original script was the Maharajah of Howduyustan, the guy that Scrooge had a rivalry with in Barks' classic tale of the giant Cornelius Coot statues (*Walt Disney's Comics* 138, 1952). I always loved to use an old Barks character from my childhood whenever I could find an excuse to do so. But in this case my editor decided that Barks' Maharajah was not really as *evil* as my Maha needed to be, so I replaced him with a new character.

D.U.C.K. SPOTTER'S GUIDE: Check the swirls in the water in the lower-right corner of panel one.

Above and overleaf: three sketches offering an alternative opening to "The Treasure of the Ten Avatars." Don decided against using the relatively good-natured Maharajah of Howduyustan as his villain for Scrooge's adventure in India.

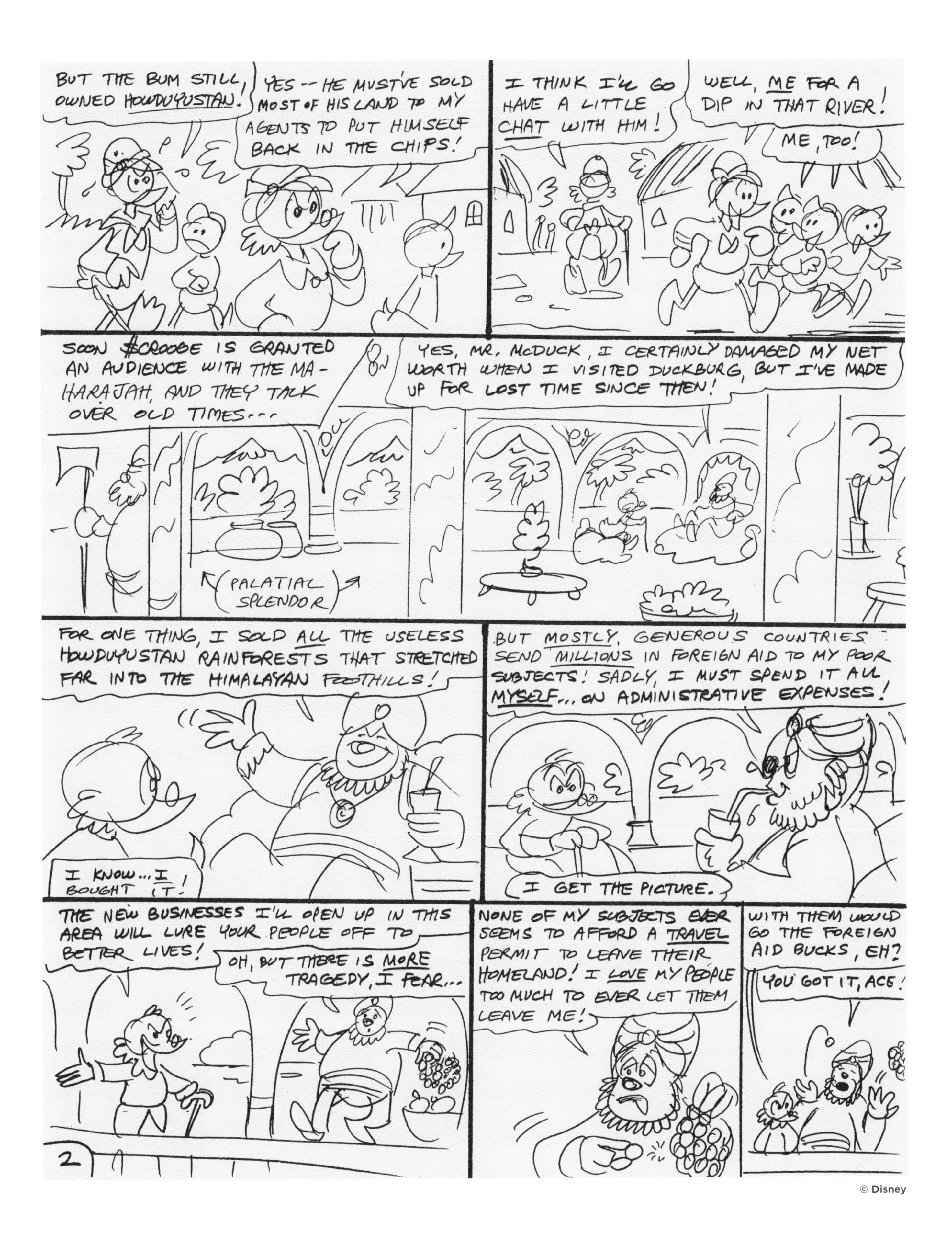

BUT THE BUM STILL OWNED HOWDUYUSTAN!
YES -- HE MUST'VE SOLD MOST OF HIS LAND TO MY AGENTS TO PUT HIMSELF BACK IN THE CHIPS!
I THINK I'LL GO HAVE A LITTLE CHAT WITH HIM!
WELL, ME FOR A DIP IN THAT RIVER!
ME, TOO!
SOON $CROOGE IS GRANTED AN AUDIENCE WITH THE MAHARAJAH, AND THEY TALK OVER OLD TIMES...
YES, MR. McDUCK, I CERTAINLY DAMAGED MY NET WORTH WHEN I VISITED DUCKBURG, BUT I'VE MADE UP FOR LOST TIME SINCE THEN!
(PALATIAL SPLENDOR)
FOR ONE THING, I SOLD ALL THE USELESS HOWDUYUSTAN RAINFORESTS THAT STRETCHED FAR INTO THE HIMALAYAN FOOTHILLS!
I KNOW... I BOUGHT IT!
BUT MOSTLY, GENEROUS COUNTRIES SEND MILLIONS IN FOREIGN AID TO MY POOR SUBJECTS! SADLY, I MUST SPEND IT ALL MYSELF... ON ADMINISTRATIVE EXPENSES!
I GET THE PICTURE.
THE NEW BUSINESSES I'LL OPEN UP IN THIS AREA WILL LURE YOUR PEOPLE OFF TO BETTER LIVES!
OH, BUT THERE IS MORE TRAGEDY, I FEAR...
NONE OF MY SUBJECTS EVER SEEMS TO AFFORD A TRAVEL PERMIT TO LEAVE THEIR HOMELAND! I LOVE MY PEOPLE TOO MUCH TO EVER LET THEM LEAVE ME!
WITH THEM WOULD GO THE FOREIGN AID BUCKS, EH?
YOU GOT IT, ACE!
2

YOU BUM! FIND A WAY TO MAKE MONEY WITH-OUT STEALING IT!
THAT'S EASY FOR YOU TO SAY, BIG SHOT!
MY SUBJECTS ARE THE ONLY RESOURCE IN HOWDUYUSTAN! THAT'S WHY I SOLD OFF ALL THAT USELESS, HILLY FOREST!
BAH! I CAN FIND RICHES ANYWHERE!
STILL THE PREACHY BRAGGART, EH, McDUCK! I'D LIKE TO SEE YOU GET CUT DOWN TO SIZE BY THAT LEAFY WASTELAND!
SIP
SMASH!
TRY ME!
IF YOU CAN GO INTO THAT GREEN NO-THINGNESS AND FIND TWO RUPEES TO RUB TOGETHER, I'LL... I'LL LET MY SUBJECTS GO WORK ON YOUR LAND!
THAT'S A DEAL! SO IF YOU'LL EXCUSE ME, MAHARAJAH, I'LL BE—
!
UNCA SCROOGE! UNCA SCROOGE!
COME QUICK! WE FOUND SOME-THING REALLY INTERESTING DOWN IN THE RIVER!
SWAT!
SWAT!
OH, SO?
LET'S GO HAVE A LOOK!
(GULP) McDUCK MIGHT DO IT TO ME AGAIN!
I'D BETTER FOLLOW!
SHORTLY
THERE WAS AN ANCIENT STONE COLUMN IN THE RIVERBED! PEOPLE HAVE BEEN WASHING CLOTHES ON IT FOR AS LONG AS ANYONE REMEMBERS!
IT MUST HAVE ORIGINALLY STOOD HERE ABOVE WHERE THAT UNDERGROUND SPRING IS BUBBLING!
WHERE IS IT!
(DOING LAUNDRY)
3

A MATTER OF SOME GRAVITY *p. 61*

Well, there's not a great deal to say about this story—it sorta speaks for itself. I found these shorter "gag" stories not really my cup of tea, but I did them about once a year just to take a break from the *intense* level of work I put into those long adventure sagas that appealed more to me, despite their complexity.

These short stories actually seemed more difficult to me... it was tough to come up with a single plot idea that was simple, yet had enough logical comedic possibilities to sustain itself for about ten pages of hijinks. Carl Barks did it masterfully for 25 straight years... but then, that's why they call him Carl Barks, eh?

This idea of a Duck story set on its side had been in my notes for years. I think I'd gotten the idea from the memory of a reprint I'd once seen of a *Little Nemo in Slumberland* newspaper strip of the early 1900s, by Winsor McCay, wherein Nemo and friends climb through the rooms and hallways of a sideways palace. If one turns the page so the rooms look normal, then the pull of gravity appears abnormal. The comic strip scholars in the audience will surely know the Sunday page(s) to which I refer—and our editor, David Gerstein, has promised to include an example below for your edification.

Readers will notice that once Magica De Spell uses her magic spell that twists Scrooge's and Donald's personal gravity to a ninety-degree angle, the *upper* half of each page is shown from our normal point of view, while the *lower* half of each page is shown in the enchanted Ducks' frame of reference. That was fun to draw.

And readers seemed to enjoy it as well. This story was so popular that I did a sequel to it a year or two later titled "Forget It!" which had the same type of plot—with Magica enchanting the Ducks, grabbing the Number One Dime, then leading Scrooge and Donald on another merry chase across town to the Duckburg airport (no witches' brooms for *my* Magica). That story was perhaps even more popular than this first one!

D.U.C.K. SPOTTER'S GUIDE: Oh, I was lazy this time. In the story's opening panel, the dedication is simply written on the label on the bottom drawer of the file cabinet.

MOUSE SPOTTER'S GUIDE: At Page 70, panel 4, you can see Mickey's head on a comic book cover.

INSANE DETAILS TO LOOK FOR: At Page 63, panel 5, you'll spot an "Oso Safe"—a safe bearing the brand name first used by Carl Barks in "The Lemming with the Locket" (*Uncle Scrooge* 9, 1955). It's oh-so-safe, get it?

An episode of Winsor McCay's *Little Nemo in Slumberland*, published in newspapers in 1908. "Befuddle Hall" was the infamous palace where—as here—strange twists in gravity and logic turned Nemo and his pals inside, outside, and upside down. Image courtesy Egmont Serieforlaget AS.

THE VIGILANTE OF PIZEN BLUFF
Uncle Scrooge 306, October 1997.
Color by Susan Daigle-Leach and Scott Rockwell.

D.U.C.K. SPOTTER'S GUIDE:
The dedication is part of the rocks to the right of Scrooge's left foot.

Legendary sharpshooter Annie Oakley, 39 years old, in 1899.
Image courtesy US Library of Congress.

THE VIGILANTE OF PIZEN BLUFF *p. 77*

This was the second extra chapter I did to supplement the original twelve-part *Life and Times of Scrooge McDuck* series, this episode usually being referred to as "Chapter 6B." But it's the first such story to use a new framing sequence featuring Scrooge's old traveling trunk of memories. In the subsequent *Life of Scrooge* tales, the nephews' curiosity about interesting items in the trunk would be the catalyst for their great-uncle to then tell them of that past adventure in a flashback.

I was well aware that I had skipped dealing with three Barksian facts about Scrooge's early life while doing those original twelve chapters. One fact was that Scrooge had once been a gold prospector in a wild-west town called Pizen Bluff (as told in an untitled Barks story in *Uncle Scrooge* 26, 1959). Another fact was that an old prospector had once given Scrooge a map to "The Lost Peg Leg Mine" (*Donald Duck* 52, 1957), but—thinking the mine was all in the old man's imagination—Scrooge threw the map away. And the third unused Barksian fact was that Scrooge had once "outfoxed the Daltons," authentic famous bad guys of the old West, as he bragged in "Only a Poor Old Man" (*Uncle Scrooge* 1/*Four Color* 386).

I'd decided to skip telling the full tale as part of that first series since it would have been yet another "young Scrooge as a cowboy" story, and I'd already done several of those. So this was a "clean-up" episode. But as proof that I already had this story in mind as far back as the original *Life of Scrooge*—and knew it would involve Scrooge's meeting with the Dalton Gang in Pizen Bluff—just refer to the pages of Matilda McDuck's scrapbook shown in the splash panel (as it always was in those original twelve chapters) of Chapter VII.

For this story I decided to team young Scrooge up with a number of real-life American heroes, villains, a showman, and a Native American: Buffalo Bill and Annie Oakley, the Dalton Boys, Phineas T. Barnum, and an Indian named "One-Who-Yawns" (better known as Geronimo!). All of them are drawn as accurately as possible, albeit with those darn black noses that the editor always insisted on. As always, I employed my mania for historical accuracy, partly because I thought it made for a more enjoyable story, but also for the sheer personal challenge of it. Therefore, I had to first make certain that all these historical figures could have been in Arizona in 1890... and fortunately they

"The Vigilante of Pizen Bluff" was first published in Europe as a three-part serialization, created by replacing the top halves of story pages 9 and 17 with these specially drawn recap panels. Color by Susan Daigle-Leach and Erik Rosengarten.

could! Bill and Annie had just returned from a lengthy European tour and Barnum was on a Western vacation in that very year! The Dalton Boys were still active. And Geronimo was supposedly on a reservation in Florida, but maybe he slipped away for a few months, eh? Prove he didn't! (No, please don't.)

Scrooge's main co-star in "Vigilante" is his own Uncle Angus "Pothole" McDuck, last seen in Chapter II of the main *Life of Scrooge* series as the person who gives Scrooge his first job in America. At the end of that old Chapter II, I told of how Uncle Pothole went on to become one of the main writers/heroes of the popular late nineteenth century "dime novels"; this Chapter 6B involves Pothole's success and fame in that career.

This story was meant to be a prequel to two more adventures—one would be another episode of the *Life of Scrooge*, and the other would be Scrooge's present day search for the Lost Dutchman Mine, referred to in the last panels. I eventually completed the Lost Dutchman Mine adventure (titled "The Dutchman's Secret"; see *Don Rosa Library* Vol. 8), but I never got around to telling the story of how Scrooge's Uncle Pothole completed his plans—alluded to in the final page of the flashback portion—of inventing the world's first comic book!

D.U.C.K. SPOTTER'S GUIDE: In panel one of the story, look at the photo on the lower right of the right page of the open scrapbook.

INSANE DETAILS TO LOOK FOR: As noted above, all details about Pizen Bluff come from an untitled story in *Uncle Scrooge* 26 (1959)—including the observation that the "ramshackle buildings" look "like they oughtta blow away in the wind" (page 89). In the *US* 26 story, that's exactly what they do.

In the opening scene, Scrooge's memorabilia trunk includes a peace pipe from Carl Barks' "Land of the Pygmy Indians" (*US* 18, 1957) and a boomerang from my earlier *Life of Scrooge* Chapter VII, "The Dreamtime Duck of the Never Never" (see *Don Rosa Library* Vol. 4). Scrooge's horse Hortense, of course, is in many *Life of Scrooge* stories.

A LITTLE SOMETHING SPECIAL *p. 101*

In many ways, this may well be my favorite story of my own works! If it has one obvious flaw, that could be that it's too packed with material! Granted, even my average

Carl Barks' "Lost Peg Leg Mine" (*Donald Duck* 52, 1957) featured Scrooge recalling a valuable gold mine map that he shouldn't have thrown away. In Rosa's "The Vigilante of Pizen Bluff," we actually see Jacob Walz giving Scrooge the map—and Scrooge unwisely discarding it.

stories are rather overly plotted with an abundance of facts and events and 50% more panels per page than any other Duck comics. With this story I was trying even harder than I normally do to jam as much plot and humor into a story... but I couldn't help it! I was given the job of creating the "official" 50th Anniversary Scrooge McDuck story, and the only way I could do such a job on my favorite comic character was to *over*do it. Again.

For the "anniversary stories" I did, normally I would choose to create another "secret origin" tale. But that idea wouldn't work here. In my *Life and Times of Scrooge McDuck* series I'd already told of Scrooge's early life and how he came to Duckburg. And I couldn't do a story that claimed Scrooge was only "fifty years old"—he's obviously far older than that. Then it struck me that my stories take place sometime in the 1950s, and it was stated in that *Life of Scrooge* series that Scrooge arrived in Duckburg in 1902. So I could do a story taking place in 1952 about Duckburg's commemoration of the 50 years since Scrooge arrived there. Ideal!

As I say, I tried hard to make sure this was a story good enough to match the special occasion. I knew I needed to bring every one of Barks' Duckburg heroes and villains into the plot, even including Scrooge's parents and sisters in pictures hanging in his office. I made sure I mentioned lots of classic Barks adventures such as those set in Tralla La and Plain Awful, and I even gave the giant Cornelius Coot statue—from one of Barks' best ten-pagers (*Walt Disney's Comics* 138, 1952)—a key role in the plot. I made sure that each Barks character had some *important* part to play in the story, and did not simply stand around and watch. I made the very destruction of Duckburg itself be one of the master-villain's evil plans... how much more villainous could he be?! I even let Donald Duck give a speech into which I inserted some of my own personal

A LITTLE SOMETHING SPECIAL
The Adventurous Uncle Scrooge McDuck 2, March 1998.
Color by Scott Rockwell.

D.U.C.K. SPOTTER'S GUIDE:
The dedication is on four flags beneath the Cornelius Coot statue.

SO! WASTING YOUR TIME READING THOSE STUPID SUPER-HERO COMICS AGAIN, EH?
WISTFUL UNION
SUPER SNOOPER
SNATCH!

Years before "A Little Something Special," an earlier Rosa use of Super Snooper—Huey, Dewey, and Louie's favorite comic book hero—came in "Super Snooper Strikes Again" (1993; see *Don Rosa Library* Vol. 3).

thoughts about Barks' most famous character (bottom of page 118). And I finally gave a clue as to what I thought would be Scrooge's ultimate destiny.

D.U.C.K. SPOTTER'S GUIDE: Look in the stack of papers on Miss Quackfaster's desk in the first panel.

MOUSE SPOTTER'S GUIDE: On page 103, Scrooge is offered an autographed picture of a rather silly-looking Mickey.

INSANE DETAILS TO LOOK FOR: At the time I created this story, my editors told me that I was not allowed to use Ludwig Von Drake as they considered him "officially dead"—they didn't like the character, and had an editorial policy of not using him at Egmont. But I like Ludwig! Barks even used him in a one-page Scrooge gag in 1961 ("Flowers Are Flowers," published three years later in *US* 54), and I wanted to make sure he wasn't left out of this special story. So I snuck in a rear-angle glimpse of him on the main stage during the contest ceremony—the editor never noticed!

On page 103, nutmeg tea comes from "A Spicy Tale" (*US* 39, 1962), and Super Snooper from the untitled ten-pager in *Walt Disney's Comics* 107 (1949). On Page 105, Plain Awful is the land of square eggs from "Lost in the Andes" (*Four Color* 223, 1949), and Tralla La the lost paradise-world from *Uncle Scrooge* 6 (1954).

On page 113 Miss Quackfaster faints at the sight of a Beagle Boy suddenly appearing before her. But why would she faint at the sight of a Beagle Boy? They weren't such fearsome villains. Keep in mind that this Beagle Boy is still wearing Gladstone Gander's clothing.

I especially enjoyed doing the fight sequence between Scrooge and the archvillain atop the giant Cornelius Coot statue—this was based on a very similar scene between Bob Cummings and Norman Lloyd atop the Statue of Liberty's torch in one of my very favorite Alfred Hitchcock movies, 1942's *Saboteur*! But let's discuss that surprise master-villain... well, I can call him by name since this text appears after you've read the story... Blackheart Beagle, Scrooge's oldest enemy (not counting the Whiskerville clan back home in Scotland). At the time of this story, I figured (my) Scrooge McDuck to be 85 years old. But he had first met Blackheart back in 1880 while working on his Uncle Pothole's riverboat. And at that time Blackheart already had three fully grown sons, so he must have been at least 40 years old. Therefore, at the time of this story, Blackheart would be over 110 years old! So how do I explain that? It's really very simple. You see, there's a... er... excuse me, there's someone at the door. I'll get back to you...

GYRO'S BEAGLETRAP *p. 130*

One of the shortest stories I ever concocted was this little-seen piece. I was asked by a magazine to create a one-page gag that would incorporate into the art—somewhere—a parody of the magazine's running-man emblem, which I used in the final panel. If the hole in the wall was a sensible shape, there would have been *no gag*... it would simply have been gratuitous slapstick!

ATTACK OF THE HIDEOUS SPACE-VARMINTS *p. 131*

This story has two things in common with "The Incredible Shrinking Tightwad" (see *Don Rosa Library* Vol. 6), which I'd done the year before. First, it's another Duck version of a 1950's sci-fi B-movie... no movie in particular, but just the typical invasion-by-icky-monsters-from-outer-space movie. However, in this version, it's the Ducks who are considered the "icky monsters," and it's a family of hillbilly aliens who spout all the usual B-movie cliché dialogue that would normally be given to humans!

The second similarity to "Tightwad" is the use of a prop from an old Barks story... in this case, the moon-rocket invented by Gyro Gearloose for Scrooge's use in an untitled 1958 adventure (*Disneyland Birthday Party* 1). But I had another reason to reuse that rocket other than the mere fact I *enjoy* using Barks characters or memorabilia that I recall from my childhood—my editor had asked me to do an "outer space" story, but I had a slight problem with that idea. I didn't think these characters should have the ability to rocket about the universe in spacecraft at a moment's notice. Space travel in a Duck story should be treated as a very unique and difficult concept, as Barks handled it in his stories. (Please don't remind me of later stories like "Interplanetary Postman" [*Uncle Scrooge* 53, 1964]... I'd say Unca Carl was running out of ideas by then.) I don't even think Gyro should be able to whip up a spaceship without a *little* extra effort. So, my best answer was to reuse a spaceship that had already been introduced into Barks'

ATTACK OF THE HIDEOUS SPACE-VARMINTS
Drawn in 1997; first printing in Egmont *Walt Disney's Hall of Fame: Don Rosa – Book 7*, 2008. Color by Scott Rockwell.

D.U.C.K. SPOTTER'S GUIDE:
The dedication is not included.

Gyro's unique moon-rocket in "Attack of the Hideous Space-Varmints" originated in Carl Barks' untitled Uncle Scrooge story made for *Disneyland Birthday Party* 1 (1958).

Duck Universe, thereby not quite violating my attitude that outer space is not a proper setting for these characters.

But beyond that, I still had to find a way to get the Ducks' moon-rocket as far away from earth as the asteroid belt (between Mars and Jupiter) without it taking them many months to reach the area. A little *Star Trek*-type warp-drive took care of that, courtesy of alien technology... in this fashion, I didn't need to have Gyro inventing something that I believed was beyond even his capabilities.

I guess my view of these Ducks is very "down to earth." I don't think Scrooge or Donald should have adventures in outer space or traveling through time; I regard Gyro as a "nuts and bolts" inventor rather than some futuristic nuclear physicist; and I regard Magica De Spell as an amateur sorceress rather than a omnipotent master of witchcraft (you'll never even see her riding a broom in my stories).

Anyway, I thought this was just about the right sort of space-opera story for Ducks. But it's too bad my European readers couldn't read the aliens' hillbilly dialogue in my original English... it's sorta fun. (I wonder how the translators handled it... *Don Rosa Library* editor David Gerstein tells me they *do* have rural dialects in Europe!)

And perhaps I should point out that I know I have misrepresented the asteroid belt, drawing it as if it was as densely arranged as the rubble in Saturn's rings. There are only about 3,500 known asteroids in the belt, and when you consider the belt follows an orbital path of many millions of miles, drawing it accurately would have made for a rather visually nonexistent belt—not to mention a rather dull story.

D.U.C.K. SPOTTER'S GUIDE: Look at the meteor collision in the lower right of the first panel and you'll see the dedication.

MOUSE SPOTTER'S GUIDE: When Scrooge's rocket takes off from the moon on page 152, it leaves behind a rather special souvenir of its visit.

INSANE DETAIL TO LOOK FOR: Scrooge's Rolls-Regal Horseless Shay—the vintage car stored in the barn on page 135—comes from Barks' "Chugwagon Derby" (*Uncle Scrooge* 34, 1961).

Below and right: "Attack of the Hideous Space-Varmints" was first published in Europe as a three-part serialization, created by adding these specially-drawn caption boxes to the opening panels of story pages 9 and 17.

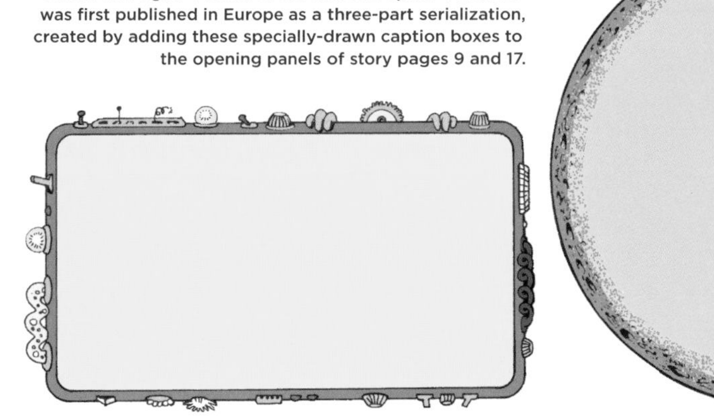

THE LAST LORD OF ELDORADO
German *Walt Disneys Onkel Dagobert von Don Rosa* Album 22, September 1999 (within which—due to a publisher's error—the actual "Eldorado" story did not appear). Color by Sanoma and Scott Rockwell.

D.U.C.K. SPOTTER'S GUIDE:
The dedication is hidden in the long feathers on El Dorado's headdress.

THE LAST LORD OF ELDORADO *p. 155*

This was planned to be a very special story. It marked the tenth anniversary of the first Duck story I wrote and drew for Gladstone Publishing, "The Son of the Sun" (1987; see *Don Rosa Library* Vol. 1). That tale had pitted Scrooge against Flintheart Glomgold to find the lost treasury of the Incan Empire. So, as my anniversary story, I thought it would be interesting to again have Scrooge and Flinty face off, again in South America, and again for a fabled lost golden treasure of an ancient civilization. But this time it would be for a treasure for which Carl Barks never had Scrooge search—the supposedly greatest treasure of the Americas, the treasure which was the reason for most of the original exploration of this hemisphere, the lost City of Gold, Eldorado.

As you probably know, back in *Four Color* 422 (1952), Barks *did* have Donald meet up with El Dorado (sic), the Gilded Man. This was the lord of the city of Eldorado, but no mention was made in Barks' story of the city or the gold. Moreover, Barks situated the Gilded Man in British Guiana on the eastern coast of South America, which is the wrong neighborhood for him. But this is an understandable historical error—Barks' research probably told him that Guiana is where Eldorado was supposedly located, but he must not have known that that was a *different* Guiana than the twentieth century version. In the sixteenth century, the name Guiana (or Guyana) referred to a territory covering almost *all* of the northern third of South America, and Eldorado would actually have been located somewhere in what is now Colombia. Therefore, I could do a new Eldorado story without conflicting with the Barks tale. Barks' *Man* of Gold must have previously retired from his original namesake hometown and moved to the future site of British Guiana, perhaps looking for a nice seaside retirement home. So I could still do a story about the search for the *City* of Gold, back in Colombia. The facts that my research uncovered about the three renegade treasure-hunting armies of 1539 revealed the most amazing true story I'd ever come upon! And every detail I tell of in this adventure is authentic… even including that there was a secret deal struck by these armies before they returned to Europe to try to claim what they found. The only thing we don't know is what it *was* that they found, because they would never tell their superiors.

And don't suppose that is all there was to this actual true-life adventure. Beyond the parts I mention, the hunt for Eldorado went on for decades—with the German bank and the King of Spain trying to find Quesada's secret; with more expeditions, battles, beheadings and kidnappings. England got into the act later, when first Queen Elizabeth and then King James sent Sir Walter Raleigh on two different expeditions to South America on his promise that he could find Eldorado for England. He sailed to South

Rosa's Lance Pertwillaby has a 1973 bridge misadventure that anticipates Donald's in "The Last Lord of Eldorado." *The Pertwillaby Papers* © and courtesy Don Rosa.

"The Last Lord of Eldorado" was first published in Sweden as a two-part serialization, created by replacing the top half of Page 16 with this all-new recap panel. Color by Digikore Studios.

America, kidnapped Quesada's son, tried to force him to lead an expedition to Eldorado, but Quesada Jr. escaped during an Indian attack. Sir Walter returned to England and was beheaded for his poor treasure-hunting abilities. Just like a movie plot, eh?

But this is actually where my problem with this story lies. It's not bad, but I just couldn't seem to create a story that was as *amazing* as the actual facts! Speaking of actual facts, the true Lake of Eldorado is supposedly known—not Lake Teusaca as I claim in my story for my purposes, but Lake Guatavita in the same area. Treasure hunters tried draining this lake many times—in 1545, 1625, 1801, and 1823—and at times salvaged some of the golden treasures that lay in its depths. In 1904 the lake was finally drained, exposing the slimy, muddy bottom. But this mud then solidified into a concrete mass, and the treasure hunters could not penetrate it with their primitive equipment. Ultimately, in 1965, the Colombian government declared the lake a historical site, and forbade any further attempts to retrieve the billions of dollars in gold that are believed to be sunk deep in the lake's muddy bottom.

This story might be regarded as a triple-sequel. It is part two of "Treasure Under Glass" (1991; see *Don Rosa Library* Vol. 3), and part two of the rivalry between Scrooge and Flintheart begun in "The Son of the Sun," and also part two adding onto Barks' "Gilded Man" classic.

Donald's predicament on the rope-bridge is an old bit that I reused from my fan-cartoonist days. This was a sequence that I used in my original version of "The Son of the Sun" plot, which I did as a comic strip in 1973—those physics calculations that the nephews perform came from that strip as well, done back when I was a civil engineering student and working on such physics problems every day (but not as well as the nephews do!). A couple of the relevant strips appear on the previous page.

D.U.C.K. SPOTTER'S GUIDE: In the first panel of the story, look in the waves in the lower left corner.

MOUSE SPOTTER'S GUIDE: Mickey doesn't actually appear, but he's *mentioned* on page 181.

NOT-SO-INSANE DETAILS TO LOOK FOR: Scrooge's copy of a 17th-century salvage chart—and numerous other details pictured on page 156—are what make this story a follow-up to my earlier "Treasure Under Glass." Scrooge's and Glomgold's "race to find the gold of the Incan empire," meanwhile, was their challenge in "The Son of the Sun." See? Not so insane this time. •

KLONDIKE GAZETTE
DUCK HITS JACKPOT!
GLASGOW
PARIS
DAWSON
CAPE TOWN
PERTH

The Rosa Archives

This Should Cover It All!

(Additional Covers and Posters, 1996-1997)

By Don Rosa

Earlier on in this volume you've seen the "Don-Rosa-story-specific" covers that I did for the early *Life of Scrooge* stories. To be precise: if I did a cover for one of the chapters near the time of its first printing, then Fantagraphics has run that cover either alongside the chapter itself, or alongside my "Behind the Scenes" annotative text.

But what about all the covers done not for my *own* stories, but for Barks classics and other projects? And what about additional special art I created? That's what *this* gallery is for.

Turn the next few pages for a spin through these "non-Don-Rosa-story-specific" covers and other drawings. Or look below for my comments on many of them:

WEINACHTSALBUM *p. 209* • *Weihnachtsalbum* is German for "Christmas album," which means that this cover was drawn for a volume that (surprise!) included several Christmas stories, starting with a Barks favorite about Christmas on an island in the South Seas (*Christmas in Disneyland* 1, 1957). I wanted to do a cover based on that old tale, but the editor preferred that I do a gag cover. I don't particularly like gag covers because I'm not able to come up with a plain old simple-yet-funny gag. Thus, I'm not even sure if people understood the supposed joke here. Scrooge is stingy, right? And the presents he gives out are pretty strange and useless, right? And he... oh, well, let's just forget about it and go on to the next one.

TRALLA LA *p. 210* • Gladstone Publishing was going to reprint Barks' story about Tralla La (*Uncle Scrooge* 6, 1954) and asked me for a Rosa cover to go with it. Showing both the parachuting Duck family and the beautiful valley of Tralla La at the same time proved to be pretty difficult. Scrooge and the others look like they're about to land on some steep cliffs on the side of the valley! I also showed Scrooge removing the bottlecap from his medicine—an ill-fated act that, in the story, actually happened while he was still on the plane.

***UNCLE SCROOGE* 300** *pp. 211-213* • The front cover of Gladstone's *Uncle Scrooge* 300 (1996) featured a simplified version of the first illustration you see here, depicting every major hero and villain to appear in a Carl Barks Uncle Scrooge story (!!!). A complete version of the image appeared inside the issue.

The *US* 300 centerfold, meanwhile, featured the landscape illustration titled "Anything But Those." Originally made on a request from a friend, this illustration uncharacteristically includes treasures referring to my own stories as well as those of Carl Barks.

From left to right, the comic books depicted are:

• Uncle Scrooge *Four Color* 456 ("Back to the Klondike," 1953)

• US *FC* 386 ("Only a Poor Old Man," functionally *Uncle Scrooge* 1, 1952)

• *Walt Disney's Comics and Stories* 31 ("The Victory Garden," first Carl Barks ten-page story, 1943)

• *Uncle Scrooge* 219 ("The Son of the Sun," my debut, 1987)

• Donald Duck *Four Color* 9 ("Donald Duck Finds Pirate Gold!," Carl Barks' first Duck comic book work, 1942)

***PICSOU* 300** *p. 215* • *Picsou* is the excellent monthly French Scrooge magazine, and for their 300th issue, I created a giant foldout poster. I think this is the single largest drawing I ever did for publication, and in contrast to the covers—which always needed some free space at the top for the book title logo—here I could fill up the whole image area. I tried to include all of the Duckburg cast including the bad guys, as well as one generic pig villain to represent all other enemies Scrooge ever had to face. Despite the crowd of characters, the resulting poster still had the top staying pretty much empty after all. Otherwise, I'd have had to put characters on ladders and scaffolds or coming down on parachutes.

TWO IN ONE *p. 218* • My friend and then-freelance Egmont writer, David Gerstein—today our *Don Rosa Library* editor—had written this story that was drawn by Daniel Branca, featuring one of Magica's devious plots in which she created clones of herself and other creatures. When Gladstone published the story, David asked me if I could supply them with a cover, which I happily agreed to. The staging was based in part on a sketch David drew for me.

THE DUCK WHO FELL TO EARTH *p. 219* • The German Egmont branch asked me for a cover for this short adventure from 1990. I took some artistic freedom to show Scrooge in the same picture as the falling Donald and put him outside of the cockpit that he never actually leaves in the story. For me, the little details are always the funniest things in such a big illustration, and what I like best about this is how Scrooge's glasses are floating around in his helmet without him being able to grab them. Ha-ha.

German *Walt Disneys Weinachtsalbum* 1, 1996; first American printing on *Uncle Scrooge and Donald Duck* 2, March 1998. Color by Susan Daigle-Leach.

D.U.C.K. SPOTTER'S GUIDE: The dedication is on the ribbon of the package that's still in Santa Scrooge's bag.

TRALLA LA
Uncle Scrooge Adventures 39, July 1996; color by Susan Daigle-Leach and Scott Rockwell. Illustrating a story written and drawn by Carl Barks (*Uncle Scrooge* 6, 1954).

D.U.C.K. SPOTTER'S GUIDE:
Look in the rice paddies in the bottom middle, directly next to one of the parachuting nephews' hands.

Uncle Scrooge 300, October 1996; color by Susan Daigle-Leach and Scott Rockwell.
The illustration appeared in a simplified version on the front cover and in this complete version on an interior page.
See page 214 for a key to the characters shown.

D.U.C.K. SPOTTER'S GUIDE:
The dedication is part of the pattern on the marble column.

ANYTHING BUT THOSE!
Uncle Scrooge 300 centerfold, October 1996; color by Scott Rockwell.
See overleaf for a key to the treasure items shown.

D.U.C.K. SPOTTER'S GUIDE:
The dedication is not included.

UNCLE SCROOGE 300
FRONT COVER • KEY

1 Gu, the Abominable Snowman ("The Lost Crown of Genghis Khan," *Uncle Scrooge* 14, 1956)
2 Hassan Ben Jaild ("McDuck of Arabia," *US* 55, 1965)
3 Maharajah of Swingingdore ("The Tuckered Tiger," *US* 9, 1955)
4 Boss Martian ("Lost Beneath the Sea," *US* 46, 1963)
5 Dan McShrew ("The Loony Lunar Gold Rush," *US* 49, 1964)
6 An asteroid Indian ("Island in the Sky," *US* 29, 1960)
7 A giant robot robber ("The Giant Robot Robbers," *US* 58, 1965)
8 Fanny Featherbrain ("Isle of Golden Geese," *US* 45, 1963)
9 Slyviper ("Crown of the Mayas," *US* 44, 1963)
10 Copperhead McViper ("Ghost Town Railroad," *US* 56, 1965)
11 Queen Cleopickerel ("Hall of the Mermaid Queen," *US* 68, 1967)
12 Ducky Bird ("Ghost Town Railroad")
13 King of Bir Sheba ("McDuck of Arabia," *US* 55, 1965)
14 "Hashknife" Katie Mallard ("Ghost Town Railroad")
15 Larkie Agnes ("The Golden Fleecing," *US* 12, 1955)
16 Pintail Duck ("Back to Long Ago," *US* 16, 1956)
17 Royal Guardian ("The Prize of Pizarro," *US* 26, 1959)
18 Odin ("Mythtic Mystery," *US* 34, 1961)
19 "Hound of the Whiskervilles" (*US* 29, 1960)
20 "The Phantom of Notre Duck" (*US* 60, 1965)
21 Lah Deedah ("Tralla La," *US* 6, 1954)
22 El Jackal ("The Mines of King Solomon," *US* 19, 1957)
23 Barko ("North of the Yukon," *US* 59, 1965)
24 Pablo ("That's No Fable!," *US* 32, 1960)
25 Matey McDuck ("Back to Long Ago!," *US* 16, 1956)
26 Longhorn Tallgrass
27 Soapy Slick ("North of the Yukon")
28 A faceless person ("The Many Faces of Magica De Spell," *US* 48, 1964)
29 Glittering Goldie
30 Cura De Coco witch doctor ("A Spicy Tale," *US* 39, 1962)
31 Jivaro medicine man ("The Money Champ," *US* 27, 1959)
32 Flintheart Glomgold
33 Gladstone Gander
34 Horseshoe Hogg ("The Great Steamboat Race," *US* 11, 1955)
35 A Casbah pygmy ("Pipeline to Danger," *US* 30, 1960)
36 and unnumbered small green figures: male "Micro-Ducks from Outer Space" (*US* 65, 1966)
37 Huey Duck
38 Beagle Boy 176-167
39 Brutopian Ambassador ("A Cold Bargain," *US* 17, 1957)
40 Princess Teentsy Teen (female Micro-Duck)
41 Lawyer from McEagle, McEagle, McHawk, McCrow and McChicken ("Heirloom Watch," *US* 11, 1955)
42 King of Tangkor Wat ("City of Golden Roofs," *US* 20, 1957)
43 Opu Nui ("The Menehune Mystery," *US* 4, 1954)
44 Argus McSwine (aka John the Con, Porkman De Lardo, etc.)
45 "The Lemming With the Locket" (*US* 9, 1955)
46 Muchkale ("The Twenty-Four Carat Moon," *US* 24, 1959)
47 Donald Duck
48 "The Queen of the Wild Dog Pack" (*US* 62, 1966)
49 Peeweegah Chief ("Land of the Pygmy Indians," *US* 18, 1957)
50 Magica De Spell
51 The king of Atlantis ("The Secret of Atlantis," *US* 5, 1954)
52 Professor Dustdiver ("Cave of Ali Baba," *US* 37, 1962)
53 Louie Duck
54 Stone ray professor (*US* 8, 1954)
55 Fermy ("Land Beneath the Ground!," *US* 13, 1956)
56 Bruto Castrova ("Swamp of No Return," *US* 57, 1965)
57 Chisel McSue ("The Horse-Radish Story," Uncle Scrooge *Four Color* 495, 1953)
58 Monsieur Mattressface ("The Fabulous Philosopher's Stone," *US* 10, 1955)
59 Chief Boogerbooboo ("Bongo on the Congo," *US* 33, 1961)
60 Dewey Duck
61 Soy Bheen, AKA Prince Char Ming ("Treasure of Marco Polo," *US* 64, 1966)

ANYTHING BUT THOSE! • KEY

1 Sun Disk ("Son of the Sun," *Uncle Scrooge* 219, 1987)
2 "Crown of the Mayas" (*US* 44, 1963)
3 Vulcan's hammer ("Mythtic Mystery," *US* 34, 1961)
4 Spanish armor ("The Prize of Pizarro," *US* 26, 1959)
5 "The Lost Crown of Genghis Khan" (*US* 14, 1956)
6 The Candy-Striped Ruby ("The Status Seeker," *US* 41)
7 Bombastium ("A Cold Bargain," *US* 17)
8 Jade elephant tail ("Treasure of Marco Polo," *US* 64)
9 "Heirloom Watch" (*US* 10, 1955)
10 Bottlecap ("Tralla La," *US* 6, 1955)
11 Stone coins ("The Treasury of Croesus," *WDCS* 601-603)
12 Scrooge's Number One Dime
13 1916 quarter ("The Secret of Atlantis," *US* 5, 1954)
14 Golden egg ("Isle of Golden Geese," *US* 45, 1963)
15 Locket, "The Lemming with the Locket," *US* 9 (1955)
16 Square egg, "Lost in the Andes" (Donald Duck *Four Color* 223, 1949)
17-21 Comics (see page 208)
22 Goose Egg Nugget, "Back to the Klondike" (US FC 456, 1953)
23 First Woodchuck Guidebook, "Guardians of the Lost Library" (*US Adventures* 27, 1994)
24 Terry Fermy Trophy, "Land Beneath the Ground" (*US* 13, 1956)
25 Bullion, "The Flying Dutchman," *US* 25 (1959)
26 Jewels, "Mines of King Solomon" *US* 19, 1957)
27 Plaque, "His Majesty, McDuck" (*USA* 14, 1989)
28 Golden fleece, "The Golden Fleecing" (*US* 12, 1955)
29 Medallion, "The Curse of Nostrildamus" (*US* 235, 1989)
30 Peace pipe, "Land of the Pygmy Indians," *US* 18, 1957)

Pin-up page in French *Picsou* 300, January 1997; first American publication on *Walt Disney Treasures* 2, 2008. Color by Susan Daigle-Leach.

D.U.C.K. SPOTTER'S GUIDE: The dedication is in the top knobs of the Junior Woodchuck flagpoles.

Pin-up page in Italian *Zio Paperone* 94, July 1997; color by Disney Italia, featuring Scrooge's coat in its traditional Italian color scheme of blue with red trim. The image was drawn to celebrate Scrooge's 50th anniversary that year.

D.U.C.K. SPOTTER'S GUIDE:
The dedication is not included.

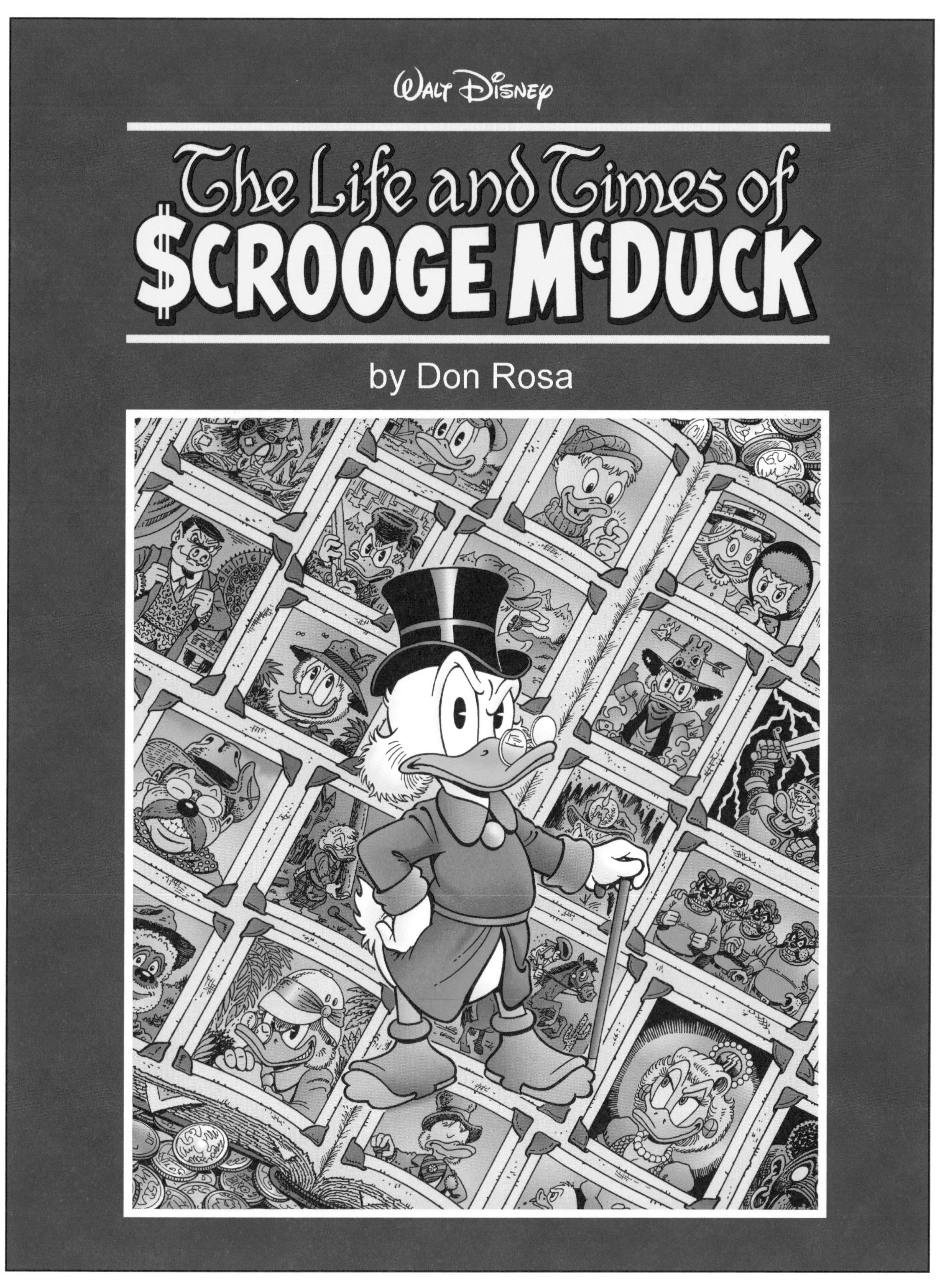

THE LIFE AND TIMES OF SCROOGE McDUCK
Danish *Joakim Von And: Her er dit liv*, 1997; first American printing in Gemstone *Life and Times of Scrooge McDuck* collected edition, 2005. Color by Susan Daigle-Leach.

D.U.C.K. SPOTTER'S GUIDE:
The dedication is in the leaves on the photo of Scrooge wearing a tropical helmet.

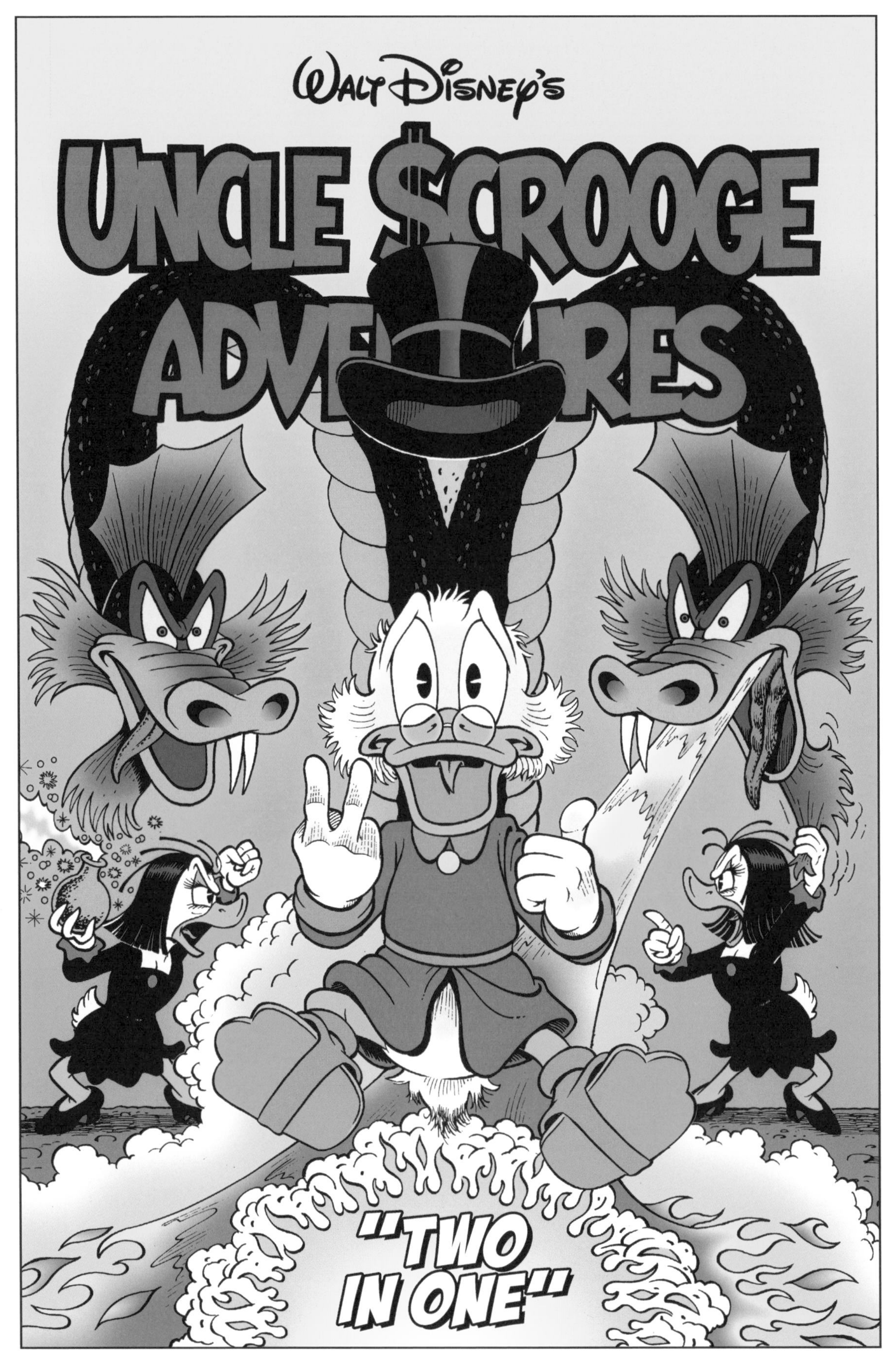

TWO IN ONE
Uncle Scrooge Adventures 44, March 1997. Layout by David Gerstein and Don Rosa; color by Susan Daigle-Leach. Illustrating a new story by David Gerstein and Daniel Branca.

D.U.C.K. SPOTTER'S GUIDE:
The dedication is not included.

THE DUCK WHO FELL TO EARTH
German *Walt Disneys Onkel Dagobert von Don Rosa* Album 14, September 1997.
Color by Scott Rockwell.

D.U.C.K. SPOTTER'S GUIDE:
The dedication is on Donald's butterfly net.

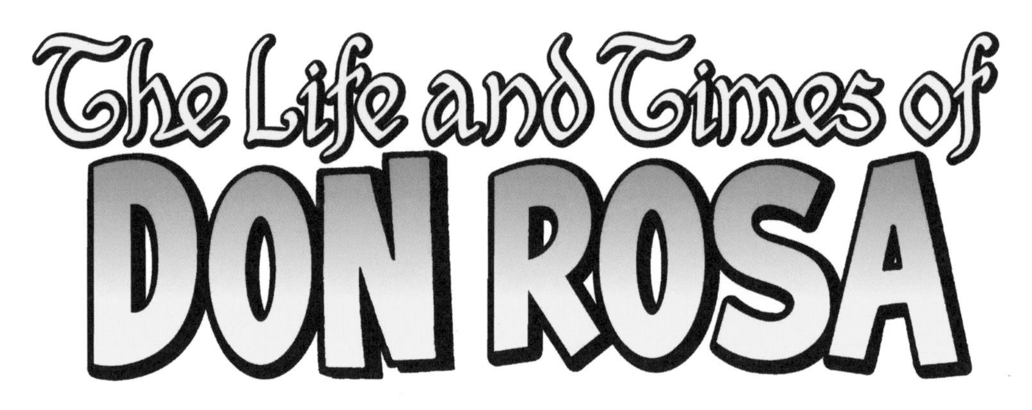

PART 5: "Of Ducks and Don and Destiny"

Previous parts of this mini-autobiography have described my life up to when I started creating Duck comics for the vast Egmont publishing company. Soon I had completed several years worth of projects for them, including my *Life and Times of Scrooge McDuck* series. From that point on it becomes more difficult to tell my tale in a linear narrative. I just kept plugging away at creating Donald and Scrooge stories as best as I could, year after year. As I mentioned in previous texts, I knew I was now working for the world's biggest and most successful producer of Disney comics. And I was working on the stories of Donald Duck, the main character in that comic universe, indeed the world's most popular comic book character due to the work of Carl Barks. I was a member of a large stable of artists and writers; but I knew that unlike the others, I had no training or experience in creating comics for such a mass audience. Nevertheless I hoped to find a small niche to fill in that comic production.

© Disney

The Clan McDuck in a special vignette drawn for Finnish *Aku Ankka* 51/1997. The more that Rosa told of Scrooge's European family and past, the more a family of European Duck aficionados came to embrace him.

But almost immediately, something totally unexpected began happening. Despite my overly complex plots and the crudity of my art, my stories seemed to be attracting an undue amount of reader attention. I've been theorizing for over twenty-five years about the reasons for that, and perhaps my observations can be the subject of another chapter of this mini-biography. But now I will try to describe to you what it feels like to become suddenly world famous doing something you love to do.

Aside from any possible qualities of my stories, I think there is another reason why I became so personally popular with publishers and readers. For over sixty years, European audiences have loved these comics to an inordinate degree! Donald Duck is a national hero in many European countries. But Carl Barks had been retired for decades and never traveled, and the modern creators—though very talented—lived on other continents and often worked in studio groups. One person thought up a plot. Another person wrote the script. One or two different artists drew the comic. This was a job to them. A job they did very well, but just a job.

Then I came along. I did the entire job from start to finish. I had a life-long deep passion for what I was doing; I was an inveterate collector and "scholar" of comic book history, and I loved to talk to other comics fans about all types of comics (and movies and TV)—*especially* Carl Barks' Ducks! And I was willing to travel. And I *spoke English*, a universal language. In other words, in the world of Disney comics, I was a celebrity waiting to happen.

In me the publishers finally had an all-encompassing spokesman for their comics: thrilled to find a continent filled with Barks fans like myself, and anxious to meet and talk to them. Within just a few years I was being invited to visit book fairs and comics festivals across Europe, being interviewed on national television, dining with mayors and governors, receiving international awards for my comics... it was sudden and unexpected fame like being a lottery winner. And I admit it—my comics might have been popular, but it was the publishers and reporters and fans who made me into this so-called celebrity. More on the fiction of "celebrity" in a moment.

And I started getting mail. *Lots* of mail. From both children and adults, in equal amounts. Because I was (and am) a fan myself, first above all, I answered every single letter I received. People would ask for drawings. I would fill every single request at my own expense of time and overseas postage—if I was asked, I did the drawings in full color (I

Can't see the queue! Rosa visits Helsinki, Finland in 2008.
Photo © and courtesy Don Rosa.

just hoped not many fans would ask for full color!). But my enthusiasm for creating comics of Barks' characters, and for the appreciation I received from my fellow comics fans had no limit. Eventually, just answering my daily fanmail was taking me two to three hours each day! I was making three or four trips to Europe each year... I never thought I'd see Europe even once. As of 2017 I have made over 100 separate or combined visits to fifteen different European countries, often on weeks-long signing tours, plus a half-dozen trips to South America. And every single trip has been absolutely free of charge—as I said, it's like being a lottery winner. (Well, except no monetary pay-off is involved. Only lots of nice travel to meet lots of nice Duck fans.)

Soon during these visits to Europe I was being recognized at airports or while walking down the street. In restaurants I'd see other diners giving me the eye, and I was almost always recognized by the young waiters (for whom I always do sketches). On occasion, in return for a few quick drawings that he can hang on the wall, the restaurant manager will tear up the entire check for the group, or at least hand out free desserts or drinks.

The most amazing restaurant story I recall took place in Finland some fifteen years ago—I had just arrived for another signing tour for the publisher. We were having lunch at a restaurant when people at another table recognized me with particular amazement—they were there treating a friend to a birthday lunch and giving her a gift of a Don Rosa hardback book. I added an autograph to the gift.

The mayor of Oslo personally gave me a tour of the magnificent Oslo city hall. I had coffee with the governor of Pernambuco, Brazil, and have dined with so many mayors in Germany or Scandinavia that I have lost count. My favorite such occurrence was when I attended a lavish

A most dedicated exhibit, featuring a complete Money Bin in honor of Don Rosa, built for the comics festival of Oporto, Portugal, in 1997. Photos © and courtesy Don Rosa.

"state dinner" with the mayor of Gijón, Spain, held in the ballroom of the city hall (actually a former imperial palace). This was like a scene such as you'd see in a movie with each dish delivered by two liveried waiters... one to carry the dish, the other to set the dish on the table. But even more memorable—during dinner I told the mayor I was currently working on a story taking place in 1903 Panama, but I could find no references for Spanish colonial military uniforms of the period. So, a thrill awaited me after dinner—the mayor took me downstairs and unlocked the city's National History Museum and showed me the displays of Spanish uniforms!

Another thrill is when a comics festival or the sponsoring city puts on a display of my work. There have been many, but I recall some special ones.

Magica De Spell, who lives on Mount Vesuvius, is naturally a mascot of Naples. At a comics festival held there in their famous Nuovo Castle they had a display of my art around the main entry hall—including a twelve-foot-tall poster of Magica's face from my cover art for "Forget It!" (see *Don Rosa Library* Vol. 8), and in the center of the hall the Number One Dime she so craves on a marble pedestal under a glass dome. Meanwhile, at the Parco Nazionale del Vesuvio headquarters on Mount Vesuvius, they had a huge public display of very clever exhibits of scenes from my stories; this was to announce their desire for me to design a "Magica's Sorcery Shop" hut that the park service planned to build somewhere on Vesuvius!

There were large exhibits of my art at other festivals and events. There was an exhibit of the life of Scrooge McDuck that filled a pavilion tent the first time I was a guest at the huge comics festival in Angouleme, France—they had constructed all sorts of displays of Barks' and my art in authentic Scottish or Yukon settings with many amusing props. But the very best such art exhibit was definitely when I was a guest at the comics festival in Oporto, Portugal. They had walled off a section of the convention hall, and all around the insides of this wall was painted the Duckburg skyline. In the center of this area was a raised platform simulating a grassy hilltop, and on this hilltop was built an enormous facsimile of the McDuck Money Bin at least fifteen feet tall! On one side of this structure, away from the always-locked main entrance, there was an unexploded bundle of (fake!) dynamite sticks near a large jagged hole "blasted" in the Bin wall—obviously the work of the Beagle Boys, whose footprints were all around. When guests entered this opening, they could view on the interior walls a display of my original art mixed with McDuck paraphernalia such as (again) that Number One Dime on its pedestal, bags of cash, a top hat and cane on a hat rack, a intruder-defense control panel, and so forth. Taking up the center of the area, sunk into the raised flooring, was an enormous swimming pool of money: thousands of fake coins, with a diving board on one side. And to top it off, disappearing into the center of the money pool was Scrooge himself from the waist down, frozen in the act of diving into his money! I actually wept when I saw this tribute!

After I created the "Quest for Kalevala" story (see *Don Rosa Library* Vol. 8) to combine the two most important aspects of Finnish culture—the *Kalevala* and Donald Duck—the Finnish Egmont affiliate then took me on a promotional signing tour around Finland. I was on every local and national TV talk show. There were articles about me on the front pages of every newspaper, even political and science journals. When I did a book signing at a department store in a shopping mall, the crowd did not stop at jamming that one store; the queue of fans snaked through the entire mall, causing all the other merchants to complain. I had security guards to help me get through crowds. I was the most famous person in an entire country for one week! This is amazing stuff for a boy from Kentucky.

My wife Ann seldom can accompany me on these tours, but sometimes she will see my appearance on a European talk show on YouTube. And she tells me she is amazed that I am so completely relaxed, even though I am on national television. But I explain that it's easy! Nervousness on such an occasion would come from being worried what people will think of me or how I'll come across. But in Europe I *know* everyone *loves* me... *not* because I'm me, but due to my close association with Barks' famous and beloved Ducks! And yet I could never appear on the *Today Show* or CNN... I'd be a nervous wreck! I mean, in America I'm nobody! Virtually no one remembers Barks' Ducks here.

I try very hard to prevent my ego from being affected by this "celebrity" thing, but sometimes it gets difficult. During a visit to Mount Vesuvius, on the rim of the crater, I was spotted by a school group from Norway. Touring Delphi with the Greek publisher, I was recognized by a Danish Duck fan. On a remote, nearly deserted beach in Mexico I was recognized by a yet another Danish fan. In the massive crowd at the Stuttgart Oktoberfest I was recognized by tourists from Finland. But my favorite such instance was when I was hiking deep in the jungle on the island of St. John in the American Virgin Islands, exploring the ruins of a nineteenth-century sugar mill high on a jungle hilltop—and a tourist from Sweden recognized me!!!

On these occasions it is my greatest delight to sign autographs and do sketches for these new friends. Then these nice fans try to tell me how thrilled they are to have recognized me and spoken to me and gotten such souvenirs. And I always tell them, "If you think you are the one who got the biggest thrill out of this, you're quite mistaken!"

I asked before—can you imagine how it feels to be such a celebrity when traveling somewhere? It feels absolutely *surreal*!!! And consider that here at home my neighbors don't even know who I am, yet in Europe people on the street stop me and ask for autographs. I never get used to it.

Celebrity seems to make some people—like certain movie or rock stars—become quite self-important and arrogant. I only feel embarrassed! It's not that I'm shy; it's more like I feel like I'm impersonating someone else, and eventually I'll be discovered as an imposter. I've seen photos of myself being interviewed in front of huge crowds at department store signings and such, and my ears are bright red! As another embarrassment, I personally despise standing in a queue for anything, and yet I have been the cause of thousands of people standing in queues for up to five or six hours just to get my autograph and shake my hand. I want to stop and talk to each one of them for twenty or thirty minutes, and do them a nice drawing in return for how wonderful their appreciation makes me feel. I am bombarded with mixed feelings: gratitude for how they are treating *me*, and shame in how little time I have for each of *them*. I learned that the only way I can handle being the focal point of such huge crowds of fans is by always sitting in a position from which I cannot see the length of the queue or all the eager faces, and I give my total attention to the single new friend directly in front of me.

I try to find some philosophical lessons to learn from these amazing experiences—the most obvious one to me is that "celebrity" is a manufactured fiction. I meet fans who are so *nervous* to meet me in person that they are struck dumb. This really makes me feel bad for us both. I try to assure such nice people that it's no big deal—I am only a comics fan, a Barks fan, like they are. I try to explain or prove how this entire "celebrity" concept is all in their minds, put there by the hoopla cooked up by the well-meaning publishers and reporters and bookstores. I want to take them for one instant back home to Kentucky with me, and show them how nobody there cares who I am—so they can realize "Say, he's just a normal person like everybody else!" Then maybe they could relax and we could talk just like two fellow comics fans.

But I will never be anything less than eternally grateful to all the European comics fans who certainly make me feel like a celebrity! It's their appreciation of my work that kept my enthusiasm alive for over two decades. It's thanks to them that I was able to face the downsides of working in my field for many extra years. •

© Disney

Celebratory vignette in *Walt Disney's Comics and Stories* 612, May 1997. This image—which accompanied a faux Scrooge autobiography in print (!)—marked the first time in North America that a Rosa rendering was published using the artist's original colors.

About the Editors

DAVID GERSTEIN is an animation and comics researcher, writer, and editor working extensively with the Walt Disney Company and its licensees. His published work includes *Mickey and the Gang: Classic Stories in Verse* (Gemstone 2005); *Walt Disney Treasures – Disney Comics: 75 Years of Innovation* (Gemstone 2006); and *The Floyd Gottfredson Library of Walt Disney's Mickey Mouse* (Fantagraphics, 2011-present). David has also worked with Disney in efforts to locate lost Oswald the Lucky Rabbit cartoons and to preserve the *Mickey Mouse* newspaper strip.

GARY GROTH has been publishing Don Rosa since 1970. Oh, and he also co-founded Fantagraphics Books in 1976. Fantagraphics is still going strong and he's still publishing Don Rosa. Life can't get any better than that.